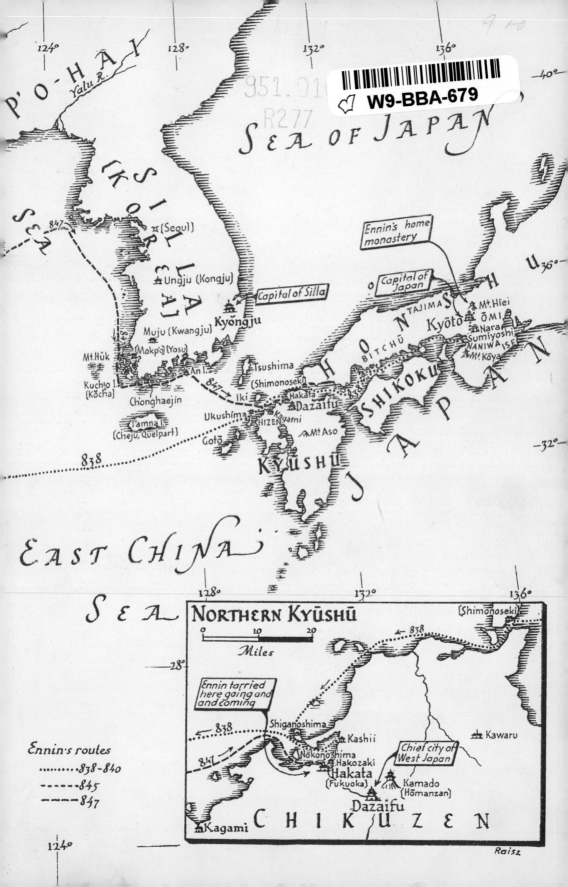

SEA OF JAPAN

P'O-HAI

Yalu R.

(SILLA)
(KOREA)

× (Seoul)

Ungju (Kongju)

Muju (Kwangju)

Kyŏngju

Mokp'o (Yosu)

Mt. Hŭk

Kuchio I.
(Kŏcha)

Chonghaejin

An I.

T'amna
(Cheju, Quelpart)

Gotŏ

Kagami

Tsushima
(Shimonoseki)

Iki

Hakata
Dazaifu

Ukushima
HIZEN

Mt. Aso

Capital of Silla

Ennin's home
monastery

Capital of
Japan

H O N S H Ū

TAJIMA

Kyōto

Mt. Hiei

ŌMI

Nara
Sumiyoshi
NANIWA
Mt. Kōya

ISE

J A P A N

BITCHŪ

SHIKOKU

KYŪSHŪ

EAST CHINA

SEA

847

838

NORTHERN KYŪSHŪ

0   10   20
Miles

838

Shimonoseki

Ennin tarried
here going and
and coming

838

Shiganoshima

838

847

Kashii

Nokonoshima
Hakozaki

Hakata
(Fukuoka)

Dazaifu

Chief city of
West Japan

Kamado
(Hōmanzan)

Kawaru

Kagami

C H I K U Z E N

Ennin's routes
.... 838–840
– – – – 845
— — — 847

Raisz

ENNIN (Jikaku Daishi)
An Idealized Portrait of the Twelfth Century

ENNIN'S
Travels in T'ang China

ENNIN'S
Travels in
T'ang China

BY

EDWIN O. REISCHAUER

PROFESSOR OF FAR EASTERN LANGUAGES

HARVARD UNIVERSITY

The RONALD PRESS COMPANY *New York*

To
Adrienne

Preface

Ennin, a Japanese Buddhist monk, crossed the sea to China in the year 838 and during the next nine and a half years kept a detailed diary of his travels through the vast T"ang Empire until he finally returned to Japan in 847. The lengthy record of his wanderings and of his tribulations and triumphs is not only the first great diary in Far Eastern history; it is also the first account of life in China by any foreign visitor.

Ennin, who is more commonly known in Japan by his posthumous title, Jikaku Daishi, was a major religious figure in his day, but among his countrymen only historians and churchmen still remember his name, and his diary, the *Nittō guhō junrei gyōki*, is little known except to research scholars. It is, however, one of the important documents of history, a primary source unique for its time, describing in rich detail a nation and a people then in the forefront of world history.

Some twenty years ago, while a graduate student rounding out my training in Japan, I started translating Ennin's diary with the hope of bringing it to the attention of scholars in the West. The work stretched out because of many long interruptions for other scholarly and nonacademic activities and was completed only recently. The full translation, supported but also encumbered by close to 1,600 explanatory footnotes, is appearing in a companion volume under the title *Ennin's Diary—The Record of a Pilgrimage to China in Search of the Law.*

As the work of translation progressed, I came to realize that Ennin's diary was of interest to others besides scholars. In the present age in which we are experiencing the painful process of amalgamation into one world, a great historical document of this sort, although medieval in time and Far

vii

Eastern in place, is a part of our common human heritage, with significance beyond these limits of time and space. It is the report of an important traveler in world history and an extraordinary, firsthand account of one of the way stations on man's long and tortuous journey from his lowly, savage beginnings to his present lofty but precarious position.

I have written this book not only for those with a specific interest in the Far East, but also for those with a more general interest in the broad record of human history. For the most part I have simply winnowed and arranged the numberless entries of Ennin's diary so that the material would form a clearer picture, or rather a series of pictures of the various aspects of life in China. In a few chapters, however, I have drawn on some other sources to round out pictures that the diary leaves incomplete. The first chapter describes the diary and its historical setting. The second chapter, which recounts Ennin's life as a whole, is based primarily on two biographies written in the ninth and early tenth centuries. Much of the third chapter, which tells the story of the Japanese embassy that Ennin accompanied to China, is based on contemporary records of the Japanese court. The first part of the seventh chapter, describing the sweeping persecution of Buddhism that Ennin encountered in China, is based on a variety of contemporary Chinese works, and a part of the next chapter, in particular the section about the Korean merchant prince, Chang Pogo, is drawn from Korean annals and a few Chinese and Japanese sources. The rest of the book comes almost exclusively from Ennin's diary, and much of it is in Ennin's own words—that is, in the twentieth-century English equivalents I have used for the mixture of ninth-century Chinese colloquial and classical idiom which he used.

In the Preface to *Ennin's Diary* I have expressed my thanks to some of those who aided me in preparing the translation. I wish in addition to thank my father-in-law, Dr. George H. Danton, and Dr. James R. Hightower, Dr. Edward A. Kracke, Jr., and my father, Dr. A. K. Reischauer, for most helpful criticisms of the manuscript for this book. I also wish to repeat my thanks to my wife not only for her invaluable aid but also for her sympathetic understanding of the time and effort consumed in the preparation of these printed pages.

E. O. R.

Cambridge, January, 1955

Contents

V

VI

VII

VIII

IX

ENNIN'S
Travels in T'ang China

I

Ennin's Diary

As we journey in our minds to distant times and places, we welcome nothing so gladly as the companionship of an observant traveler whose feet trod in reality the roads we follow in our imagination, and who can supplement the dry chronicles with the sights, the sounds, and the breath of life now long vanished. In visiting China in the days of the Mongol conquest, we have long enjoyed the company of the Venetian merchant, Marco Polo. We may now find an even more trustworthy guide to an earlier China of still greater cultural brilliance in the Japanese Buddhist monk Ennin, who is known to some by his posthumous title of Jikaku Daishi.

More than four centuries before Marco Polo made his famous overland journey eastward to Cathay in search of commercial riches, Ennin made the perilous voyage westward across the sea to China in search of new Buddhist texts and further enlightenment in his faith. While pursuing his religious goals, he traveled through various parts of China for more than nine years, and during most of this time he kept an extraordinarily detailed and scrupulously accurate diary, which contrasts sharply with the vague generalizations and sometimes faulty impressions of the Italian trader whose memoirs of his eastern travels were to startle Europe so many years later.

The essential difference between these two great travelogues can be illustrated by their respective accounts of the city of Yang-chou, the large commercial and administrative center near the lower reaches of the Yangtse River, where the paths of the two wanderers crossed, though many years apart. Near the end of the thirteenth century Marco Polo

1

spent three years in Yang-chou, but all that he chose to relate of those years he compressed into the following brief statement:

On leaving the city of Tinju, one travels for one day to the south-east, through a very fine country, where there are many towns and villages. Then one reaches a great and noble city called Yanju. And you must know that it is so large and powerful that it has twenty-seven other cities dependent upon it, all of them large, wealthy, and thriving with trade. In this city resides one of the Great Kaan's twelve barons, for it has been chosen as one of their twelve seats. They are idolators. They have paper currency, and are subject to the Great Kaan. And Messer Marco in person, he of whom this book speaks, held the government of this city for three years by order of the Great Kaan. They live by trade and handicrafts, for great quantities of equipment for horsemen and men-at-arms are made here. For you must know that in this city, and all around in its district, are stationed many troops.

There is nothing else worth mentioning. And so we will leave this place, and tell you of two great provinces that form part of that of Manji.[1]

Ennin arrived in Yang-chou in the summer of 838, not long after reaching China, and almost daily during the eight months he spent in that city he recorded in his diary the small incidents of life around him. For instance, on New Year's Eve he jotted down, "At sunset clerics and laymen together burned paper money, and after midnight the lay households burned bamboos and as they exploded shouted 'Banzai.' In the streetshops there were all sorts of foods in extraordinary profusion." Again, he recorded a single incident of his stay in Yang-chou in the following graphic terms:

There is an Imperial order prohibiting [the use of] copper, and throughout the land the sale or purchase of it is not allowed. It was explained that there was [such a regulation] as a rule once every six years. The reason for the prohibition is that they fear that, if the people of the empire always make copper utensils, there would be no copper for minting cash.

On the seventh day of the eleventh moon, Chen-shun, a monk of the K'ai-yüan-ssu, privately sold broken pots to a merchant to the amount of ten pounds weight. When the merchant went out with his iron, he ran into some police inspectors at the monastery gate and was arrested and brought back. The five inspectors came and said, "Recently the Minister of State has prohibited [the use of] iron, and one is not allowed to sell or buy it. How then is it that you have sold some?" Chen-shun replied that he did not know that its sale was prohibited. Then the officer in charge and Chen-shun prepared documents asking for a decision, and the officials pardoned him. Thus we learned that within the jurisdiction of Yang-chou the sale or purchase of iron is not permitted.

MARCO POLO AND ENNIN

Marco Polo's fame as a traveler has spread the world over, but only an occasional scholar has heard of Ennin, even in his native land of Japan. The Venetian's account of his wanderings, by stirring men's imaginations, helped to shape the course of history, while Ennin's record of his travels has gone virtually unread and unknown to this day. Yet Ennin long preceded the Italian to that great land and left what is in some ways an even more remarkable record of his peregrinations. The illiterate Marco Polo, years after his travels were over, recounted his adventures orally and in broad and sometimes hazy outline, but Ennin's day-by-day diary of his varied experiences is a unique document for its time in world history.

Marco Polo, coming from a radically different culture, was ill-prepared to understand or appreciate what he saw of higher civilization in China. He was virtually unaware of the great literary traditions of the country and, living in a China which was still in large part Buddhist, comprehended little of this religion other than that it was "idolatrous." Ennin, coming from China's cultural offshoot—Japan—was at least a stepson of Chinese civilization, educated in the complicated writing system of the Chinese and himself a learned Buddhist scholar. Marco Polo came to China as an associate of the hated Mongol conquerors; Ennin, as a fellow believer, entered easily into the heart of Chinese life. He saw China from within, the Venetian from without; he saw it with understanding eyes, Marco Polo with the eyes of a "barbarian."

While Marco Polo's memoirs have enjoyed incomparably greater renown and influence than Ennin's diary, the Japanese monk as a person was far more famous in his own day. Marco Polo was a minor figure, a traveling merchant like many others, and, except for the accidental recording of his story at another's hand, he probably would have been lost in the anonymity of history. And his life, fascinating though it has proved to generation after generation of vicarious adventurers, was spent on what was to prove one of history's blind alleys. The overland trade in which he and his uncles participated was soon to fade away and with it the early overland contacts between West and East. The Mongol Empire, which he served in China, was the largest land empire man has ever created, but it also was soon to disappear, never to be restored.

Ennin, on the other hand, was a great and honored man of his age, who moved down the less romantic, though more significant, main road of history. He was in the forefront of the intellectual movements of his day. As the leading churchman of his generation in Japan, he played a great role in introducing new aspects of Buddhism to Japan and in helping to fashion it into the religion which has remained dominant there ever since.

Ennin actually was taking part in an even greater movement in world history—the spread of higher civilization to the outer edges of Europe and Asia. The classical civilizations of the world had been developed in an earlier age and had culminated in the great empires of Rome in the West and Han in the Far East. In a much later age and one in which we still live, Western civilization spread across the seas to all corners of the earth, coming into contact and then into drastic and still indecisive conflict with the civilizations of Asia. But between these two major phases of world history, perhaps the single greatest historical development was the

spread of the higher civilizations to the limits of the old
world. While Mediterranean civilization was seeping northward into North Europe, Chinese civilization was spreading
southward into South China and parts of Southeast Asia and
northeastward into Manchuria, Korea, and Japan. In Europe
the process was slow and at times hardly perceptible; in
Japan it was rapid and clearly discernible—a great flood of
cultural influences flowing strongly throughout the period
from the late sixth century until the middle of the ninth.
Coming at the end of this era, Ennin stands out as one of the
last great individuals of this phase of history in East Asia.

NINTH CENTURY CHINA

The two Chinas which Ennin and Marco Polo observed
were naturally quite different, separated as they were by four
centuries. Marco Polo's China may have been of greater
interest—at least superficially. China, the most populous,
the richest, and the most advanced nation on earth, had been
conquered in its entirety for the first time in history and
formed the most important vassal land in the huge but loosely
coordinated empire carved out by the horsemen from Mongolia.

The China which Ennin saw was less dramatic and, for
that very reason, more significant in the broad pattern of
history. In the Western world the classic unity of Rome,
once shattered, was never successfully restored. In China the
rapid disintegration of the classic empire of Han in the third
and fourth centuries closely paralleled the slower collapse of
Rome, but subsequently their historical paths diverged. In
the late sixth century the Chinese succeeded in re-creating
the political unity of late classic times, and in the glorious
dynasty of T'ang, which lasted from 618 to 907, China
achieved new heights of political and cultural development.
The empire was larger than ever before, more prosperous,
and better ruled. An advanced system for the selection of
administrators through examinations was developed which
produced a type of civil servant that, through changing

dynasties, successfully ruled a united China for the greater part of the next millennium, until the system finally foundered less than a century ago. Trade, both internal and by sea with the outside world, grew at a rapid rate and resulted in spectacular economic growth. In culture, too, this was a period of rich development. Printing is one significant example of progress in this field, for it was developed in China in late T'ang times, centuries before it was dreamed of in the West.

When Ennin was in China the T'ang dynasty was decaying politically. Throughout Chinese history there has been a tendency for dynasties, after an initial century of growth and expansion, to fall prey to the weaknesses of size and age. The burdens of empire increased, while efficiency in administration declined. The result was rising governmental expenses, coupled with decreasing income for the state. At the same time the Imperial line usually degenerated, and factionalism among the Emperor's ministers increased, until eventually the whole political structure collapsed.

This is the so-called dynastic cycle of China's past—and perhaps the administrative cycle to be perceived in all bureaucratic governments. In any case, the dynastic cycle was well along in Ennin's day. The revolt in 755 of An Lu-shan, a T'ang general and court favorite of Turkish origin, started a decade of civil war and barbarian incursions which all but snuffed out the dynasty. China was shorn of many of its imperial conquests and was left permanently on the defensive against the nomads of the north and west. The remaining century and a half of T'ang rule were characterized by desperate efforts at fiscal reform and military defense and by a gradual disintegration of central control. The civil bureaucracy became divided into hostile personal factions, and the court eunuchs formed another clique which at times competed with the bureaucrats for control of the state through palace intrigues and bloody *coups d'état*. Meanwhile regional commanders (*Chieh-tu-shih*), who enjoyed full civil and military authority over large areas of the empire, became increasingly independent of the capital, until finally in

907 the refusal of these satraps to recognize the authority of the central government brought an end to the dynasty and ushered in a half century of political division.

Ennin saw China in one of its periodic stages of dynastic decline, but his detailed picture of life and government actually gains in interest and significance from this fact. First as a member of a foreign embassy, then as a foreign pilgrim and student in need of government credentials, and finally as one of the thousands of Buddhist monks caught in the greatest religious persecution in Chinese history, Ennin came into close and varied contact with government authorities of all types. He had prolonged dealings with petty administrators, down to the smallest local units; at the same time he had the chance to meet and talk with the two greatest political figures of the day—Li Te-yü, the leader of the dominant faction of scholar-bureaucrats, and Ch'iu Shih-liang, a powerful and fantastically wealthy court eunuch and general.

From hundreds of small details concerning Ennin's dealings with bureaucrats and a few dozen official documents that he copied into his diary, there emerges a picture of government in operation which is amazing for the ninth century, even in China. The remarkable degree of centralized control still existing, the meticulous attention to written instructions from higher authorities, and the tremendous amount of paper work involved in even the smallest matters of administration are all the more striking just because this was a period of dynastic decline.

Perhaps the conclusion to be drawn from this picture is that, despite the downward swing of the dynastic cycle, the ninth century was in a more fundamental sense a period of significant political growth in China. The Chinese were never able to overcome the dynastic cycle and the periodic political collapse it entailed, but by late T'ang times they had achieved such a high level of administrative efficiency that China never again underwent the type of general collapse which ensued from the downfall of Han and Rome. During the five decades of political disunity which followed the fall

of the T'ang, there was marked cultural and economic
growth, rather than decline. This also proved to be the last
prolonged period of multiple political division in Chinese
history. The Sung dynasty, which came into being in 960,
quickly restored the political unity of the T'ang dynasty as
well as its essential administrative structure, and thereafter
Chinese political unity and administrative forms succeeded
in surviving the vicissitudes of dynastic change and barbarian conquest. How well they can survive the even more dis-
ruptive invasions by "barbarian" machines and ideas in the
nineteenth and twentieth centuries is yet to be seen. But in
any case, the ninth century, while superficially characterized
by dynastic decline, was in fact part of that important
period in history when the Chinese managed to achieve such
a high degree of administrative efficiency and stability that
China became the first political unit in the world to assume
a form which is recognizable as the same country we know
today.

The economic and cultural advances of ninth-century
China were even more obvious and perhaps more important
than the political accomplishments. Declining revenues and
recurrent financial crises gave rise to stopgap measures, some
of which were to prove as significant in later Chinese history
as the great political revival and innovations of the early
T'ang. In addition, military weakness and foreign threats
stimulated the growth in late T'ang times of a nativistic in-
trospection and hostility toward the "barbarian" world,
which has proved more characteristic of Chinese thought and
culture in the last millennium than has the Buddhistic uni-
versalism of the early T'ang.

The ninth century falls in that great formative period in
Chinese history from the seventh to the thirteenth century
when the revived classicism of early T'ang was transformed
into the modern China with which the West came in contact
in recent centuries. Virtually all that is most characteristic
of this modern China was in existence at least in embryo by
the ninth century and came into early bloom under the succeeding Sung dynasty—the philosophy of Neo-Confucian-

ism, the encyclopedic scholasticism of modern times, the great arts of landscape painting and ceramics, new methods of taxation based primarily on the land rather than the individual, a closer integration of commercial wealth with state finances, and finally the great commercial cities and overseas trade through the ports of the south and east, which in modern times took the place of the early caravan routes briefly restored to importance in the time of Marco Polo and the Mongols. All these and a host of other factors which distinguish modern China from its classic ancestor were apparent or at least starting to emerge in the China of Ennin's time.

Ennin, of course, gives no coherent account of any of these important developments, but he sheds light on many of them. For example, his numerous references to merchants and shipping along the eastern littoral of China and the detailed descriptions of his own voyages up and down the China coast give by far the clearest picture we have of China's coastal and foreign trade at this time. Similarly, his intimate descriptions of Chinese Buddhist believers, their ceremonies, and holy places give a unique insight into Buddhism as a living religion at its highwater mark in Chinese history, and his firsthand account of the persecution which developed during his later years in China is our only detailed record of what proved to be one of those great turning points in the intellectual and cultural life of a nation.

The China which Ennin saw and described, although it has been scorned by traditional Chinese historians as an age of dynastic decline, was a China in the midst of one of its greatest periods of development and growth. Marco Polo's China, for all its outward drama, was fundamentally a more static China near the end of this great dynamic period. Ennin's China, viewed as a temporal segment in Chinese history, stands out as a time of greater significance. Viewed as a geographic segment of human society in the ninth century, it is even more outstanding, because then, perhaps more than at any other time, China led the world as the richest, most advanced, and best organized land on earth.

It is fortunate that Ennin's diary, which is a unique
record for the ninth century anywhere in the world, should
deal with China and not some other area, such as Europe,
which at that time was underdeveloped in comparison with
the T'ang Empire. If men of later ages were to have but one
such intimate account of life in the nineteenth century, they
would probably wish it to concern Europe, possibly England. For the twentieth century they might prefer the United
States or, according to one school of thought, the Soviet
Union. But for the ninth century, it is the human record in
China that is of the greatest interest to mankind.

HSÜAN-TSANG, ENCHIN, AND JŌJIN

While Marco Polo's more famous travelogue naturally
suggests itself as a first parallel to Ennin's diary, there are
other works that are actually closer to it both in spirit and
in time. The best known of these is the *Hsi-yü-chi* (*A Record
of Western Lands*) by the great Chinese monk and traveler
Hsüan-tsang, who went overland from China through Central Asia to India and back again in the years 629 to 645, at
the very beginning of the T'ang dynasty. On his return to
China, Hsüan-tsang became the outstanding churchman of
his day and one of the last important transmitters of Buddhism from India to China. Thus, he and Ennin played
closely analogous roles in two successive Buddhist waves
rolling eastward. The records of their pious travels, however,
are quite different. Hsüan-tsang has left us not a diary but a
summary account of the lands he traversed, compiled after
his return to China. While it stands out as our most reliable
record of these areas at that time and is a solid chronological
peg on which to hang our rather vague knowledge of the
middle period of Indian history, it lacks the detail and full
life-color of Ennin's diary.[2]

A closer parallel to Ennin's work is to be found in the
Gyōryakushō (*Travel Jottings*) of the Japanese monk
Enchin, a younger contemporary and rival of Ennin in the
Tendai Sect, which was the leading Buddhist group of the

day in Japan. Enchin traveled in China between the years 853 and 858, a decade and a half after Ennin. He, too, compiled a detailed record of his travels on the continent and finally, after his return to Japan, succeeded Ennin's successor as the Abbot of the Enryakuji, the great monastic headquarters of the Tendai Sect, standing on Mt. Hiei, high above the capital city of Kyōto.

But in death as well as in life Enchin was to come off second best in his rivalry with Ennin. The disciples of these two men finally broke into open hostility, splitting the Tendai Sect into two antagonistic groups, and Enchin's followers were forced to withdraw from Mt. Hiei and establish their own headquarters at the great monastery known as the Onjōji, or Miidera, at the base of the mountain. Here, as the Jimon, or "Monastic Branch" of the sect, they remained for centuries in ecclesiastic and sometimes military conflict with the Sammon, or "Mountain Branch," ensconced on top of Mt. Hiei. As a diarist, Enchin fared even worse. Although Ennin's record appears to have been preserved in its virtual entirety, only a few fragments of Enchin's *Gyōryakushō* remain.[3] These contain many items of interest, including information about the subsequent activities of two of Ennin's Japanese companions during his travels in China, but they are only fragments. While Ennin emerges as a man to be bracketed with Marco Polo or Hsüan-tsang, Enchin must be content with a place in the footnotes of history.

A better fate awaited the records of some of the later Buddhist pilgrims who went from Japan to China. Notable among them is Jōjin, a monk from the Miidera headquarters of Enchin's branch of the Tendai Sect. He left Japan on the perilous trip to China in 1072 at the relatively advanced age of sixty-two, leaving behind him a still more aged mother who, though in her eighties, proceeded to keep a poetic diary of this period of separation from her son, which is still preserved and regarded as a literary work of some merit. Jōjin proved to be an indefatigable diarist as well as an energetic pilgrim. In only a little more than a year he visited the two holy mountains of T'ien-t'ai in the south and Wu-t'ai in the

north, which had been the chief objectives of Ennin's pilgrimage, and he also spent some time at the capital where
he was showered with honors by the Sung Emperor. During
this busy time of travel and study, he found time to keep an
incredibly detailed diary.[4]

But Jōjin's work and those of the Japanese monks who
followed him to China in later centuries, while full of interesting materials, are still far less valuable than Ennin's
diary, simply because they tell of stages in Chinese history
that are much better known from native sources than is the
ninth century of Ennin. His work is not only the first great
diary by a Japanese; it is also the earliest intimate account
of life in China.

This is not to say that Chinese history is poorly docu-
mented up until Ennin's time. On the contrary, China's past
is far more fully recorded than that of any other part of the
world for the period between late classic times and recent
centuries. While relatively few primary source materials,
such as legal decisions and personal documents, have been
preserved from this period, the Chinese have always had an
even stronger consciousness of history than have the peoples
of the Occident and, as a result, have been careful to compile
and preserve a voluminous official record of their past. But,
just for the reason that the Chinese have been so conscious
of the past and also of the historical judgment of the future,
their records have tended to be extremely formalized and
polished, listing the established facts of political history
rather than portraying the life of the people.

Although the official histories of the successive dynasties
are both huge and surprisingly accurate, the wealth of information they contain has been so marvelously condensed
and compressed that all life has been squeezed out of it, and
only the bare facts remain. Philosophers and literary men
have left a vast store of historical tales of one sort or another,
but in the polished atmosphere of literary China these accounts have been transformed from actual happenings into
moralistic anecdotes. Poets and essayists have left monu-
mental collections describing their lives as well as their

thoughts and feelings, but all are cast in traditional forms and tend to be self-consciously addressed to posterity. The result usually is the portrayal of ideal literary types rather than living men. After the establishment of the Sung dynasty in the second half of the tenth century the written record left by the Chinese broadens considerably and takes on a much higher degree of verisimilitude, but only Ennin opens a wide window looking back into the daily life of the dynamic, growing China of pre-Sung days.[5]

ENNIN'S DIARY TODAY

If all this is true, then why has Ennin's diary received so little attention? It is all but unknown to the Chinese, who should be the most interested of all. Perhaps no more than a half dozen Occidental scholars have made any use of it, and only one has done more than quote an isolated line or two in connection with some specific subject under study.[6] Even in Japan, where it is well known to scholars interested in the T'ang period, it has been used only in a fragmentary way in scholarly publications and is still quite unknown to the general reading public.

The answer to this question is probably twofold. For one thing Ennin's diary has not really been accessible to most readers even in the Far East, written as it is in medieval Chinese about an age and a life that is little more familiar to the contemporary Chinese or Japanese than is ninth-century Europe to us. Moreover, Japanese historians, like those of China, still tend to view history as a record of important names and facts and therefore have usually overlooked the chief value of the diary as our first candid portrait of daily life in China.

An excellent example of the Japanese scholar's attitude can be found in the work of the great Sinologist, Okada Masayuki, who devoted the last years of his life to an uncompleted study of Ennin's diary. He brought out a photographic reprint of the earliest manuscript copy of the work,[7] which is invaluable to the serious student of the orig-

inal, and he devoted a series of authoritative and detailed
studies to certain passages in the text that serve to verify
and supplement the main events of history as they are traditionally thought of in Japan. The points he found worthy
of study were (1) an otherwise unknown abortive attempt
by the Chinese Emperor to deprive his eunuch generals of
their dominant military power at the capital, (2) a stele inscription recording the capture of some Chinese by Japanese
troops in a seventh-century Korean war in which both China
and Japan were involved, (3) some confirmatory datings of
one of many incursions into China by the Turkish Uighur
tribesmen, (4) further details on the life of Chang Pogo, a
fabulous merchant prince and king-maker of Korea, and (5)
an account of the great Buddhist persecution in China.
While all these points are of interest and the last two of
major importance, Okada entirely overlooked the still more
significant aspect of Ennin's diary as a picture of the life of
the times.[8]

This situation is reminiscent of a story related by the
famous Taoist philosopher of ancient China, Chuang-tzu. A
friend told him of a gourd seed he had received, saying, "I
planted it, and it bore a gourd so enormous that if I had
filled it with water or broth it would have taken several men
to lift it, while if I had split it into halves and made ladles
out of it they would have been so flat that no liquid would
have lain in them. No one could deny that it was magnifi-
cently large; but I was unable to find any use for it, and in
the end I smashed it up and threw it away."

Chuang-tzu, scoffing at his friend for his obtuseness, told
him of a family that had long known a secret drug which
enabled its members to steep silk floss without chapping their
hands. A stranger, however, bought the recipe from them
and, obtaining a naval command, used it on the hands of his
sailors in a winter campaign with such excellent results that
he won a great naval victory for his lord and a fine fief for
himself. Chuang-tzu then concluded, "As for you and your
large gourd, why did you not tie it as a buoy at your waist,
and, borne up by it on the waters, float to your heart's con-

tent amid the streams and inland seas? Instead, you grumble
about its gigantic dimensions and say that ladles made from
it would hold nothing." [9]

Perhaps it is unfair to apply this story to the specialists
who have used Ennin's diary only to ladle out, with no great
efficiency, a few more official facts about court history, instead of floating on it through the life of T'ang China. But
in any case, since the scholars have not made better use of
Ennin's diary, it is small wonder that others have remained
unaware of it, for, like Marco Polo's work, it can belong to
the general reader only when properly prepared for him.

Linguistically Ennin's diary is perhaps a little more
readable for the contemporary Japanese, and still more so
for the modern educated Chinese, than are the various
medieval versions of Marco Polo's account for contemporary
Europeans and Americans. In terms of its content, however,
it is less comprehensible to either Chinese or Japanese than
is Marco Polo's work to us. After all, Marco Polo attempted
to inform others about distant lands and strange places and
consequently he explained what he thought needed elucida-
tion, but Ennin was merely trying to keep his own personal
record of his travels and religious studies under most trying
and involved circumstances. Moreover, the inevitable frag-
mentation of incident in a diary and the smothering of
narrative in thousands of repetitive details, which gain significance only in the aggregate, make his diary less immediately attractive or understandable than Marco Polo's
glittering generalities. When, in addition, the text is presented to the reader in the raw—medieval Chinese heavily
larded with long-forgotten names and titles, both lay and
ecclesiastic, and studded with copyist's errors—it is not hard
to see why the general reader has left the work to those
scholars who can stomach such fare.

The very title of the diary gives some hint of its difficulties
and the esoteric veils which still surround it. It has no popular title, but is known by its cumbersome original name of
Nittō guhō junrei gyōki, or *The Record of a Pilgrimage to
China in Search of the Law*, the "Law" in this case meaning

Buddhism. The size of the diary also might discourage the casual reader. It consists of four booklets, or "scrolls," as they are called in Chinese, totaling something over seventy thousand characters. Because of the terseness of written Chinese, this is the equivalent of an English text of about one hundred thousand words.

The language of the diary is, of course, an even greater barrier than its bulk. Ennin wrote in Chinese for much the same reasons that a medieval North European monk would have written in Latin. It was only in the ninth century that the Japanese slowly evolved from the Chinese characters a phonetic syllabary with which their own language could be properly written, and it was not until the tenth century that any significant amount of Japanese prose was actually written in this medium. Moreover, Ennin, as a Buddhist cleric, would have been the last person to attempt to write in the local idiom and in this newfangled script, for he had, no doubt, received his whole formal education in classical written Chinese, in which he must have had considerable proficiency even before he went to China.

The early part of the diary makes amply clear that Ennin spoke little or no Chinese when he arrived in China, but during his nine years' stay he certainly must have picked up a reasonably good knowledge of the vernacular. As a consequence, his diary became a combination of classical written Chinese and the spoken language of modern China as it was starting to emerge in the ninth century. Ennin also copied into the text a number of documents written in the curious "officialese" of the petty local bureaucrats of the time. The language of the diary is further complicated by many strange turns of phrase and clumsy locutions, owing no doubt to the fact that Chinese after all was not Ennin's native tongue.

THE TRANSMISSION OF THE TEXT

Ennin's diary has never been easy reading, and it seems perfectly possible that centuries went by with no one reading it at all. In fact it came very close to total disappearance before it was rediscovered by modern scholars and put into print. It has been preserved in only two manuscript forms. One, known as the Tōji text from the name of the ancient Kyōto monastery which owns it, was copied by a Tendai monk named Ken'in, who completed his work in the year 1291 while "rubbing his old eyes," as well he might, for he also records that he was seventy-two at the time. The other manuscript, known as the Ikeda text, was not made until 1805 and appears to be merely a slightly emended copy of Ken'in's manuscript.

We are thrown back, therefore, on the Tōji manuscript as our one and only link to Ennin's original work. Copied with an obviously shaky hand by the aged Ken'in, it is a frail link indeed. The cursive and abbreviated calligraphy and the inevitable wormholes in so old a manuscript give rise to many doubts on specific characters, and still more serious doubts arise over the copyist's accuracy in his work. Whether Ken'in fully understood what he was copying or simply did it as a pious act of faith, I cannot say. Either he or some previous copyist of the text must have transcribed it without much understanding of what he wrote, for scores of times one comes across characters which are all too obvious errors for others they closely resemble. This same rote copyist may also be responsible for further obscurities resulting from the loss or misplacement of certain parts of the diary.

In view of all these difficulties confronting the reader, one may wonder whether the diary in its present form deserves any great credence. But this is a doubt no one who has read much of it could entertain for a minute. With all its petty inaccuracies of transmission, it rings unquestionably true from beginning to end. Copyists' errors have done little to dull its clarity, and there is not the slightest sign that any later hand has tried to touch it up. The hundreds of names of obscure places in China and the scores of little-known ninth-century titles which fill the pages of the diary could not have been marshaled without the aid of the most advanced tools of the modern scholar. Where Ennin records the hearsay reports of others, his diary contains obvious mis-

statements and errors; but where he records what he himself
did and saw, its accuracy on points that can be verified today
is truly astounding.

Ennin's geographic comments are a good case in point.
Of his scores of carefully recorded travel distances that can
be checked on detailed modern maps, only three or four seem
somewhat out of line, and this despite the fact that "20,"
"30," and "40," as written in the Tōji manuscript, and several other key numbers as well, are extremely susceptible to
confusion with each other. Of the hundreds of local names
Ennin mentions, only a handful are clearly wrong, and these
usually because of quite understandable errors of copying.
In many more cases, local names he mentions which cannot
be found in any of our modern standard reference works can
be verified through more detailed research work of a sort
quite impossible before the development of modern libraries.
If conditions in China were propitious, one could today re-
trace Ennin's steps over the greater part of his travels
throughout North China and, with nothing more than his
diary for a guide, could spend most of one's nights in the
same towns and villages where he slept and, during the daylight hours, could for the most part stay within a mile or
two of the very path he followed.

The errors of transmission in Ennin's diary are not to be
minimized, but they are infinitesimal when compared with the
willful distortions as well as the unwitting inaccuracies of the
official chroniclers and self-conscious men of letters. One
need but compare the diary with the lifeless, though sometimes fanciful, biographies of Ennin's life, some of which
were compiled soon after his death, to realize the vast gulf
which lies between a true diary and a formal record written
at a later date.

Ennin's diary has been printed four times in the past half
century in Japan, each time in one of those huge collections
of early documents and records of which the modern Japanese scholar is so justly proud, but which the average reader
leaves strictly alone on the library shelves.[10] These four
printings, while giving the diary some currency in the

scholarly world and greatly increasing its chances for continued survival, have not made it in any sense a popular work even in Japan.

Marco Polo's famous account, from the very beginning of its history, has been continually translated and retranslated, until it is now available in several variant forms in most of the leading tongues of the world. But Ennin's diary has never before been taken out of the original Chinese characters in which it was composed. The fourth of the Japanese printed editions [11] purports to be a translation, but, since it merely adds Japanese grammatical elements to the original words of the text, to read it one must know both contemporary Japanese syntax and the ninth-century Chinese vocabulary of the original.

In a companion volume to this book I am publishing an annotated translation of the whole work under the title *Ennin's Diary—The Record of a Pilgrimage to China in Search of the Law*. While I feel certain that in this English translation Ennin's work has become considerably more readable and comprehensible than ever before, it still remains somewhat heavy and in places confusing reading.[12] It is for this reason that I have written the present volume, in which I have told in condensed form the main story of the diary and have brought together the scattered information contained in it and in a few related sources on certain of the more interesting aspects of the history of the time. The specialist, I trust, will find this volume a useful aid in his approach to the diary.[13] The general reader may be satisfied with the guided tour of Ennin's world that it affords, but some, I hope, will have the curiosity to go beyond it and let Ennin himself lead them on a pilgrimage to his Holy Land.

II

Ennin: Pilgrim and Patriarch

The best known as well as the most interesting years of Ennin's life are the nine he spent in China and recorded in such detail in his diary, but contemporary historical sources and later biographies furnish a relatively reliable account of the rest of his career as well. The early Japanese court kept official annals in Chinese, modeled on those of the T'ang court. These records contain several references to the activities of Ennin and under the date of his death, which was the fourteenth day of the first moon of the year 864, devote to him a biographical entry of unusual length for annals of this sort.[1] Running to over one thousand characters of condensed classical Chinese, this biography is unquestionably our most reliable source for Ennin's life as a whole. A great many details, however, are added by another early biography dating from the first half of the tenth century, which is almost nine times longer than the one in the official annals and incorporates virtually the whole of it.[2]

THE NEOPHYTE

Unlike most of the other great Buddhist clerics of early Japanese history, who were scions of prominent families in the areas close to the capital, Ennin was born into an obscure family in Tsuga District in the Province of Shimotsuke in East Japan. At that time Shimotsuke was a remote area not far from what was still the frontier between the Japanese people and the Ainu, their hairy, proto-Caucasian predecessors in that part of Japan. His family had the name of Mibu and claimed descent from Sujin Tennō, traditionally the tenth Emperor of Japan; but, in a country in which great emphasis is put on having an impressive genealogy, such a claim need not be taken very seriously.

Ennin was born in 793.[3] As might be expected from his illustrious later career, a purple cloud hung over the house on the day of his birth. It was not observed by the family, but a certain monk named Kōchi noticed it while passing by on his mendicant rounds and, without explaining his reasons, asked the family to entrust the child to him if it grew up without blemish. The father of the family died while Ennin was still young, and, after some instruction at home in the classical literature of China, the boy, at the age of nine, was put under the care of Kōchi, where he became a devout and studious Buddhist and grew into a handsome youth five feet seven inches tall.[4]

One night Ennin saw in a dream a priest of heroic proportions. This apparition, he discovered, was the great Buddhist monk Saichō, who had introduced to Japan the teachings of the Chinese Buddhist Sect of T'ien-t'ai, known in Japan as Tendai. Because of his dream, Ennin at the age of fifteen went to the Enryakuji, the monastic headquarters of Saichō's new sect, standing near the summit of Mt. Hiei, a short distance northeast of the new capital of Kyōto. There he met the great man, became one of his favored disciples, and was given special instruction by Saichō in the *Maka-shikan*, one of the major works of Chih-i, the sixth-century founder of the sect in China. Ennin excelled his fellow students, and in 814 was officially accepted as a candidate novice. Two years later he took his vows as a monk at the great Tōdaiji monastery in the older capital of Nara. Subsequently he was selected by Saichō to be a transmitter of Mahayana Buddhism, that is, the more liberal "Greater Vehicle," as opposed to the older Hinayana or "Lesser Vehicle" of traditional Buddhism. For this purpose he was given instruction by Saichō in the *Lotus Sutra*, one of the chief Mahayana scriptures, and was also specially baptized by the master as a transmitter of the faith.

For several years after Saichō's death in 822, Ennin
preached and practiced religious rites on Mt. Hiei, until he
was finally persuaded by his colleagues to venture forth and
preach in the outside world. In the summer of 828 he lectured on the *Lotus Sutra* at the already historic Hōryūji
monastery near the old capital city of Nara. The next year
he lectured at the Shitennōji, in what is now the huge indus-
trial city of Ōsaka, and also in his native "north land." But
his religious zeal was apparently too great for his constitution, for at the age of forty [5] his body was worn out and his
eyes were dim. He retired, therefore, to a secluded spot in a
ravine on Mt. Hiei where he built a small hermitage in which
to await death. He did not die, however, and, after a few
years of a quiet life of religious devotions and a marvelous
dream in which he received a honey-like medicine from
heaven, he was fully restored to health.[6]

In 834 an embassy was appointed by the Japanese court to
go to China. When Ennin heard this news the next year, he
promptly dreamed that Saichō, although warning him of the
dangers of the trip, instructed him to go to China to search
for the Law. Shortly thereafter Ennin was appointed a
member of the embassy in the capacity of a Scholar Monk
(*Shōyaku-sō*), the senior of two categories of monks who
commonly accompanied Japanese embassies for the purpose
of further study in China, which next to India itself was the
holy land of Far Eastern Buddhism.

In going to China as a Scholar Monk, Ennin was following in the footsteps of his master, Saichō, for the latter had
gone in the same capacity with the preceding embassy in
804. It was not surprising, therefore, that Saichō again appeared to his successor in dreams to advise him, although
somewhat cryptically, on the clothing he should wear and to
tell him what he should study in China. The selection of
Ennin for the mission had probably been initiated by his
superiors in the Tendai Sect and was not only a signal honor
but also a heavy responsibility. His fellow monks at the
Enryakuji got together lists of questions regarding points
of doctrine and asked Ennin to take these to the mother

church in China for explanation and solution. He, thus, was to continue the work of the great Saichō himself by seeking in China new illumination on the sacred traditions of the sect.

THE TRIP TO CHINA

Ennin's diary affords vastly more detailed and accurate information about the nine years he spent in China than do his biographies. In fact, they are of interest for this period only because of the sometimes amusing contrast they make with the diary. The general outline they give of Ennin's stay in China is quite accurate and the names of men and places they include usually correct, but they add to the bare outline of the factual events certain elaborations of the story which do more credit to the religious enthusiasm of the authors and their pious respect for Ennin than to their historical accuracy. The biographies record incidents and conversations to which the diary makes no reference, but which are obviously intended to show that the Chinese paid Ennin far greater honor than he ever claimed for himself; they emphasize his occasional dreams of Buddhas and saintly predecessors, and interpret them as the chief turning points in his adventurous stay in China; and they transform his very modest claims of having witnessed a few mildly miraculous sights into truly wondrous stories. Where the diary tells of a dedicated but entirely realistic and even matter-of-fact pilgrim, the biographies, written only a few decades later, describe a miraculously blessed church patriarch.

The embassy which Ennin accompanied made two abortive attempts to cross to China in 836 and 837 and finally reached its destination early in the seventh moon of 838. Ennin's arrival in China, however, was scarcely auspicious. The ship on which he was traveling was wrecked on the shoals just north of the mouth of the Yangtse River, and he and his companions only reached shore after a severe and prolonged buffeting by the waves and tides. They proceeded inland by canal to Yang-chou, which is located a few miles north of the Yangtse and in T'ang times was an important regional capital and the predecessor of Shanghai as the major commercial entrepôt of the lower Yangtse Valley.

Early in the tenth moon the chief officers of the embassy and some of the accompanying monks started out from Yang-chou for distant Ch'ang-an, the capital of the T'ang Empire, located in the northwestern part of the country. Ennin, however, remained behind awaiting permission to go to Mt. T'ien-t'ai to the south in what is now the province of Chekiang. This holy mountain not only was the original home and headquarters of the Tendai monks, from which the name of their sect had been derived, but also had been the chief objective of Saichō's pilgrimage to China four decades earlier. Ennin availed himself of his enforced wait in Yang-chou to commence his studies of aspects of Buddhism still unknown to his church in Japan, while keeping an observant eye open for the secular world around him. It was at this time that he became acquainted with the great Chinese statesman Li Te-yü, who was then in supreme command of the Yang-chou region.

Ennin's somewhat impatient wait in Yang-chou was not rewarded by the expected permit to go to Mt. T'ien-t'ai. The request was rejected at the capital on the grounds that there was not sufficient time remaining before Ennin was scheduled to return to Japan with the embassy. Unfortunately, his rank as Scholar Monk worked against his cherished ambition. His fellow Tendai monk, Ensai, who up to this point had been his closest companion on the trip, did receive permission to visit the holy mountain, for he was only a Student Monk or, as the title of *Ryūgaku-sō* literally means, a "Stay and Study Monk," and therefore was not expected to return to Japan with the embassy.

It was a bitter disappointment to Ennin to have failed so completely in his pilgrimage to China, but since there was no appeal against an Imperial decision, he prepared to return home with his countrymen. He and the other Japanese who had remained behind in Yang-chou left the city in the second moon of 839, traveling north on the Grand Canal, the great man-made waterway which at this time connected the Yangtse River with the Huai River to the north and through tributaries of the latter with the Yellow River itself. At Ch'u-chou, where the Grand Canal met the Huai, they rejoined the other members of the embassy who had been to the Chinese capital. In the third moon the Japanese all embarked at Ch'u-chou for home and descended the Huai River to its mouth, a short distance south of the southern base of the Shantung Peninsula.

In the meantime, however, Ennin had come to a momentous decision. Korean traders in Ch'u-chou, who were far more familiar than were the Japanese with the laws of China and their loopholes, had suggested to him that he let himself be put ashore along the Shantung coast, where friendly Koreans would shield him from the Chinese authorities and would eventually find some way whereby he could continue his pilgrimage. But now an unexpected difficulty arose. The officers of the embassy, after much wrangling, decided to abandon their original plan of skirting the coast of Shantung northward before crossing to Japan and determined to take advantage of a favorable wind to sail eastward into the open sea from the place they then were. Ennin had no choice but to have his compatriots put him ashore with his two disciple novices, Ishō and Igyō, and his servant Tei Yūman on the desolate and mountainous coast a short distance north of the mouth of the Huai.

At this point occurred an incident which the biographies retell with much gusto. The four men on shore suddenly heard voices and saw that a strange ship had slipped into the cove so recently vacated by the Japanese vessels. Fearing that they might have fallen into the hands of pirates, they pressed all their belongings on the boatmen; however, the latter turned out to be merely friendly merchants of Korean origin engaged in the transportation of charcoal from Shantung southward to Ch'u-chou. The traders even delegated one of their number to lead the Japanese across a range of hills to the nearest village. Despite the happy ending to the incident, the biographies persist in calling these harmless charcoal merchants "pirates of fearsome mien intent on robbery," and ascribe the cutthroats' miraculous change of attitude to Ennin's act of self-abnegation in readily surrendering all his belongings.

Ennin's troubles, however, were far from over. Despite an effort to pass himself and his party off as Koreans, a judicious lie which he terms "an expedient," the four men were arrested by the Chinese authorities and taken to another ship of the Japanese embassy which happened to be in a nearby port. Ennin once again resigned himself to returning to Japan, and a few days later the ship set sail directly eastward across the sea. But this time fate intervened in his behalf. The ship was blown back to the coast of Shantung some distance to the north, giving him one more chance to try to penetrate the baffling curtain of Chinese officialdom. After seven miserable weeks of stormy weather, the ship finally reached the eastern tip of the peninsula on the seventh day of the sixth moon. The next day Ennin and his followers moved ashore to a small Korean monastery, which he calls the Mt. Ch'ih Cloister, and, with the connivance of the man in charge of the local Korean community, stayed on there when the Japanese ship finally set sail a few weeks later.

THE PILGRIMAGE

The four Japanese lived quietly in the Korean monastery through the autumn and winter of that year and, when spring came, started out on their long-delayed pilgrimage. However, their objective now was no longer Mt. T'ien-t'ai far to the south, but Mt. Wu-t'ai, in the northeastern part of the modern province of Shansi, about 520 miles air-line distance to the northwest from where they were. The local Korean monks had pointed out that this holy mountain could be reached more easily than Mt. T'ien-t'ai and was the latter's equal as a center of Buddhist learning, and Ennin had accepted their judgment.

The four Japanese set out on the nineteenth day of the second moon of 840, going first to Wen-teng, the local subprefectural capital. There, through the good offices of his Korean friends, Ennin received a permit to continue on his way. Armed thus he and his attendants proceeded next to the local prefectural capital, obtaining there another permit which allowed them to go on to the regional capital, where in due course they received a final permit to proceed to Mt. Wu-t'ai and from there to the national capital, Ch'ang-an.

On the twenty-eighth day of the fourth moon, more than two months after leaving the Mt. Ch'ih Cloister and after forty-four days on the road by his own reckoning, Ennin and his party reached the sacred region of Mt. Wu-t'ai. This was one of the greatest Buddhist centers in T'ang China and the home of a flourishing cult to Monju (Mañjuśrī in Sanskrit), the Bodhisattva of Wisdom, who had made the area sacred by several corporeal manifestations of himself in one guise or another. Mt. Wu-t'ai literally means "Mountain of the Five Terraces," and it was made up of five massive domed peaks, "looking like overturned bowls," as Ennin says. The five mountains covered a large area, and each rose far above the timber line and high above the surrounding mountains.

Ennin and his companions stayed slightly more than two months at Mt. Wu-t'ai. Much of the time was spent at two of the greatest monasteries of the region, where Ennin studied avidly under leading Buddhist scholars, and his two attendant novices took their monastic vows on one of the few platforms on which, according to Chinese law, ordinations could be performed. The Japanese made the pilgrim rounds of these and other monasteries, looking with awe at their majestic statues of Monju and other Buddhist deities and worshiping their holy relics. They also climbed each of the five terraces and with pious thoroughness visited all the many holy places on their summits and sides.

Mt. Wu-t'ai was, of course, a region of miracles, many of which Ennin carefully relates in his diary, and it was naturally here that his own modest miracles occurred. Once he alone "suddenly saw five beams of light shining straight into the hall, and then suddenly they were no more to be seen." Another time he and those with him saw "a colored cloud, shining bright and luminous," which "drifted through the air up to the summit [of the mountain] and then after a while melted away." Another time they saw at night two lights, one above a ridge and the other close to a valley, which grew from insignificant proportions to the size of a small house and then faded away.

Even the modern skeptic would scarcely begrudge Ennin such minor miracles, but his biographers were not content with these humble claims. They transformed the light he saw in the hall into a "five-colored nimbus" which eventually settled in glory on his head for all to see. Their writing brushes gave new proportions to the two lights which he saw at night, combining them in the process into one, which, according to them, "filled deep valleys and lighted up distant peaks, the single light illumining the whole of the five terraces." The biographers even add a miracle of their own invention. Lions, although never native to China, were to be expected in the Wu-t'ai region, for Monju himself was usually portrayed as riding on this noble animal of the West. Ennin records seeing carved and painted lions engaged in bearing the Bodhisattva, but his biographers grant him a more dramatic confrontation with a terrifying lion in the flesh. Twice, or even three times according to one text, the beast barred his way as he sought to continue on his rounds of the five holy peaks; but when, undaunted, he again attempted to continue on his way, he found that it had vanished.

THE PERSECUTION

Leaving Mt. Wu-t'ai early in the seventh moon, the four Japanese journeyed the length of the modern Shansi from northeast to southwest, crossed the Yellow River into what is now Shensi Province, and arrived at Ch'ang-an, the modern Sian, on the twentieth day of the eighth moon of 840. A few days later they were settled on government order at the Tzu-sheng-ssu, a monastery of the eastern half of the metropolis. Here, they came under the jurisdiction of the powerful eunuch, Ch'iu Shih-liang, who, among his duties as a high palace functionary and army general, was in charge of the clerics of that half of the city. Ennin now sought out the leading Buddhist scholars of the capital, both Chinese and Indian, and devoted himself to his studies for the next few years. Either because of his concentration on theological matters or else because the novelty of life in China was wearing off, he recorded little of the incidental aspects of his life in the capital, limiting himself for the most part to major religious festivals and hearsay reports of events of political significance.

The even tenor of Ennin's studies, however, was soon to be disturbed and then shattered. The Emperor Wu-tsung had come to the throne early in 840 and had summoned Li Te-yü from Yang-chou to be a Minister of State. Wu-tsung was interested in religion, and as the years went by he became a fanatic devotee of Taoism, at this time Buddhism's chief rival faith in China. According to rumors that Ennin recorded, the Emperor was also an unbalanced person given to irrational acts. Moreover, the civil bureaucracy by the ninth century was losing the attachment it once had to Buddhism and was becoming increasingly hostile to it as a foreign religion and as an antisocial institution which withdrew good men from their normal social functions as fathers of families, tillers of the soil, and servants of the state and kept good land off the tax registers. The hostility of the bureaucracy and the Taoist fanaticism of the Emperor combined at this time to produce the most severe religious persecution in the whole of Chinese history. The Buddhist church, then at a peak of prestige and intellectual vigor in China, was dealt a blow from which it never fully recovered; the weaker foreign religions, such as Nestorian Christianity, which had won a precarious foothold at the capital, were blotted out.

Signs of the coming persecution became obvious early in 842, and in the tenth moon of that year the first edict was issued defrocking certain categories of monks and nuns and returning them to lay life and to the tax registers. Ch'iu Shih-liang did his best to oppose the anti-Buddhist measures

and gave protection to the three Japanese monks and the
eighteen other foreign clerics under his jurisdiction, including one each from Ceylon and Kucha in Central Asia and
several from India and Korea. Unfortunately for the Buddhists, the great eunuch died in the sixth moon of 843. The
next moon Ennin suffered another more personal loss when
Igyō, one of his two disciple monks, died.

   The persecution was greatly intensified in the latter
months of 844 and during the following year. Through
progressive stages all the remaining monks and nuns were
defrocked and the destruction of all the monasteries and
other Buddhist edifices was ordered, if not always executed.
As early as 841 Ennin had started to submit petitions in
which he requested permission to return to his homeland, and
in the third moon of 845 he requested in desperation to be
allowed to return to lay life. The Chinese officials apparently
paid no more attention to this request than to his earlier
ones, but two months later he and the other foreign monks
were all suddenly ordered to be defrocked and deported. As
Ennin rather wryly records in his diary, he had unsuccess-
fully applied more than one hundred times for permission to
return to his homeland, but now, because of the intensification of the persecution, he was suddenly ordered home, and
he comments, "There was both sorrow and joy."

   Ennin's friends among the officials of the capital gave him
what was, under the circumstances, a glorious and daring
send-off. The three Japanese on their trip from Ch'ang-an
to the coast traveled at first in the custody of Chinese officers but later simply under travel orders. They were forced
to go to Yang-chou, but from there they went once again up
the Grand Canal to Ch'u-chou. Failing to gain permission to
settle in that region to await a ship bound for Japan, they
proceeded on foot to the tip of the Shantung Peninsula,
arriving there on the twenty-seventh day of the eighth moon
of 845. There they found their old home, the Mt. Ch'ih
Cloister, destroyed and abandoned but were given lodging and protection by their friends in the Korean community.

In the third moon of 846 Wu-tsung died, and his successor almost immediately relaxed the restrictions on Buddhists, with the result that Ennin was able to recover his treasure of Buddhist texts and pictures which he had been forced to leave behind in the home of a Korean friend in Ch'u-chou. In the tenth moon of that year he was joined by Shōkai, a Japanese monk who had been expressly dispatched from Japan to find Ennin. Early in 847 the group of Japanese started again for the south to catch a Japanese ship reported there. On reaching Ch'u-chou, they discovered that it had sailed, but that a Korean vessel was waiting for them along the Shantung coast. Hastening back north they managed to catch up with this vessel and on the second day of the ninth moon saw the last of the coast of China. Fifteen days later, after threading through the islands of the western and southern littoral of Korea, they reached their starting point in western Japan, from which Ennin had sailed for China more than nine years earlier.

THE CHURCH FATHER

Ennin, accompanied by Shōkai and Ishō, reached Kyōto, the Japanese capital, on the twenty-ninth day of the third moon of 848. There they were greeted by an officer representing the Emperor and were given Imperial gifts, for Ennin was now no longer a wandering monk but a national hero returning in triumph from a hazardous mission to China. His colleagues at the Enryakuji flocked about him "like a cloud," rejoicing and giving praise and marveling at the religious pictures and texts he had brought back with him from China.

Ennin at once started to teach his confreres some of the new religious practices he had learned in China, and the court heaped honors upon him, giving him a patent of clerical rank shortly after his return [7] and in the seventh moon of the year appointing him to be a Court Priest.[8] This was the pattern which continued for the remaining sixteen years of his life, and during this period his biographies constitute little more than a catalogue of the ceremonies and religious practices he introduced, the commentaries he wrote on certain scriptures, the religious edifices he erected, and the honors he received from the court. But unmitigated success was no more interesting in the ninth century than it is today. These last, triumphant years of Ennin's life will hold the attention only of those who wish to know the detailed history of Buddhism in one of its less dramatic phases.

Some of the high points in Ennin's later career, however, are worthy of note. His first year back in Japan he had reproductions made of the two great *mandara* he had obtained in China. These were large paintings which portrayed the Buddhist pantheon and certain theological principles in great detail and in schematic form. In the fifth moon of 849, under Imperial auspices and at government expense, he conducted a great ceremony of baptism in which more than one thousand monks participated. When a new Emperor, Montoku, came to the throne the following year, Ennin was commissioned to inaugurate various ceremonies designed to protect the new ruler and his realm. Finally, in the fourth moon of 854 he received Imperial appointment as the Abbot of the Enryakuji, thus becoming the acknowledged head of the Tendai Sect in Japan. In 856 Ennin administered one of the esoteric forms of baptism to the Emperor and to some of his courtiers, initiating them into the mystic practices of Buddhism which he was attempting to popularize in Japan, and a few months later he did the same for the Crown Prince and other high court dignitaries.

Montoku was succeeded in 858 by Seiwa, who proved as eager as his predecessors to honor Ennin. Not long after his accession to the throne, Seiwa invited Ennin to lecture to him in person on the Buddhist doctrines, and under the venerable monk's guidance the Emperor took the Buddhist vows known as the *Bosatsu-kai*, or the "Rules of the Bodhisattva." Ennin subsequently administered these same vows to the Empress and many courtiers, including a group of 150 at one time. Meanwhile, he continued teaching his many disciples the new rites, ceremonies, and doctrines he had learned in China, writing exegetical and expository works on the scriptures

and ceremonials of Buddhism, and constructing sacred buildings, including a hall to the Bodhisattva Monju, under whose
blessing he had come during his pilgrimage to Mt. Wu-t'ai.
But Ennin was now growing old and tired, and increasingly
he encouraged An'e, his chosen successor as Abbot of the
Enryakuji, to take over his duties. Finally Ennin fell sick in
the tenth moon of 863 and died on the fourteenth day of the
first moon of the following year in the seventy-second year of
his life.

In a country such as Japan, in which posthumous honors
are not felt to be empty vanities, Ennin's career did not end
with his death, and some of his biographies continue without
a break for several years longer. On the sixteenth day of the
second moon, only a month after his death, an Imperial
emissary read a rescript before his grave, elevating him to
the highest ecclesiastic rank, *Hōin-daikashō*, or "Great
Priest, the Seal of the Law." How great an honor this was
can be seen from two facts. This specific rank was created
and the whole system of priestly ranks revised on this occasion, very possibly because of the court's desire to bestow
some special honor on Ennin.[9] Furthermore, neither Saichō,
Ennin's own master and the founder of the Tendai Sect in
Japan, nor Kūkai, who had accompanied Saichō to China in
804 and returned two years later with Shingon, the other
great new sect of the period, received this rank until more
than a month later.[10] Thus, although they had preceded
Ennin to the grave by forty-two and twenty-nine years respectively, they had fallen behind him in attaining this new
honor and even then appear to have achieved it only by
riding in on the tail of his robe.

Saichō may have been similarly beholden to his popular
disciple for the ultimate official honor he was to receive. The
posthumous title of *Daishi*, or "Great Teacher," was first
awarded by the Japanese court on the fourteenth day of the
seventh moon of 866, when Ennin was given the posthumous
name of Jikaku Daishi ("Great Teacher of Compassion and
Understanding") and Saichō that of Dengyō Daishi ("Great
Teacher, Transmitter of the Faith"). Kūkai probably owed

Ennin nothing for the posthumous name of Kōbō Daishi ("Great Teacher, Spreader of the Law") bestowed on him by the court, but he had to wait fifty-five years longer to receive it.

While the government was giving Ennin these posthumous promotions, his successors and disciples at the Enryakuji were continuing his career in another way. One by one they completed the projects he had started or planned before his death, finishing manuscripts he had begun, constructing buildings he had vowed to erect, and performing ceremonies he had intended to perform. The last comment concerning such a posthumous undertaking is recorded in the tenth-century biography of Ennin under the year 916, at which time this work itself was probably at least partially completed. This final biographical entry concerns the carving of a white sandalwood image of the Buddha Amida and the copying of a certain scripture in golden characters, two pious acts Ennin had vowed to perform before his death.

ENNIN IN HISTORY AND IN PERSON

This account of Ennin's life and his many accomplishments gives little concept of him either as a man or as a figure in history. His biographies convey the pious awe of their authors but none of Ennin's personality; and his religious accomplishments as recorded by them, while obviously impressive to his near contemporaries, dwindle into apparent triviality when viewed from the distance of a millennium. Ennin was not the founder of his sect or even the first Abbot of the Enryakuji. Between his death and our own time, more than 240 other monks have held this same post. One does not wonder that in the popular mind Ennin has gradually disappeared among the misty throngs of history, while only Kūkai and Saichō among the Japanese men of religion of his age still stand out as discernible individual figures.

But Ennin probably deserves a better fate than this at the hands of history. Wholly aside from the chance preservation of his diary, which in itself gives him ample claim to lasting fame, his career had far more historical significance than his biographers knew how to describe. Where Saichō and Kūkai innovated, he developed and consolidated, and without his efforts much of what they first taught in Japan would perhaps not have borne the rich fruit it did. It was from Ennin first of all and from a host of other lesser figures that these two great popular heroes of Japanese Buddhism drew the added luster which has kept the light of their fame shining brightly through the ages.

To say this is not to belittle the work of either Kūkai or Saichō. The latter broke with the tradition of the so-called Nara Sects, which had been dominant in Japan during the eighth century and founded his own religious center on Mt. Hiei. Even more remarkable, during a brief stay in China of less than a year he was able to acquire sufficient mastery of the major doctrines and works of the Tendai Sect in all their eclectic vastness and syncretic complications to be able to introduce them with success in Japan. Kūkai similarly broke with the previous tradition of Japanese Buddhism, introduced the esoteric mysteries of the Shingon Sect which he had found enjoying sudden popularity in China, and founded his own religious center amid the forested grandeurs of the summit of Mt. Kōya, some distance south of the capital district.

Ennin as the second major Tendai leader to visit China had a chance in his longer stay on the continent to learn many aspects of the teachings of the sect that Saichō had inevitably overlooked during his brief visit, but Ennin's chief contribution to the sect in Japan was the addition of the whole esoteric aspect of Buddhism. Kūkai had already introduced the esoteric cults to Japan through his Shingon Sect, and Enchin, who followed Ennin to China a few years later, returned with the same mystical practices. This duplication of effort was perhaps the seed for the future rivalry between the disciples of Enchin and the successors of Ennin at the home monastery on Mt. Hiei, but it also serves to indicate the tremendous popularity of the esoteric cults at this time in China, which no doubt is the reason why Ennin chose this aspect of the religion for his primary efforts.

Ennin thus brought back with him little that was strictly new to Japanese Buddhism, but his contribution lay in his successful combination of the Tendai philosophy with the esoteric cults and his vigorous propagation of what he had learned. Kūkai's Shingon was centered in the mountain fast-nesses south of the plains of the capital district, but Ennin brought the esoteric mysteries to Mt. Hiei within sight of the capital, where the court came to know them at first hand and embraced them with immediate enthusiasm. The majestic ceremonies, the rich symbolism, and the glorious artistic ap-purtenances of the esoteric cults appealed at once to the Japanese courtiers, who for long had been accustomed to the elaborate pageantry of secular authority.

The result was not only a triumph for the esoteric prac-tices first brought to Japan by Kūkai but also for the Tendai Sect first introduced by Saichō. The latter had exhausted his energies in breaking away from the Nara Sects and in com-bating their still overweening power. Ennin continued his master's fight and, by broadening the appeal of the Tendai teachings, brought the struggle to a triumphant conclusion, winning unparalleled favor from the court for the Tendai Sect and establishing it as the unquestioned leader among the Buddhist churches of the day.

It was the half-esoteric but wholly triumphant Tendai of Ennin, rather than the originally exoteric sect of Saichō, that was to dominate the religious life of the next few cen-turies. It was the Enryakuji developed by Ennin as much as the original monastery founded by Saichō that was to be-come the great mother church of all later Japanese Bud-dhism and the religious home from which the later sectarian founders were to emerge. Ennin's esoteric mysteries cer-tainly appealed as much to the aristocrats of the time as did the syncretic doctrines introduced by Saichō, and when the great religious awakening of the popular faith sects of the twelfth and thirteenth centuries came, their leaders derived as much from the symbolic acts of faith popularized by

Ennin as from the philosophic doctrines introduced by his predecessor. Thus, Ennin stands out in the history of Japanese Buddhism, not as the romantic figure that Kūkai has become or the intellectually appealing individual that we now see in Saichō or some of the later Buddhist leaders, but still as one of the most significant molders of the religion that has dominated Japan for over a thousand years.

But whatever may be the true proportions of Ennin the historical figure, the exact dimensions of Ennin the man are hard to ascertain. His pious biographers regarded him with the same distant awe they would have shown for one of the Buddhist deities he worshiped. Even his own writings do not tell us all we should like to know about his personality. He was a scrupulously accurate and delightfully detailed diarist, but he was no Boswell determined to make posterity his confidant.

We can, nevertheless, draw some conclusions from the diary, his other works, and his biographies about what type of man he was. While his was not a mind of brilliant originality and creativeness, he must have possessed extraordinary ability. His many writings and his whole career attest to this, but what is truly remarkable is that he achieved all this even though he came from an obscure background in the remote eastern frontiers of Japan. In ninth-century Japan birth meant everything in most walks of life and almost everything even in the clergy, the only hierarchy open to a man of humble origin. Saichō, for instance, was born in the capital region of a family of continental extraction, while Kūkai came from an aristocratic family on the island of Shikoku in western Japan. Ennin, in rising from nowhere to reach the highest honors open to a Japanese commoner, accomplished something that few men in Japanese history have ever achieved.

Character was perhaps as important to Ennin in his rise to clerical supremacy as was intellectual ability, and character he seems to have had in full measure. No one could have shown greater determination than he during his years of adversity in China, and no one could have had more loyal disciples and friends. Ennin made no effort to conceal his human frailties. He was often discouraged, sometimes timid, and not always above a judicious lie, but there is not the slightest indication that his faith and religious devotion ever faltered for an instant or that he once lost his courteous equanimity in the face of his many tribulations.

Ennin's whole life was spent, as far as we know, without a single quarrel. Even when his former traveling companion, Ensai, appropriated for his own purposes twenty-four ounces of gold sent by the Japanese court to support Ennin in his studies in China, the latter let no trace of irritation show in his diary, and this despite the fact that Ensai presumably was already degenerating into the ill-tempered and hypocritical scoundrel Enchin was to encounter some years later in China. Even in success Ennin's saintly character seems not to have changed. As the greatest churchman of his day, he apparently remained as simple in his faith, as fully devoted to his work, and as blameless in his relations with others as he had been as a humble pilgrim and eager traveling scholar.

The picture of Ennin's personality is at best shadowy and incomplete, but there seems to emerge a major figure showing a rare balance between energy, intellect, and character— a man of outstanding ability, as saintly in conduct as he was determined in action, and driven throughout by a strong unswerving faith in his religion. He apparently was not a man of creative imagination who blazed new trails of the intellect, but he was one who through the strength of his own determination and the inspiring example of his character led his fellow men in the less spectacular but perhaps more difficult task of developing the new lands which others had discovered.

III

The Embassy to China

It was a fortunate accident of history that Ennin went to
China as a member of an official Japanese embassy to the
T'ang court. The first third of his diary, in telling his own
story, also constitutes a record of the adventures and vicissitudes of the embassy on the high seas and in China, giving
us our only detailed account of a foreign embassy to China
during this early stage in international relations. Again by
good fortune this particular embassy happened to receive
fuller treatment in the Japanese annals than any other early
mission abroad. The *Shoku Nihon kōki* (*The Later Record
of Japan Continued*), which covers these years of Japanese
history, has many scattered notices about the embassy from
its first appointment to its final termination, and these,
when added to Ennin's detailed account of its activities
abroad, give a remarkably complete picture of what a Japanese embassy to T'ang China was really like.

Today embassies and diplomatic relations in general may
suggest pompous superficiality. For the most part missions
abroad have little to do with a country's inner development
and, instead of shaping international relations, tend to be
merely the surface manifestation of the strains and stresses
arising at the points of more vital contact between nations.
But this was by no means the situation in the Far East in the
ninth century. Embassies were the heart and soul of the
foreign relations of the T'ang Empire and the embodiment
of the whole principle of international relations as conceived
by the Chinese. To the early Japanese they meant even more.
They were their chief contact with the outside world and the
greatest source of knowledge about the continental civiliza-

39

tion which was rapidly changing Japan from a remote barbarian land into an integral part of the civilized world.

INTERNATIONAL RELATIONS IN THE
EARLY FAR EAST

In ancient times the Chinese thought of their country as the unique land of civilization surrounded by the "four barbarians," that is, the lesser breeds inhabiting the lands of the four cardinal points of the compass. Actually this was not an altogether inaccurate picture of the Far East, at least until early T'ang times. The peripheral peoples of their world, the Chinese felt, participated in civilization only in so far as they recognized the political and cultural suzerainty of China and voluntarily established tributary relations with her. The barbarians were supposed to come periodically with their tribute to the Chinese capital, more frequently if they were close and therefore important barbarians, less often if they were remote and thus less significant. In exchange for their tribute and obeisance, they would be given presents and sometimes official investiture by the Chinese Emperor and, returning with these, would bring to their distant and benighted homelands some of the blessings of civilization.

The exchange of tribute in the form of local products for Imperial gifts of silk goods and other Chinese manufactures constituted a type of international barter, which was, in fact, not an inconsequential part of the total trade of the Far East at a time when international commerce had not yet assumed great proportions. Far more important than the economic aspects of the tributary embassies, however, was their political significance. Tributary relations were the only form of international contact officially recognized by the Chinese. A land which was not tributary to China was, with some justification, assumed to be either so remote and insignificant as to be beyond the pale of civilization or else in a virtual state of rebellion against China, whether or not it was engaged in actual hostilities. Thus, tributary em-

bassies to China were the symbol of the only international
order of the day in the Far East and also in some cases almost the sum total of China's contacts with certain of its
more distant neighbors. Under later dynasties the tributary
system was to become more fully and rigidly schematized at
the same time that it was becoming less important economi-
cally and less realistic politically. In T'ang times, however,
it was already in spirit and in general practice the system
which, according to official theory, embodied China's relations with the outside world until the middle of the nineteenth century.

The Japanese, like most of the peripheral nations of T'ang
times, readily fitted into this tributary relationship with
China. From time to time they sent embassies to the T'ang
court, bearing tribute to the Chinese Emperor and receiving
in return his gifts and investiture. Actually the Japanese
had had fitful relations with the Chinese for some time before the advent of the T'ang dynasty. The Japanese histories contain a few vague references to the exchange of
early envoys, and the dynastic histories of China record with
considerably greater exactitude the occasional coming of
embassies from Japan.

The earliest Japanese mission mentioned in the Chinese
records came to China in 57 A.D. On this occasion the Emperor of the Later Han dynasty granted the emissary from
the land of Nu in Japan a seal of investiture for his master.[1]
Oddly enough, a golden seal inscribed "King of Nu of Japan,
[Vassal of] Han," was accidentally unearthed in 1784 by a
peasant redigging an irrigation ditch in the old capital district of Northern Kyūshū in West Japan, which was the
traditional contact point with the continent. We cannot be
sure that this was the same seal mentioned in the Chinese
sources, nor do we know who the "King of Nu" actually was.
In 57 A.D. Japan was not a unified kingdom, and the Chinese
sources describe it as being divided up into a number of
small tribal units, each under the rule of a hereditary high
priest or high priestess. The "King of Nu" was presumably
one of these many sacerdotal chieftains, and there is no way

of knowing whether or not he was an ancestor or relative of the hereditary line of chieftains that by the fifth or sixth century had evolved into the Japanese Imperial family.

The next Japanese embassy, which according to the Chinese histories came to the Later Han in 107, presented 160 slaves. In the first half of the third century several more embassies are reported to have reached the northern dynasty of Wei in a China that was then divided, and in the fifth century still more came to Nanking, the capital of the southern dynasties of the period. It is not known which if any of these embassies represented the group that was gradually establishing itself as the central government of Japan, nor is it certain that these were all really official embassies. Many so-called embassies to China were actually nothing more than groups of private traders seeking official recognition and the better trading opportunities that were afforded the recognized representatives of some foreign ruler. This probably was the case in 166 A.D. when some merchants, presumably from western Asia, turned up on the southern borders of China and posed as an embassy from Marcus Aurelius of Rome. The credentials of some of the early embassies from Japan may have been equally bogus.

JAPANESE EMBASSIES TO THE SUI AND T'ANG

After a lapse of more than a century, Japanese embassies to China were suddenly renewed in the early seventh century, but now on a more permanent basis, on a much larger scale, and with far more significant results than ever before. In part this was because China, after close to four centuries of almost uninterrupted political division and disruption, was once again a powerful, unified empire. Even more important was the fact that Japan itself was by now at least a loosely unified kingdom and already in possession of enough of the continental culture, including the Chinese system of writing, to be able to learn from China more rapidly than in earlier times. In fact, after centuries of slow and largely unconscious borrowing from the continent, the Japanese were at last beginning to be consciously aware of the benefits to be derived from a greater knowledge and mastery of both the physical and the intellectual aspects of Chinese civilization.

A few decades earlier, in 552, the small but rapidly rising court of the Japanese ruler had had the problem of cultural borrowing from the continent brought to its attention when a gift of Buddhist images, scriptures, and other holy articles from the Korean kingdom of Paekche occasioned a dispute among the aristocratic court families over the desirability of accepting these symbols of a foreign religion. A brief civil war in 587 finally decided the issue in favor of the Soga family, which had championed the acceptance of Buddhism, and the still small and weak central government of Japan made its first hesitant steps toward what eventually became a wholesale and enthusiastic adoption not only of Buddhism but also of the political institutions of the Chinese and whatever else the Japanese were able to borrow from the superior continental civilization.

The first great champion of the foreign religion and Chinese political institutions was Prince Shōtoku, who dominated his times as Crown Prince for his aunt, the Empress Suiko, though his early death in 622 robbed him of the chance to rule in his own name. Two of Prince Shōtoku's greatest achievements were the founding of Buddhist monasteries and the issuing in 604 of a so-called "Constitution in Seventeen Articles." This in reality was a series of moral injunctions and political admonitions embodying Confucian principles for the most part but also indicating the author's devotion to Buddhism. Another and by no means the least of the Prince's achievements was the dispatching of embassies to China to learn more about the land which he and his associates had chosen as the model for the Japan they planned to build.

In 607 Prince Shōtoku sent Ono no Imoko at the head of an embassy to the short-lived Sui dynasty, which had reunited China a few decades earlier. The message which the Japanese envoy bore to the Chinese Emperor was addressed

from "the Son of Heaven in the land where the sun rises to
the Son of Heaven in the land where the sun sets." [2] This
brash claim of equality with the Chinese Emperor and the
insulting suggestion of superiority in geographic location
may have been due to the Prince's ignorance of Chinese
theories of international relations, but most Japanese historians have seen in it his consciousness of the national
dignity of Japan. Certainly the islanders of Japan, like
those of England and the other former barbarians of North
Europe, developed a national consciousness far earlier than
most of the other peoples of the world, perhaps as compensa-
tion for the obvious and embarrassing fact that their countries were far younger and at first far weaker than the lands
from which they had derived almost the whole of their higher
civilization. But there were to be few signs of such nascent
national consciousness in Japan until some six centuries after
Prince Shōtoku's death. His act of national self-assertion, if
such it was, left little trace on the course of Sino-Japanese
relations during the next three centuries, and the Japanese
soon accepted their tributary status without cavil.

The Chinese, in any case, would have tolerated nothing
less. As the *Sui History* records, the Emperor "was displeased" with the wording of the Japanese message and informed his officials that "the letter from the barbarians was
discourteous." Perhaps the written reply from the Chinese
court was couched in such terms that Ono no Imoko felt it
expedient not to show it to his masters in Japan, and this
may have been the story behind his surprising report to the
Japanese court that Koreans had robbed him of the Chinese
Emperor's reply on his way home.[3]

However indignant the Sui Emperor may have been over
the Japanese *faux pas*, he seems to have been anxious to
bring Japan within his tributary system, for he paid the
Japanese the compliment of a return embassy in 608. The
Japanese ruler, as reported in the Chinese records, rendered
full honors to the Sui envoy, speaking of the Japanese as
"barbarians" and "an uncivilized people" and begging for
information about "the great civilized country of Sui."

When the Chinese ambassador departed, Ono no Imoko was again dispatched to accompany him to China and to take tribute a second time to the Sui court. The message from the Japanese this time, as recorded in the Japanese histories,[4] began, "The Emperor of the East pays his respects to the Emperor of the West," which was not much better from the Chinese point of view than the earlier message, but the diplomatic Ono no Imoko may have seen fit to lose this letter too, for the *Sui History* makes no mention of it.

A few years later, in 614, still another embassy was sent to the Sui court. The Sui, however, collapsed soon thereafter and in 618 were superseded by the T'ang. The first Japanese embassy to the new dynasty was dispatched in 630 and arrived at the Chinese court the next year.[5] A Chinese envoy sent in return to Japan in 632 got into a dispute with the Japanese court and "came home disgruntled, without having conveyed the message from his Sovereign." [6] In 653 two separate Japanese envoys were dispatched to China, each accompanied by more than 120 Buddhist monks and other students and attendants, but one of the two expeditions was lost on the high seas. A third embassy to the T'ang reached China in 654, and a fourth went in 659, but this time one of the ships was blown far to the south, where its luckless occupants were slaughtered almost to a man by savages. The other more fortunate members of the embassy reached China safely but were detained there by the Chinese until 661 so that the Chinese plans for an attack on the Korean kingdom of Paekche in 660 should not leak out prematurely.

A fifth embassy left Japan in 665, perhaps to accompany a Chinese envoy back to his homeland; and a sixth, dispatched in 669, is probably the embassy that brought with it some bearded Ainu bowmen of whom the Chinese records speak with wonder. The chief envoy of the next embassy to the T'ang, which went to China in 702, was Awada no Mabito, who so impressed the Chinese that they took the trouble to record in their official histories that he "was a scholar and adept at composition, and his personal deportment was refined."

Still another embassy, 557 strong, went to China in 717, accompanied by the scholar Kibi no Makibi and the monk Gembō, both of whom remained behind in China to study. They finally returned to Japan in 734 on one of the ships of the following embassy, which had gone to China in 733. Two of the three other vessels of this embassy were wrecked on the return voyage. Back in Japan Kibi no Makibi and Gembō became key figures in the transmission of the higher secular and religious learning of China, which they had acquired during their long stay there.

The redoubtable Kibi no Makibi again went to China with the next embassy, which left in 752 and returned two years later. This embassy brought back the great Chinese Buddhist leader Chien-chen, who is known as Ganjin to the Japanese. This venerable monk, who at the time was sixty-seven years old and was blind, had failed in five previous attempts to reach his chosen missionary field of Japan, but this time he succeeded and became the founder of the Ritsu or Rules Sect there. A student, Abe no Nakamaro, who had originally gone to China with the embassy of 717, also attempted to go back to Japan with the mission returning in 754, but his ship was blown far to the south. His friend, the great Chinese poet Li Po, thinking him dead, dedicated a poem to him, but Nakamaro survived and managed to make his way back to China, where he made his home for the remainder of his life, achieving high court office and eventually becoming Governor of Annam, the northern part of the modern state of Vietnam.

Some of the members of the next embassy, which left for China in 777, were also lost at sea on the return voyage the succeeding year, and the following embassy too was wrecked in its first attempt to reach China in 803, although it succeeded in crossing over to the continent the next year. It is chiefly remembered as the embassy on which Saichō and Kūkai went to China.

The next embassy, which finally reached China in 838,[7] was the one to which Ennin was appointed. It is even more memorable as the last to go to the T'ang and for that matter

the last mission to be dispatched abroad by the Imperial
court of Japan until the nineteenth century. When another
embassy was proposed in 894 and the famous scholar and
statesman Sugawara no Michizane was appointed as Ambassador, the latter raised doubts as to the value of sending
a mission to China in view of the declining fortunes of the
T'ang and the dangers of the voyage, and the whole venture
was abandoned. The T'ang dynasty by that time was indeed
in prolonged death throes. But there was a more basic reason
why the Japanese decided to abandon this embassy and
failed to restore official relations with China when a new
dynasty had established itself. Japan too was changing. By
the late ninth century the Japanese were engaged in modify-
ing and adapting what they had learned from China to fit
their own needs. The higher civilization of China, which had
been so enthusiastically borrowed over the past three centuries, was being transformed into something distinctly
Japanese. The work of the time was adaptation and assimila-
tion, not the borrowing of new institutions and learning, and
for the Japanese the embassies had lost their chief *raison
d'être*.

THE MEMBERS OF THE EMBASSY

The Japanese embassies to the Sui and T'ang varied
greatly in their fortunes, but the composition and official
procedures of the later embassies at least were quite uniform.
We know relatively little about the organization of the earlier
embassies, except the names of their top two or three officers
and the fact that some embassies sailed on one and others
on two ships. A great deal more is known about the composition of the last six embassies, beginning with the one of 717.
These all had four vessels and also four categories of top
officers, which corresponded to the usual four categories of
officers in charge of most of the many branches of the central
and provincial governments. The embassy Ennin accompanied seems to have been quite typical of these later embassies both in its organization and procedures and, since it

is by far the best known, it affords an excellent example of this interesting and significant aspect of Far Eastern history.

Ennin's embassy first came into being on the nineteenth day of the first moon of 834, with the appointment of the top four categories of officers, an Ambassador (*Taishi*), a Vice-Ambassador (*Fukushi*), four Administrative Officers (*Hangan*), presumably one for each of the four ships, and six Secretaries (*Rokuji*). The choice of Fujiwara no Tsunetsugu as Ambassador was significant for several reasons. He was a member of the Fujiwara, that vast noble clan which was in the process of winning complete domination over the Imperial court. In addition, Tsunetsugu was the seventh son of Fujiwara no Kadonomaro, who had led the previous embassy to China in 804. And finally, Tsunetsugu was thought to be the type of man to impress the Chinese favorably, for he was a scholar in the field of Chinese literature and an accomplished calligrapher.[8] The Vice-Ambassador, Ono no Takamura, was similarly a man of literary distinction, for he was an outstanding poet and well versed in Chinese studies. Moreover, for a Japanese he must have been a veritable giant: his biographers claim that he was six feet two inches tall.[9]

Appointments to the subordinate posts of the embassy seem to have been made piecemeal over the next two years, since those for which the dates are known were all made many months after the choice of the Ambassador and his chief associates. There were also subsequent appointments to some of the top posts, perhaps as replacements for men who had dropped out. In all, the *Shoku Nihon kōki* names thirty-nine officers and learned men appointed to the embassy, though not all of them actually reached China; and Ennin in his diary mentions by name eighteen of these men and thirty-two others in addition, although most of the latter were merely subordinate members of the embassy.

There were several other categories and subcategories of officers besides the top four. Three men were appointed at one time or another as Acting Administrative Officers (*Jun-*

hangan). One of these, Nagamine no Takana, had become a full Administrative Officer within a few months after his appointment;[10] a second, Yoshimine no Nagamatsu, was probably a spot replacement for an Administrative Officer who died in China; but a third, Fujiwara no Sadatoshi, who was already an Acting Administrative Officer in 835, long before the embassy sailed for China, still had the same title when he returned from the continent in 839. We also have the names of three Acting Secretaries (*Jun-rokuji*), who possibly were replacements for some of the original six Secretaries.

These higher officers of the embassy appear to have been relatively young men. The Ambassador was thirty-nine when appointed, the Vice-Ambassador thirty-three, the Administrative Officer Sugawara no Yoshinushi thirty-two in 834, the Acting Administrative Officer Fujiwara no Sadatoshi twenty-eight in that year, and the Acting Administrative Officer Yoshimine no Nagamatsu only twenty-one, although he may not have been appointed to this post until five years later. Only one of the higher officials of the embassy whose ages we know was of comparable age to Ennin, and this was the Administrative Officer Nagamine no Takana, who was forty-two, only one year younger than Ennin, when he was appointed to the embassy in 835.[11]

The officers who ranked next to the Secretaries and Acting Secretaries were Ship's Masters (*Chijōsenji*). The literal meaning of the title, "Ship's Loading Master," suggests that they may have been officers in charge of the cargo and tribute articles. This supposition is strengthened by the fact that one of the six Ship's Masters whose names we have is described by Ennin while in China as the Supervisor of the National Tribute Articles (*Kan-kokushin*).[12] Another point of interest about these Ship's Masters is that three of them were said to be men of continental origin and therefore presumably had some special knowledge of continental ways. Two claimed descent from immigrants from the southeastern Korean kingdom of Paekche, which had disappeared in the seventh century, the other from an Emperor of the Later

Han dynasty of China. Of only one other member of the embassy is it recorded that he was of continental origin, and this was a Secretary who claimed descent from immigrants from the North Korean kingdom of Koguryŏ, which had disappeared at the same time as Paekche.[13] The Ship's Masters apparently had neither navigational nor administrative control of the vessels of the embassy. Ennin happens to mention a Ship Captain (*Senshi*) and an Acting Ship Captain,[14] who probably were the actual skippers of two of the vessels. In addition each ship also had a Ship's Commander (*Sendō*), who was normally the highest ranking member of the embassy on board and had the over-all command of the vessel and its personnel.

Among the other members of the embassy were Scribes (*Shishō* or *Shi*), three of whom are named in our texts, and Interpreters (*Osa*), of whom four are named, including one who was the former Buddhist monk Erei, returned to secular rank and position under his original name of Ki no Harunushi.[15] From Ennin's diary we see that another category of Interpreters, never mentioned in the Japanese records, played a much larger role abroad than did the Japanese linguists. These were three Korean Interpreters, or rather Silla Interpreters (*Shiragi Osa*), for the South Korean state of Silla had unified the whole of the Korean Peninsula almost two centuries earlier. These Koreans, one of whom was a monk and each of whom accompanied one of the three ships that finally reached China, obviously had the requisite knowledge of routes and contacts in China as well as a command of the necessary languages, and they, rather than the Japanese Interpreters, seem to have been used for most embassy negotiations while abroad.

Ennin's diary also gives some idea of the various types of petty officers and subordinate personnel on the embassy. He mentions an Officer at Large (*Zasshi*), a Boatswain (*Kako no Chō*), and a Military Attaché (*Sangun*),[16] the latter perhaps being in charge of part of the military complement of the mission. He also mentions several personal attendants, who seem to have varied in status in accordance with the rank of the men they served. Awada no Ietsugu, who was the Ambassador's attendant, appears to have been a painter and had the court post of Provisional Professor (*Gon no Hakase*) of the government University (*Daigaku*).[17] On the other hand, an attendant of a Scribe and three men who were attendants of the Administrative Officer Nagamine no Takana, were of such lowly status as to have had no surnames. The same was true of a diviner on board one of the vessels.[18]

The bulk of the men on board the ships of the embassy apparently fell into the categories of archers, sailors, artisans, and porters. Ennin at one point writes of more than fifty artisans, porters, and archers of the first ship, another time of sixty archers and sailors from the same ship, and still again of thirty-six master carpenters, general carpenters, ship's carpenters, and founders from the first and fourth ships.[19] From these figures it would seem that the first ship alone had a complement of at least ninety men belonging to these various categories and may have had considerably more, for none of Ennin's enumerations was necessarily a complete listing. The rather aristocratic Japanese surnames of the five archers Ennin mentions by name and the post of one of these men in the Imperial Body Guards of the Left (*Sakon'e*) indicate that these men had some claim to gentle birth. The names of the three sailors recorded by Ennin are much less aristocratic.[20]

In many ways the most important members of the embassy were the learned men, both clerics and laymen, who were going to China for the study of some special field of knowledge or the arts. Although they were not in the normal chain of command, the more important among them were equal in rank and status to the higher officers of the embassy, except for the Ambassador himself. From the Japanese histories and Ennin's diary, we know the names of eight Buddhist clerics who were appointed to the embassy as Scholar or Student Monks of one or the other of the several sects then known in Japan, and also the names of four others who were disciples of these monks. Among the lay scholars and artists who happened to be mentioned by name were a Student of History

(*Kiden-ryūgaku-shō*), a Physician (*Ishi*), a Scholar and a Student of the Calendar (*Koyomi-shōyaku* and *Koyomi-ryūgaku-shō*), a Student of Astronomy (*Temmon-ryūgaku-shō*), a Master of Astrology (*Onyō-shi*), a man called both a Director of Music (*Onjō-chō*) and a Master of the Reed Organ (*Shōshi*), and a relative of the latter who had the two titles of Master of Painting (*Gashi*) and Master of Court Music and of the Reed Organ (*Gagaku-tōshō-shi*). No doubt there were many other artists, musicians, and scholars with the embassy whose names have not been preserved. Ennin, for example, once mentions three Japanese painters without giving their names.[21]

Several of the officers of the embassy also doubled as scholars and students of the arts. The Ambassador and Vice-Ambassador were, of course, both men of letters, and a certain Tomo no Sugao, who first appears in Ennin's diary simply with the title of Scholar (*Shōyaku-shō*) and happened to be an expert chess player, ended up in command of one of the returning vessels. As has already been mentioned, the Ambassador's attendant, Awada no Ietsugu, was a painter as well as a scholar. One of the Ship's Masters was also versed in a Chinese text referred to as the *Classic of Medicine* (*I-ching*) and eventually became a court physician.[22] And the member of the embassy who was to achieve the greatest fame as a musician was the Acting Administrative Officer, Fujiwara no Sadatoshi, who came of a long line of lute (*biwa*) players and himself became a court musician. According to his biography, while in China Sadatoshi paid a famous teacher of the lute, Liu Erh-lang, the truly inordinate sum of two hundred ounces of gold for lessons on the instrument and so impressed his teacher with his skill that the latter not only gave him dozens of scrolls of music and two fine lutes but also his daughter in marriage. This last was a bonus indeed, for Sadatoshi's bride was a skilled musician herself and taught him several more pieces.[23]

Between officers, learned men, archers, sailors, and the other common folk, the embassy was unquestionably a very large expedition. Actually it is said to have set out in 836

with 651 men on board the four ships, and we know that the
third ship alone at the time it was lost was still carrying 140
men after some had been drowned.[24] Some time after the return of the embassy to Japan, 391 men who had made the trip
to China were put on a special honors list.[25] Some of these
men may have been included posthumously, but most of them
presumably had made the round trip safely. However, only
the men of the first and fourth ships and a fraction of the
men of the second ever got back to Japan. According to news
Ennin received in China, only thirty-odd men from the second ship returned home safely.[26] This would suggest that
some of the survivors and perhaps some replacements for
the men of the third ship had been added to the regular
complements of the other three vessels, and that these in
their successful crossing to China in 838 may have each carried about 180 men.

PREPARATIONS

The selection of personnel for the embassy was by no
means the hardest part of organizing it. There was also the
problem of equipment. For one thing the four ships had to
be constructed for the expedition, and for this purpose a
chief officer and a vice-officer were appointed Ship Construction Officers (*Zōhakushi*) within a fortnight of the
selection of the Ambassador. Later in the year two other
men, for unspecified reasons, were substituted for the original two officials, and the new vice-officer was designated the
master carpenter of the project.[27]

At the same time that the Ship Construction Officers were
appointed, two other dignitaries were designated as Costume
Officers (*Shōzokushi*), whose duty it was to provide suitable
apparel for the members of the embassy. Where and how
they did their work we do not know, but we do learn that
about a year later Dazaifu, the administrative headquarters
in North Kyūshū, was ordered to provide one hundred bro-
cade-decorated suits of armor, one hundred helmets, and four
hundred pairs of pantaloons for the use of the embassy.

Meanwhile other officials and government bureaus were no doubt busy preparing the tribute articles and other goods to be taken to China, but all we know about this aspect of the preparations is that the Empress' Household Department (*Kōgōgūshiki*) was temporarily used for the making of silk cloth for the embassy.[28]

Another aspect of the preparations, of which we hear a good deal more, was the giving of promotions of rank and office to the various higher members of the embassy. Some promotions, particularly those announced early in the first moon as part of the regular New Year's honors list, may have been purely routine, but most of them appear to have been special rewards to compensate for the dangerous assignment the men had received.

The ranking system of the Japanese court was highly complex. There were nine major ranks, but each of these was subdivided into Senior and Junior Ranks, and these, except for the highest, were further subdivided into Upper and Lower Grades. The Ambassador, for example, at the time of his appointment held the Junior Fourth Rank Upper Grade, and the Vice-Ambassador the Junior Fifth Rank Lower Grade. On the seventh day of the first moon of 835 the latter was raised one grade to the Junior Fifth Rank Upper Grade and exactly a year later to the Senior Fifth Rank Lower Grade, while the Ambassador was promoted at the same time to the Senior Fourth Rank Lower Grade. Similar promotions of one grade at a time are recorded for various other officers of the embassy, and at one point eight priests of the embassy were raised one clerical rank.[29]

In addition to higher court ranks, the officers of the embassy were also given promotions in the government posts they held concurrently with their embassy assignments. In most cases these promotions probably meant increases in salary rather than new duties. The Ambassador, for instance, at the time of his appointment was a Counsellor (*Sangi*) of the Council of State, the Controller of the Right (*Udaiben*), one of the two chief liaison officers of the Council of State, and also the acting Governor (*Kami*) of Sagami, a province

in East Japan. On the thirteenth day of the fifth moon of
834 this last post was changed to Provisional Governor of
the province of Bitchū in the Inland Sea region and less
than two months later to Provisional Governor of Ōmi, not
far from the capital. These were both promotions, because in
each case the new province was closer to the capital than the
one before, and in the last case it was a richer province as
well. Subsequently, the Ambassador was also shifted from
Controller of the Right to Controller of the Left (*Sadaiben*),
which again was a promotion, because the left takes pre-
cedence over the right in the Far East. After his first unsuccessful attempt to reach China, he was given a further
promotion to the post of Provisional Governor General
(*Sochi*) of Dazaifu.[30]

Similar promotions of concurrent posts are recorded for
many of the other officers of the embassy, and in some cases
men without previous court rank or office were given appointments commensurate with the positions they held with
the embassy. Thus, the members of the embassy between the
ranks of Scribe and attendant were all given patents of court
rank at one point, and the monk Erei, on the day that he was
made an Interpreter of the embassy, was at the same time
given the Senior Sixth Rank Upper Grade and appointed
concurrently to be the Provisional Magistrate (*Jō*) of
Tajima, the third ranking office in that province.[31]

In addition to their regular promotions, the Ambassador
and Vice-Ambassador were also granted still higher but
purely temporary ranks in order to give them greater prestige while in China. Fujiwara no Tsunetsugu was raised to
the dizzy height of the Senior Second Rank and Ono no
Takamura to the Senior Fourth Rank Upper Grade. The
temporary nature of these honors was emphasized by the
fact that they were presented orally. The two men also were
given special honors in another way. The Ambassador's previously rankless mother was given the Junior Fifth Rank
Lower Grade "in accordance with old precedent," and the
equally rankless family god of the Ono family was granted
the same rank at the Vice-Ambassador's request.[32]

There were still other ways by which the court bestowed favors on some of the members of the embassy. Several were granted more aristocratic names, by no means an unimportant matter in highly aristocratic Japan, and a few were given permission to move their official family residences, usually to the capital. The change of family name was complicated by the fact that each aristocratic family at this time had not only its specific surname but also a *kabane*, which was a hereditary rank originally indicative of functional status. Thus, the Ambassador's full name was Fujiwara no Ason Tsunetsugu. Ason, which means "Courtier," was the *kabane* of the whole Fujiwara family and of many other noble families as well.

We have records of the change of *kabane* or of *kabane* and surname for eleven members of the embassy and records of a shift of residence for three of these same men and also for the embassy Physician. Significantly, all four of the men who are said to have been of foreign origin, three of the Ship's Masters and one of the Secretaries, were among those who changed their family names in one way or another. Since two of the other seven were Scribes, two musicians, one the Master of Astrology, one an Acting Secretary, and the last an Interpreter—in other words, men holding positions demanding a good knowledge of the Chinese language or of a Chinese art or science—it is possible that they were all of continental origin and therefore may have possessed less aristocratic surnames and *kabane* than those of their purely Japanese colleagues.[33] An interesting example of a double promotion in name is afforded by the Secretary of Korean descent. At the time of his appointment to the embassy his full name was Matsukawa no Miyatsuko Sadatsugu, Matsukawa having been his surname, Miyatsuko his *kabane*, and Sadatsugu his personal name. A few months later the surname and *kabane* were changed to Takamine no Sukune, and still later, but before the embassy set sail, he had another promotion in *kabane*, becoming finally Takamine no Ason Sadatsugu.[34]

Special rewards and honors were not limited to members of the embassy. Consideration also had to be given to the vari-

ous Shintō deities who were to aid and protect the embassy in
its hazardous mission. The first god to be mentioned in connection with the embassy, however, was rewarded for services
already rendered rather than for hoped-for protection. This
was Yamizo-kogane-no-kami ("The Gold God of Yamizo")
of the far northern province of Mutsu, who early in 836 was
granted two households in fief for having answered the
prayers of the local officials by granting a greatly increased
production of gold with which to defray the costs of the
embassy.[35]

A few days later a general holiday was called at the court,
and offerings were made to the gods of heaven and earth on
behalf of the embassy. A little later the envoys themselves
made offerings at the great Kamo Shrine in the capital, and
subsequently offerings were again made to the famous deities
of the whole land on behalf of the embassy. Finally, at the
end of a rescript announcing a routine series of promotions
in court rank for several major deities, issued only a few days
before the departure of the mission, a special prayer was appended to the request for protection of the Imperial line
which usually concluded such a document. This special
prayer read, "And further, deign to look with kindness and
pity upon the envoy to China, the Counsellor of the Senior
Fourth Rank Lower Grade, Fujiwara no Ason Tsunetsugu,
that he may be without disaster of wind or wave on his way,
and grant that he return safe and sound." [36]

As the date for departure drew near, there was a flurry of
final court ceremonies. On the ninth day of the second moon
of 836 the more important members of the embassy were
given an Imperial audience in the main hall of the palace,
and, after a court dignitary had read an Imperial edict to
them, they were all presented with Imperial gifts. The
Ambassador received one hundred bolts of figured silk and
twenty lengths of a linen-like cloth, and the Vice-Ambassador, the Administrative Officers and Acting Administrative
Officers, the Secretaries, the Ship's Masters, the Interpreters,
and finally the Scholar Monks, were given progressively
smaller amounts of the same gifts, the priests receiving only

ten bolts of silk apiece and none of the other cloth.[37] The
next court audience for the envoys, held on the ninth day of
the fourth moon of 836, was, in accordance with precedent,
not graced by the Emperor's presence, but the members of
the Council of State, from the Ministers of State (*Daijin*)
down to the Counsellors, were all there.

Then came a farewell banquet given by the Emperor himself on the twenty-third day of the same moon. A typically
Far Eastern feature of this event was the compulsory composition of poems on the somewhat obvious subject of "a farewell banquet for the envoys to China." The participants in
the mass exercise in poetry composition were those of the
Fifth Rank or higher, which was the dividing line between
officially recognized courtiers and lesser functionaries. The
Emperor, too, composed a poem, which he gave to the Ambassador, who placed it in the bosom of his robes and withdrew to his place executing a few ceremonial dance steps.

A more remarkable feature of the banquet, which is described in detail by the court chroniclers, was the Ambassador's toast to the Emperor, performed in the usual Far
Eastern manner by the exchange of wine cups. This was a
great honor for Tsunetsugu, requiring the Emperor's express permission, which was granted only because of his
ambassadorial status. After the exchange of cups, done
through the intermediary of servants, Tsunetsugu knelt to
drink his cup and then withdrew to his seat, performing the
usual ceremonial dance steps. Again, Imperial gifts were
granted to the two chief envoys, an outfit of clothing for
each and in addition two white silk mantles and two hundred
ounces of gold dust for the Ambassador and two red silk
mantles and a hundred ounces of gold dust for the Vice-
Ambassador. Apparently the evening was a complete success,
for all were reported to have left the banquet "profoundly
drunk."

Five days after the banquet the two chief envoys were
jointly granted "the sword of authority" (*settō*), which, according to the Imperial proclamation accompanying it, gave
them the authority to handle any murder or lesser offense

committed by their subordinates. On this occasion the two
men were again given Imperial gifts of clothing. The final
act of ceremonial preparation for the embassy occurred on
the tenth day of the fifth moon of 836, when patents of new
ranks for eight members of former embassies who had died
abroad were entrusted to the envoys with the expressed hope
that these would comfort the spirits of the dead heroes and
probably with the unexpressed hope that the latter would
watch safely over their successors in the perilous mission to
China. Among the eight so honored were the student, Abe no
Nakamaro, who received the Junior Second Rank, and Fujiwara no Kiyokawa, the Ambassador whom Nakamaro had
accompanied on his ill-fated attempt to return to Japan in
754, who was raised to the Junior First Rank.

THE FIRST ATTEMPT TO REACH CHINA

The envoys were now ready to leave, and two days later,
on the twelfth day of the fifth moon of 836, a representative
of the Emperor bade them farewell at the port of Naniwa at
the head of the Inland Sea, presenting them with an Imperial
rescript of consolation and gifts of wine and food. The next
day another official gave them the farewell message of the
Council of State, reminding the two chief envoys of the full
authority they held over their subordinates. The same day
the envoys boarded their ships, the Ambassador going on the
first vessel and the Vice-Ambassador on the second, and the
next day the ships cast off on the relatively safe voyage down
the Inland Sea to North Kyūshū.

Four days later a violent storm hit Kyōto, and the court,
apprehensive about the safety of the embassy, sent a messenger of inquiry to the ships, which were then harbored in
the vicinity of the modern port of Kōbe, across the bay from
Naniwa. The first messenger failed to get through because of
floods, but a second succeeded, apparently finding the ships
undamaged. A few days later special offerings were made by
the court to the tumuli of four former rulers associated with
overseas expeditions, with a humbly worded request that

these most awesome Imperial ancestors look with kindness
and pity on the envoys and bring them safely home again.
The four were the Emperors Kōnin and Kammu, who had
dispatched the two preceding embassies, the Emperor Tenchi,
under whom two embassies had been sent to China in the
seventh century, and the Empress Jingō, who reputedly had
led an expedition of conquest to Korea in the early part of
the third century.

Still not content with these divine measures, the court took
a more mundane step to insure the safety of the embassy by
dispatching a minor official named Ki no Mitsu as envoy to
the Korean state of Silla with a request that, if the Japanese
should be blown off course to the coasts of Silla, the Koreans
should aid them and not detain them.[38] The seventh century
embassies to China had usually skirted the Korean coast on
the way to China, staying in sight of land most of the way,
but since the unification of Korea by the hostile kingdom of
Silla, the Japanese had been avoiding the Korean coast by
attempting the more hazardous crossing directly westward
from North Kyūshū to China. But even then there was always
a good chance that the ships would be blown to Korea, and
the mission to Silla, therefore, was a reasonable precaution.
Naturally the Japanese note from the Council of State to the
Korean government diplomatically ignored the long-stand-
ing enmity between the two countries and opened with the
bland statement, "Though our old friendship remains un-
changed, we now renew our neighborly amity."

The great concern of the court over the safety of the
embassy was by no means unjustified. The ships and navigational skills of the Far Easterners of the ninth century were
perhaps adequate for short coastal hops in sight of land but
scarcely for crossing the five hundred miles of open sea between Japan and China. The compass was not to come into
use in these waters for perhaps another three centuries; the
ponderous junks of the time could only sail down wind; and
worst of all, the Japanese did not seem to have the basic
meteorological knowledge needed for navigation in their part
of the world. This time, as on several previous embassies, the

departure of the envoys from Kyūshū was not made early enough to avoid the dread season of typhoons, which usually lasts in this region from mid-August to October.

It was not until the second day of the seventh moon, which fell on August 17, 836, according to our calendar, that the four ships finally set sail from North Kyūshū for China. On the very day word of their departure reached the court from Dazaifu, a second and obviously faster messenger also arrived with a report that the first and fourth ships had been blown back to northwestern Kyūshū. A few days later a message arrived by horse relay from Dazaifu that the second ship too had floated back to the northwestern tip of Kyūshū. Then came the still less pleasant news that sixteen men from the third ship, riding on "planks bound together as a raft," had floated ashore on the island of Tsushima in the straits between Japan and Korea. Subsequently nine more men were reported to have floated ashore in northwestern Kyūshū on another raft, and finally word was received that the wreck of the ship itself had floated ashore in Tsushima with only three men still on board.[39]

Among the twenty eight survivors from the third ship was the Shingon Scholar Monk Shinzai, who in a report to the throne gave the details of the disaster. During the storm the rudder had snapped, waves washed over the vessel, and some of the men were drowned. Then the ship drifted helplessly with the currents. Finally the Administrative Officer, Tajihi no Fumio, who was in charge as Ship's Commander, decided that, since the 140 men still on board would all die of thirst if they remained with the crippled vessel, they should break it up to make rafts, and this they did, though most of the rafts were never heard of again. It is not surprising that Shinzai, after this inauspicious start, decided to drop out of the embassy.

The news of the failure of the attempted crossing gave rise to a rapid exchange of messages between Kyōto and North Kyūshū. On reaching land, the Ambassador had sent two letters in quick succession to the court. The Emperor immediately replied, sending him words of consolation and informing him that since the ships "are no longer whole and must be refitted, you should wait until they are repaired before crossing the sea." At the same time a notice was sent to the Vice-Governor (*Daini*) of Dazaifu, ordering him to repair the ships and promising to send carpenters for the purpose. In this document Dazaifu was also instructed to place lookouts in the Chika Islands, an ancient name for the Gotō Archipelago west of Kyūshū, to search for the other ships and render them aid.

The Ambassador replied to the Emperor, assuring him in ornate but humble terms that Tsunetsugu and his subordinates were faithfully carrying out the Imperial wishes. He also said that, while at sea, he and his men had given up all hope of life and had expected to find burial in the bellies of fishes and that, even though they had survived, their spirits were half dead with mortification at their failure, and therefore, untalented and unworthy though they were, they had received the Emperor's magnanimity with great consolation.

The day after word was received of the return of the second ship an Imperial message was also sent to the Vice-Ambassador, ordering him to repair the loss of the small boats and the damage to his ship, after which he was again to attempt to carry out his mission in company with the Ambassador. Meanwhile Dazaifu, because of a food shortage brought on by droughts and pestilence, had petitioned the throne to have all the members of the embassy return to the capital, leaving behind only an Administrative Officer and a Secretary to supervise the repair work. This was ordered by the court, though it was specified that the two chief envoys were free to remain at Dazaifu or return to Kyōto as they saw fit. Subsequently, Dazaifu was again ordered to send men to isolated islands and uninhabited spots to look for survivors from the third ship. Finally, on the fifteenth day of the ninth moon the two chief envoys re-entered the capital and respectfully returned the "sword of authority," thus concluding the first attempt to reach China.

It was reserved, however, for Ki no Mitsu, the envoy to Silla, to take the final curtain call of this unhappy first act.

This hapless individual had not even left for Silla before the whole purpose of his mission had become outdated, for word of his departure from Dazaifu was received in Kyōto at the same time as the report of the finding of the last three survivors from the third ship. Once he arrived in Korea his mission turned into a complete fiasco, as he was forced to admit in his report to the Japanese government after his return to the capital. The Koreans, whose reply to the Council of State is quoted in full in the Japanese records, found fault with almost everything about Mitsu and the message he brought. In particular they took exception to the discrepancy between his claim to be an envoy of good will and his very specific request for aid to the ships of the embassy to China. Their questioning of the unfortunate envoy only produced further confusion. The Silla officials even chose to believe that Mitsu and his documents were simple frauds and sternly warned the Japanese against such duplicity.[40]

Where the fault lay is hard to determine now, but there is no doubt who took the blame. The lowly Mitsu was made the scapegoat for the humiliating incident. The court accused him of having lost sight of the real purpose of his mission in an effort to magnify his own importance and blamed him for a lack of sufficient finesse to straighten out the misunderstanding. This may have been in part true, but a more fundamental reason for the fiasco was probably the basic hostility that existed between Silla and Japan. In the first place the Japanese request appears to have been somewhat casual and perhaps even a little disrespectful, and in any case the reply from Silla shows an ingrained hostility that one minor Japanese official could scarcely have assuaged. The Japanese government wisely made no further efforts to enlist Korean aid on behalf of the embassy to China.

THE SECOND ATTEMPT

In the meantime preparations had started for a second crossing to the continent. In the autumn of 836 the same two men who had been primarily responsible for the construction of the embassy's ships were put in charge of the repair of the remaining three,[41] and early in the new year the ceremonial preparations for departure began. The first day of the second moon, as in the year before, was declared an official holiday, and the envoys made offerings to the gods of heaven and earth. On the eleventh day of the next moon came the Imperial banquet with all the courtiers again ordered to compose poems. The theme this time was almost identical with that of the year before, "a farewell banquet for the envoys to China on an evening in spring," but there was an unforeseen variation in the procedures. The courtiers were to present their poems at sunset, but the Ambassador was already too drunk by that time to take part and had to retire.

Two days later the envoys had their court audience and after another two days were given "the sword of authority" with the same accompanying message as the year before. The Ambassador received the sword, placed it on his left shoulder and, with the Vice-Ambassador walking in front, withdrew. A few days later the Ambassador left Kyōto for Dazaifu and was soon followed by the Vice-Ambassador. The court, however, continued its spiritual preparations for the crossing. A delegation was sent to make offerings at the Great Ise Shrine of the Sun Goddess, the progenitress of the Imperial line, and a little later the first ship of the embassy, which we learn had the name Taiheira, was granted the Junior Fifth Rank Lower Grade.[42]

The envoys had set out from the capital much earlier than the year before, but once again they appear to have delayed their departure from Kyūshū too long. Word was received at the capital on the twenty-second day of the seventh moon, which fell on August 26, 837, in our calendar, that the three ships had set sail from the northwestern tip of Kyūshū but that the first and fourth had been driven back to the island of Iki off the north coast of Kyūshū and the second ship with great difficulty had managed to come ashore in the Gotō Archipelago. Once again the ships appear to have been too damaged to permit the envoys to continue on their way, and the Governor of the Province of Buzen was put in charge of their repair, with the Provisional Governor of Chikuzen and the Administrative Officer Nagamine no Takana as his two assistants.[43] The second attempt to reach China had ended almost as dismally as the first.

PREPARATIONS FOR THE THIRD ATTEMPT

After two such disastrous failures, the Japanese naturally assumed that the gods must be against them, and they therefore redoubled their spiritual efforts in preparation for the third attempt to cross to China. Hitherto the court had relied on the native Shintō deities. Now it turned in addition to the more universally powerful gods and scriptures of Buddhism. In the spring of 838 an Imperial rescript was issued, citing the misfortunes of the embassy but expressing the conviction that "faith will be rewarded." The document concluded with an order to each of the nine provinces of Kyūshū to select one man apiece, aged twenty-five or more, who was devoted to Buddhism, observed the Buddhist scriptures, and was also of blameless character, to make offerings and perform religious rituals until the embassy should return safely from China. These nine men were to be assigned to four of the greatest Shintō shrines of Kyūshū, but they were to perform their worship in the official Buddhist monasteries which had been erected in each province a century earlier and in the Buddhist establishments associated with the shrines.[44] Another Imperial edict a little later gave orders that the Buddhist text known as "The Scripture of the Dragon-King of the Sea" should be read throughout the land "from the day the embassy to China departs until the day it returns to Japan." [45] Because of the common association of dragons with water, this scripture naturally could be counted on to have special efficacy in a dangerous ocean crossing.

On the twenty-eighth day of the fourth moon the Emperor sent a message to the envoys, who apparently had not returned to Kyōto after their second false start. In it he reminded them that the season of reliable winds was commencing and expressed his distress that they were not yet ready to leave. He also dispatched a high court officer to look into the reasons for their delay. Four days later a letter arrived from the envoys attributing their difficulties to spiritual opposition and asking, "How are we to succeed unless we receive divine grace?" The letter concluded with a request that another famous Buddhist scripture, the *Daihannya-kyō*,[46] be read throughout the land. On that very day the court ordered that lectures be held on "The Scripture of the Dragon-King of the Sea" and also that the *Daihannya-kyō* be read in all parts of Japan beginning in the middle ten days of that moon and continuing until the day the embassy should return. The ceremonial reading of scriptures usually consisted of the intoning of selections, such as the opening and closing lines of each chapter. This pious act as well as the lectures on the other scripture were, of course, to be performed by the monks of the official government monasteries in the various provinces.

Fortified by these spiritual aids, the embassy doggedly set sail a third time. The first and fourth ships seem to have gotten a slightly earlier start than in the two previous years, for, according to Ennin, those on board had their last glimpse of the westernmost islands of Japan on the twenty-third day of the sixth moon, which fell on July 18, 838, in the Western calendar. Word of the departure of the second ship did not reach the capital until twenty-four days after news of the sailing of the other ships had been reported there. This delay was probably occasioned by the Vice-Ambassador's sudden refusal to go. A month earlier the officer whom the Emperor had sent to look into the departure of the embassy had reported that Ono no Takamura was unable to leave because of illness. This, however, turned out to be an illness of convenience, and later in the year the true story came to light.[47]

The Vice-Ambassador had probably begun to entertain misgivings about his mission after the disaster of 836, for there is a significant difference in tone between the expressions of consolation in the Imperial message to Tsunetsugu at that time and the Imperial reminder to Takamura to per-

severe in his assignment. But the real trouble started after
the failure of the second attempt. The Ambassador's first
ship was damaged more severely this time than the Vice-
Ambassador's second ship, and Tsunetsugu therefore decided to exchange vessels with his second in command. He
pointed out in a petition to the throne that, when the ships
were first built, the Ship Construction Officials had themselves determined their order, which was not in accordance
with old precedents, and with the court's permission he re-
determined their sequence through divination, with the grati-
fying and probably not unexpected result that the less
damaged second ship was renumbered as the first. Takamura
refused to submit meekly to this thinly disguised trickery,
arguing that the best of the ships had originally been designated as the first and that it was not fair to force him to exchange his good fortune for another's less lucky lot.

The Ambassador no doubt realized that the disagreement
would eventually come to the court's attention, and it was
probably for this reason that, when he sailed, he left behind
a statement of abject devotion to the Emperor, in which he
assured his ruler that, although he had but a single life, he
was ready to undergo ten thousand deaths in behalf of his
sovereign.[48] Takamura too took up his talented brush and
wrote a "Ballad of the Way West," in which he attacked the
whole purpose of embassies to China and in so doing was said
to have insulted the memory of former Emperors. In any
case, the retired Emperor Saga saw the piece and was in-
furiated by it. The judgment meted out to Takamura late
in the year was that, although he merited death by strangu-
lation for having refused to carry out his mission, his punishment was to be mitigated one degree to banishment to the
island of Oki off the northern coast of western Honshū.
Twelve days later he was deprived of his patent of court
rank.

Takamura was not the only member of the embassy who
preferred possible execution and certain disgrace to another
bout with the stormy East China Sea. Four lesser officers,
one of the Ship's Masters, the Scholar of the Calendar, the

Student of the Calendar, and the Student of Astronomy, all fled the ships before they sailed. Their sentences of decapitation were mitigated one degree to exile to the island of Sado off the western coast of northern Honshū.[49]

THE CROSSING

With the departure of the three ships in the summer of 838, the embassy sailed for the time being out of the pages of the Japanese histories. In the spring of 839, however, the court issued an order for the continued reading of the two chosen Buddhist scriptures in the monasteries of the land.[50] Meanwhile, Ennin, on board the first ship of the embassy, had taken up his writing brush and commenced his diary. His first entry, dated the thirteenth day of the sixth moon, records that the members of the embassy again boarded the first and fourth ships, perhaps somewhere near the modern city of Shimonoseki at the western end of the Inland Sea. Four days later a ten-hour run down the coast brought them to the vicinity of Hakata Bay near Dazaifu. On the twenty-second they cast off again and, sailing for thirty hours, reached the northernmost island of the Gotō Archipelago, where on the twenty-third they dropped those who had come this far to see them off and then set out across the open sea, borne by a northeast wind.

The first two nights at sea the two ships kept in touch through fire signals, which were "like stars in appearance," but by the dawn of the third day the fourth ship was no longer in sight. The wind shifted to southeast, but this was still quite satisfactory. The first day out the Ambassador made a drawing of the Bodhisattva Kannon, while Ennin and his companion monk, Ensai, read scriptures and prayed. All the way across, the Japanese paid great attention to the bamboos and reeds floating in the sea, the birds which came and went, and the changing color of the water in the hope of gaining some indication of their position from these phenomena. On the third day the water turned light green, on the fifth whitish green, and the next day the color of yellow mud. This they surmised was water from the Yangtse River, and, when they came out again into light-green water, the Korean Interpreter, Kim Chŏngnam, expressed the fear that they might have passed by the entrance to the canal system which led from the coast north of the Yangtse to the great city of Yang-chou.

Shortly after noon that same day they found themselves once again in muddy water and soundings showed fifty feet of water and then only about forty. After some debate it was decided to proceed cautiously, but high waves had blown up meanwhile, and early in the evening, while still out of sight of the low-lying shore, the ship grounded on a shoal. The men immediately lowered sail, and when they found the vessel still battered by the waves, cast loose the rudder and cut down the mast. This lessened the impact of the waves somewhat, but Ennin records:

. . . When the waves came from the east, the ship leaned over to the west, and when they came from the west, it inclined to the east. They washed over the ship [to a number] beyond count. All on board put their faith in the Buddha and in the [Shintō] deities, and there was none but did pray. The men were desperate, and all from the head of the mission down to the sailors stripped and bound their loin cloths fast about them. Since the ship was about to break in the middle, we rushed to stern and bow, and each of us looked for a place that remained intact. Because of the shock of the waves the structural joints [of the ship] were all pulling apart, so they fastened ropes to the right and left railings and pulled them together, striving to find a way to survive. Bilge water filled [the ship], which thereupon settled onto the sand bottom, and the official and private goods [in the hold] washed about in the bilge water.

The next morning the tide receded, leaving the ship partly buried in the sand. The Japanese proceeded to strengthen the hulk to withstand the next high tide. Unfortunately there is a small hiatus at this point in the diary, but from later statements it seems clear that the Ambassador and a large proportion of the group on board set out for shore in the

small boats. Ennin was one of the thirty-odd men who remained with the ship, and on the night of the first day of the
seventh moon, two full days after the original grounding,
he records that they at last saw a light which they realized
must be on shore. The next morning the ship was refloated
by the tide but after drifting to within sight of land it ran
aground again. Once more the situation was serious and
Ennin writes:

. . . The current, which was strong and swift, then dug out
the mud at the side of the ship, and the mud boiled up. The
ship eventually fell over and was about to be submerged. The
men were terrified and struggled to climb onto the side of the
vessel. All bound their loin cloths about them and tied themselves with ropes here and there [to the ship]. Tied thus in
place, we awaited death. Before long the boat again fell over,
[this time] to the left, and the men consequently shifted to the
right side [of the ship]. When [the ship] would fall over, we
would change place, and in time [these shifts] mounted up in
number. . . . The men lost heart and wept and made vows.

At this desperate juncture a boat came into sight, manned
by six Chinese and guided by an archer from the party that
had gone ashore. The Japanese transferred themselves and
the tribute articles from the ship to the Chinese boat and at
last reached land, where they lodged in a village of border
guard troops. On inquiry, Ennin discovered that this day
was also the second day of the seventh moon in China, although the year was known to the Chinese as the third year
of the K'ai-ch'eng period, and he also learned that they were
just north of the mouth of the Yangtse in the territory of
Yang-chou. The following day he and his companions were
rejoined by the Ambassador and the rest of the men from the
first ship, and Ennin heard their harrowing experiences in
reaching dry land and finding their way to a "salt bureau,"
which was one of the few signs of civilization in this swampy
and sparsely populated coastal area.

It was on this same day that the first word was received of
the whereabouts of the fourth ship. From subsequent notices

it would appear that it too had become stranded on the tidal flats not very far from the first ship, though it had remained in somewhat better shape. At first the men were able to stay with the ship, but, when it began to show signs of breaking up, the Administrative Officer in charge moved ashore to the home of a fisherman. Many of the men, however, still remained on board, and five of these died of "body swellings." Finally ten Chinese boats came to their rescue, and these in time removed the ship's cargo by making daily trips to the stranded vessel when weather permitted. But it was not until the twenty-fourth day of the eighth moon, almost two months after they had first been washed ashore in China, that the men from the fourth ship were able to catch up with the Ambassador's party at Yang-chou.[51]

The second ship, which had left Japan later than the other two, naturally did not reach China as soon. The first word Ennin had of its arrival was a letter dispatched from the Korean Interpreter on board that vessel to Kim Chŏngnam, the Korean Interpreter of the Ambassador's ship. Ennin saw this letter on the tenth day of the eighth moon, but only a month later did he learn that the Vice-Ambassador had not come to China and that the ship was under the command of the Administrative Officer, Fujiwara no Toyonami. The second ship had arrived at Hai-chou, a port near the the southern base of the Shantung Peninsula, and apparently had escaped damage, for it alone of the three vessels was able to sail for Japan the next year. A group from the second ship must have joined the other higher officers in their subsequent trip to the capital, for Toyonami himself was reported to have died on the way, and the monk Kaimyō, whom Ennin met on board the vessel the next year, was probably the Scholar Monk of the Hossō Sect whose difficulties at the capital he describes.

The ship itself and the majority of its complement of men, however, seem to have remained at Haichou over the winter, and it was there that Ennin was to find them in the fourth moon of 839 shortly before their departure on the return voyage.[52]

BY CANAL TO YANG-CHOU

The men from Ennin's ship spent their first few days ashore drying their effects and hiring boats for the canal trip to Yang-chou while waiting for the Chinese government to establish contact with the embassy. Finally, on the ninth day of the seventh moon an official, uniformed representative of the local military garrison, accompanied by eight soldiers and attendants, arrived and welcomed them with wine and cakes and a musical entertainment, after which he returned to his headquarters. Three days later the impatient Japanese dispatched an Interpreter and an archer to the local sub-prefectural town in an effort to hasten the arrival of the boats that were to pick them up; after waiting two more days thirty members of the embassy, including the higher officers, decided to wait no longer and started out on the canal trip to the subprefecture on whatever boats they had at their disposal.

Some of their impatience may have been due to the extreme discomfort of life in the swampy delta region. The heat was oppressive, and there were frequent thunderstorms. Worse still were the ubiquitous mosquitoes, which Ennin claims were "as large as flies" and "hurt like needle pricks." Before long some of the men also began to suffer from dysentery. Ennin himself escaped some of the discomforts of the military village by moving to a nearby monastery, where the higher officers were staying, and he was soon joined there by Ensai, who had contracted dysentery.

Eventually, on the seventeenth day, more than thirty small boats arrived from Ju-kao-chen, the modern Ju-kao-hsien, which was about forty miles west of where they were and the first town of any size on the way to the city of Yang-chou. Early the following morning most of the Japanese started out on forty-odd boats tied together in twos or threes and all connected in a long line drawn by two water buffalo. The canal they were following was said to date back more than two centuries to the Sui dynasty, and it was "over twenty

feet wide and straight without bends." Their first night
along the way they stopped at a place where Ennin heard
the sound of drums and noted in his diary, "It is the custom
of this land to have watchmen who, when night comes, beat
drums in order to guard government property."

Ennin felt that their progress on the canal was quite swift,
but on the third day an officious local dignitary decided that
they were going too slowly and ordered the boats split up
into groups of three, each of which was to be pulled by
seven sailors. But this soon exhausted the men, and so the
original train of boats drawn by the water buffalo was restored. Late the same day they reached Ju-kao-chen, where
they found the Ambassador and his party waiting for them.

Since Ju-kao-chen was the headquarters of a garrison
command, the Ambassador had been able to establish preliminary contact with the Chinese government through it.
One result was the decision made a few days earlier that the
local Chinese officials were to take charge of the wreck of the
first ship and its cargo and that all the remaining Japanese
were to come on to Yang-chou. Another result was that the
Chinese government had started supplying the embassy with
daily living provisions, as it was bound to do for any bona
fide foreign embassy. The Ju-kao-chen officials explained
their dilatoriness in this respect as the result of a misappre-
hension regarding the identity of the group. They had believed that Japan and Korea were in the same place, and,
since there were always many Koreans on these shores, they
had paid the embassy little attention, but, now that they
realized that Japan was "different and far distant from
Korea," they were accepting it as a tributary embassy and
had sent on word of its arrival to higher authorities.

On the twenty-first day the whole party started out from
Ju-kao-chen, soon leaving behind the rows of "rich and
noble houses" which lined the canal at that point. The area
the Japanese now traversed was once again sparsely inhabited, and they went miles at a time without seeing a house,
but two sights along the way impressed Ennin greatly. One
was the carefully guarded flocks of white ducks and white

geese along the waterway, sometimes as many as two thousand in a flock. The other was a long train of "boats of the salt bureau laden with salt, with three or four, or again, four or five boats bound side by side and in line," which "followed one after the other without a break" for several miles. Such a sight was to be expected in this major salt-producing region, but the Japanese quite naturally were amazed.

It took the party two and a half days to reach the sub-prefectural town of Hai-ling-hsien, the modern T'ai-hsien, about thirty-seven miles west of Ju-kao-chen. Here the higher officers spent the night in a monastery, where the local officials presented them with copper coins, but Ennin stayed on his boat and recorded that "all the people of the subprefectural town crowded around, struggling to look at us." The next morning the monks of the Chinese monastery made a call on the Japanese clerics, but the local officials paid the embassy scant courtesy, sending only military officers to see it off.

The Japanese, however, seem to have had their minds on more immediate matters. Ennin records that "the men were suffering from dysentery, and the boats did not progress evenly. A boat going in front would stop and thus become a unit in the rear, and men bringing up the rear would forge ahead." But, despite these difficulties, they managed to reach Yang-chou, about twenty-eight miles to the west, after two days' travel. Before entering the city they stopped briefly at a monastery where a memorial service had been held by the previous Japanese embassy on behalf of its Vice-Ambassador, who had died on the trip. Then, after sending a messenger to inform the local officials of their arrival, the Japanese threaded their way through the throngs of boats of all sizes which crowded the waterways around Yang-chou and finally stopped opposite the north wall of the city.

THE EMBASSY IN YANG-CHOU

The higher officers went ashore on the night of their arrival in Yang-chou, which was the twenty-fifth day of the seventh moon, but Ennin and Ensai did not move to the of-

ficial inn on the south side of the river until the next afternoon. The inn must have been commodious, for the two monks
were given separate rooms. Both the Ambassador and Ennin
waited until the first of the next moon to start the main business which faced them in Yang-chou. Early that morning
the former made his first call on the Regional Commander,
Li Te-yü, and that afternoon Ennin and Ensai in a letter to
the Ambassador requested permission to go to Mt. T'ien-t'ai,
the headquarters of their sect. In this note the monks also
asked that each be assigned a sailor to "perform the menial
tasks in our search for the Law." The Ambassador granted
the request, for in the document he forwarded to the Chinese
authorities two days later he asked for travel permits not
only for Ensai and Ennin, but also for the latter's disciples,
the novices Ishō and Igyō, his servant Tei Yūman, and for
a novice and servant attached to Ensai.

Li Te-yü was less accommodating and seems to have taken
a rather stiff attitude in all his dealings with the embassy. On
the fourth he returned the gifts of Japanese products which
had accompanied the request and, perhaps as a warning
against bribery, cut down the daily provisions of the embassy. He also insisted that the Japanese petition be re-
worded and simplified to exclude all names except those of
the two principals. On the ninth day a Chinese officer who
had been made Commissioner in Charge of the Japanese
Embassy (*Kou-tang Jih-pen-kuo shih*) called on the two
monks, and, probably on the strength of this visit, the latter
hopefully weighed their baggage the next morning and reported the results to the embassy officers. But their hopes for
a speedy departure were dashed that very afternoon by news
that Li Te-yü was petitioning the throne in their behalf and
they would have to await the arrival of an Imperial order
before starting for Mt. T'ien-t'ai.

The Ambassador realized that Ennin, as a Scholar Monk
due to return with the embassy to Japan within a few months,
could ill afford to wait for permission to arrive from the
capital, and he therefore requested that Ennin be allowed to
start, while Ensai, who as a Student Monk had no fixed

limit to his stay in China, remained temporarily at Yang-chou. Li Te-yü, of course, rejected the request and instead decided to place the monks and their followers in one of the major monasteries of the city, the K'ai-yüan-ssu. Official orders for the move came through on the twenty-second; the monastery's reply was reported the next day; and the day after that Ennin and his companions took up residence at the K'ai-yüan-ssu.

In the meantime the embassy had been in contact with the Chinese officials over some other matters which Ennin happened to record in his diary. On the seventeenth a Ship Captain had died. The preceding day, the Commissioner in Charge of the Japanese Embassy and a representative of Li Te-yü had come to the inn to make a record of the stricken man's baggage, and, although the Japanese officers were permitted to hand the baggage over to the man's personal retainer, a minor Chinese functionary supervised the matter and "attended to the buying of a coffin and to the burial."

Another more complicated incident had grown out of a vow the Ambassador had made on shipboard that, if he reached shore safely, he would have pictures drawn of certain Buddhist deities which would be the same height as his own body. On the first day of the eighth moon, Ennin had visited the K'ai-yüan-ssu to arrange for the drawing, and two days later an artist was sent to the monastery to copy some paintings there. To the surprise of the Japanese, he was denied entry, because "for some reason the regulations do not allow foreigners to enter monastery buildings at will." The Ambassador, perhaps seeing in this another sign of Li Te-yü's somewhat unfriendly attitude, decided to postpone the fulfillment of his vow until the next spring, though his stated reason for this decision was that "divination had shown that there was a taboo against it." Ennin, on receiving this information, prayed at the front gate of the K'ai-yüan-ssu and entered into negotiations with the monastery officers. It was perhaps because of his efforts that a few days later Li Te-yü gave his permission for the making of the drawings. The Ambassador, however, stuck to his decision, and no more is heard about the matter until the next spring, when he succeeded in having some of the pictures painted while at Ch'u-chou, after which he held a large Buddhist ceremony and made offerings to the completed pictures. At the same time he renewed his vow to have the remaining pictures painted, stating that, although he had not fulfilled his vow because his public duties since reaching land had been numerous and the difficulties of travel too great, he promised to draw these pious pictures the day he reached Japan.[53]

Ennin's wait for word from the capital was not rewarded by the expected permission to start on his pilgrimage. On the thirteenth day of the ninth moon he learned that a reply had come from Ch'ang-an, and a few days later he was informed of its contents by the embassy officers. The court had decided that the embassy would have to renew the request after reaching the capital and that meanwhile Ennin and Ensai should remain at Yang-chou. The Ambassador, on hearing this, protested the decision to Li Te-yü, who assured him that the matter had already been appealed and that he expected a speedy reply.

The time was now approaching for the Ambassador's departure for the capital, and before leaving he gave Ennin a personal gift of some edible seaweed and a substantial present from the Japanese court for the monk's support in his "search for the Law" in the form of ten Chinese ounces of gold dust, which is the equivalent of a little more than thirteen of our ounces. The Administrative Officer, Nagamine no Takana, told the two monks that he would take personal charge of their petition at the capital if they would write out the particulars for him. He also entrusted Ennin with a mission on behalf of the embassy. If on his trip to Mt. T'ien-t'ai Ennin were to reach the borders of Ming-chou, the modern port of Ningpo in Chekiang, he was to read and then burn the patent of promotion, raising the court rank of the Vice-Ambassador of the previous embassy to China, who had died in Ming-chou. Ennin's written instructions from the embassy merely referred to an appointment to the Fourth Rank, but this obviously was the promotion from the Junior

Fourth Rank Lower Grade to the Junior Fourth Rank
Upper Grade given to the Vice-Ambassador as one of the
eight promotions for members of former embassies made by
the Japanese court more than two years earlier.

It seems probable that the embassy, too, was forced to
wait in Yang-chou until permission arrived from Ch'ang-an
for the chief officers to proceed to the capital. It is perhaps
for this reason that Ennin makes no mention of their departure until Li Te-yü held a farewell banquet for them on
the auspicious date of the ninth day of the ninth moon. The
Ambassador himself did not attend, presumably wishing to
emphasize by his aloofness the dignity of his position. Several
more weeks were to elapse before the party bound for the
capital was ready to start on the long trip by canal and road.
On the twenty-ninth Li Te-yü gave them another farewell
party, and finally on the fifth of the tenth moon they set out,
making a somewhat inauspicious start in the face of a twenty-
four-hour rainstorm.

THE IMPERIAL AUDIENCE

The trip to Ch'ang-an and the audience with the Chinese
Emperor were of course the climax of the whole embassy,
but unfortunately this is the aspect of the mission of which
we know least. The official Chinese histories merely tell us
that in 839 "tribute was again brought to the court" by the
Japanese, and one official Chinese survey of Japanese contacts with China even overlooks the embassy itself and only
records, with obvious reference to Ennin and his followers,
that during this period "monks were sent to visit our country
and make a pilgrimage to Wu-t'ai." [54] The Japanese records
tell little more about the embassy's experiences at the capital,
and only through Ennin's scattered comments on what he
learned by letter or hearsay from the men who went to
Ch'ang-an can we piece together this part of the story.[55]

It took the Ambassador fifty-nine days to reach the capital, where he arrived on the third day of the twelfth moon,
but word of his arrival came back to Ennin in only fifteen

days. In all, 270 members of the embassy, drawn from all three ships, made the trip to Ch'ang-an. Not all the higher officers were included in this number, for at least one Administrative Officer and one Secretary remained behind at Yang-chou.[56] The envoys were met at a post station about two miles east of the city by a representative of the Emperor, who transmitted the latter's inquiries. They were then lodged in the Foreign Guest Court (*Li-pin-yüan*) in the eastern half of the city.

The Imperial audience did not take place until over a month later on the thirteenth day of the first moon of 839. On that day twenty-five of the Japanese went to the palace, but apparently the Ambassador and the Administrative Officer Nagamine no Takana, who was substituting for the missing Vice-Ambassador, were the only ones allowed into the Imperial presence.[57] In all, five foreign embassies were received that day. Nan-chao, the Thai state in what is now the southwest Chinese province of Yunnan, was ranked ahead of Japan, since, having contiguous boundaries with the T'ang, it was considered of greater importance. The Japanese could not have taken much pride in being ranked ahead of the other three embassies, for Ennin records that "the princes from the other [lands] did not wear headgear and were crooked and ugly in appearance and dressed in furs and blankets."

Either at the audience or shortly thereafter the Ambassador was given titular office in the Chinese government, presumably as part of the investiture of the Japanese ruler as a vassal of the T'ang Emperor. The Japanese records are significantly silent on the investiture itself, for the Japanese seem to have maintained to themselves a pretense of equality with China, but Ennin recorded in detail the offices the Ambassador was given at Ch'ang-an and the Chinese court ranks commensurate with each post. Tsunetsugu, in addition to the several Japanese governmental posts he held, was now a "Cloud Banner General of China, Acting President of the Bureau of Imperial Sacrifices, and concurrently General of the *Chin-wu* Imperial Palace Guards of the Left."

About three weeks after the audience, there was an Imperial order that, in accordance with the precedent of the preceding Japanese embassy to China, all the Japanese who had gone to the capital and also all those who had stayed behind in Yang-chou and Hai-chou should be given five bolts of silk apiece. It was specifically ordered that the Japanese monks were to be included in this distribution of Imperial largess, although no precedent was to be found for this. Ennin received his "official salary," as he calls it, soon after news of the decision had reached Yang-chou.

On the day the Ambassador had arrived at the capital, he had presented petitions regarding Ennin's pilgrimage to Mt. T'ien-t'ai and the vessels the embassy wished to secure for the voyage back to Japan, but he was told that no petitions could be accepted before he had his Imperial audience. The Ambassador, however, persisted in his demands and was given permission to hire the ships he wanted and to leave China in the third moon of the next year, but Ennin's request was refused on the grounds that there was not enough time remaining before the embassy would be setting sail again for Japan. The Ambassador again petitioned on Ennin's behalf the day of his audience but drew a flat refusal from the Emperor, and a later appeal was equally unsuccessful.

Ennin was not the only Japanese monk to run foul of Chinese red tape. One monk who had made the long trip to Ch'ang-an was refused admittance to the capital, and his disciple monk was forced to become a lay official and serve as a retainer of one of the Administrative Officers of the embassy. Another monk was at first denied permission to reside in a capital monastery, and not until a second petition had been made was he allowed to study there for a period of fifteen days. Only one of the many lay and clerical scholars won permission to stay in China beyond the departure of the embassy. This was the Student Monk Ensai, who, the Chinese government ruled, was to be provided by the Japanese with subsistence for a period of five years. Accordingly, the embassy gave Ensai thirty-five bolts of silk, seventy-five

pads or packages of two types of silk floss, and twenty-five
Chinese ounces of gold dust.

TRADE AND COMMERCE

Trade, though not the major objective of the envoys and
definitely frowned on by the Chinese authorities, was undoubtedly an important aspect of the embassy from the point
of view of the Japanese. To their disappointment, however,
they were prohibited from selling and buying while at the
capital. Moreover, attempts to sell their goods while on the
return trip from Ch'ang-an were frustrated by the Commissioner in Charge of the Japanese Embassy. The latter did
not leave Yang-chou for the capital until more than two
months after the Ambassador, but he reached Ch'ang-an in
time to make a thorough nuisance of himself on the trip back
to the coastal region. Whenever the Japanese attempted to
trade along the way, he would strike the drums which signaled departure and would force them to move on.

The Japanese therefore decided to send a party of ten
men back to Yang-chou to attempt to trade there. The group
was under the charge of one of the Ship's Masters, Harumi-
chi no Nagakura, who had the additional title of Supervisor
of the National Tribute Articles. Nagakura and his men,
however, seem to have had scant success in Yang-chou. The
very day they arrived there, Nagakura and an Interpreter
were arrested and detained overnight for having "bought
some items under Imperial prohibition." The same day four
other members of the party "went to the market place to
buy incense and medicines, but because local officials questioned them, they fled, abandoning over two hundred strings
of cash, and only three of them got back." This was a serious
financial loss, because a string of cash consisted of one thousand round copper coins (with square holes in the middle for
stringing purposes). Awada no Ietsugu, the artist and Professor who was the Ambassador's attendant, was also detained overnight for attempting to buy things in the market
place, and we hear of a Scribe and an archer who were ar-

rested on the same charge during the next few days, though
the latter was allowed to keep his purchases. One suspects
that the three archers and sailors who had been pilloried at
about the same time for having "physically mistreated some
Chinese," may have come to blows with the latter over attempted commercial transactions.[58]

We can only guess what the Japanese were attempting to
buy and sell in China. The national tribute articles to which
Ennin makes frequent reference were no doubt gifts for the
Chinese Emperor, but he also mentions "official and private
goods," which probably were articles brought by the government and by individual members of the embassy for sale
and barter in China. The many references to gold dust for
major financial transactions show that the Japanese had
brought most of their assets in this handy form, which could
be easily converted as needed into Chinese copper coins. Some
of their wealth also seems to have been in the form of silk
stuffs and silk floss, and in addition the various "Japanese
products" which they used for minor presents included such
things as knives decorated with silver, girdles, assorted
writing brushes, rosaries of rock crystal, powdered tea,
conch shells, and edible seaweed.[59]

The only articles we know for certain that the Japanese
sought to buy in China were incense and medicines, but, since
the major presents they received as a group or individually
were silk stuffs, it would seem probable that fine silks together with the manuscripts and pictures collected by the
scholars of the embassy made up the bulk of the return
cargo. Among other minor gifts received by members of the
embassy were such obvious perishables as peaches, honey,
and pine nuts, but also certain articles such as copper coins,
knives, and powdered tea, which no doubt were well worth
taking back to Japan. In any case, we know that the embassy
returned from China laden with many goods of commercial
value, for, in addition to the articles retained by the court
and those presented to Shintō deities and Imperial tumuli,
there remained enough Chinese goods for the court to hold
a "palace market" a few weeks after the embassy's return.

On this occasion three tents were erected outside one of the palace gates, and here the surplus Chinese goods were displayed by the government officials and disposed of by barter.[60]

PREPARATIONS FOR RETURN

Since two of their three ships had been wrecked on the Yangtse mud flats, the Japanese obviously needed new vessels for the return voyage. It was only natural therefore that the Ambassador, as soon as he reached the capital, should have asked permission to secure these. The authorization must have come through quite quickly, for we learn that even before the end of 838 the Korean Interpreter, Kim ✓ Chŏngnam, left Yang-chou to select the ships at Ch'u-chou, a convenient port on the Huai River. There he arranged for the hiring of more than sixty Koreans who were "familiar with the sea routes" and the purchase of nine Korean craft, which must have been much smaller than the two Japanese ships they were to replace.[61] Early in 839, on the fourth day of the intercalary first moon, which that year was sandwiched between the regular first and second moons, thirty-six Japanese carpenters and founders were sent from Yang-chou at Kim's request to help repair the ships he had bought.

By coincidence the Ambassador and his party left Ch'ang-an that same day, arriving in Ch'u-chou on the twelfth of the next moon. On the eighteenth Ennin and Ensai moved from the K'ai-yüan-ssu in Yang-chou to an inn, and the next day, after the embassy officers had made a farewell call on Li Te-yü, all the Japanese remaining in Yang-chou boarded ten boats for the trip up the Grand Canal to Ch'u-chou. The rash of arrests for commercial crimes, however, delayed their departure, and they did not reach Ch'u-chou until the twenty-fourth. Here the monks were lodged in a monastery which, like the one in Yang-chou, was called the K'ai-yüan-ssu, for an Emperor in 738 had ordered that monasteries of this name should be established in every prefecture of the land.

Two days later a Chinese monk who had been giving Ennin instruction in esoteric rituals arrived from Yang-chou with orders that the Commissioner in Charge of the Japanese Embassy hire a boat for Ensai and his two attendants and escort them by way of Yang-chou to Mt. T'ien-t'ai. The Commissioner insisted on a speedy departure, and so the next day was devoted to packing and to farewells. The Ambassador gave Ensai the gold and silk he needed for his support, and Ennin entrusted him with the lists of doctrinal questions and a Buddhist scarf which had been given him by the Enryakuji for delivery to the mother monastery in China. The Japanese officers gave the Commissioner wine, which Ennin tritely states "was drunk in sad farewell," though the Japanese were probably only too glad to see the last of this officious Chinese, and the party set out for the journey south on the twenty-eighth.

A second Chinese monk called Ching-wen arrived from Yang-chou five days later to bid Ennin adieu. Ching-wen, who was a member of a Mt. T'ien-t'ai monastery, had originally gone to Yang-chou to see Ennin and had there told him much about the holy mountain and how he himself had seen Saichō come there thirty-four years earlier.[62] Now he announced that he would return to Yang-chou and accompany Ensai to Mt. T'ien-t'ai.

While in Ch'u-chou Ennin made his decision to attempt to stay in China even without official permission. The Korean Interpreter, Kim Chŏngnam, seems to have been responsible for the specific plan to have Ennin placed in the hands of friendly Koreans somewhere along the Shantung coast, and the Korean traders of Ch'u-chou were apparently in on the plot. This is probably the meaning of Ennin's magnificent gift of two ounces of gold dust as well as a girdle to Yu Sinŏn, the official Interpreter of the local Korean community. Yu came back with a courtesy present of ten pounds of tea and some pine nuts. Ennin had already won the Ambassador's approval of his plan, but the latter had accompanied it with a sobering warning:

. . . If you desire to remain, that is for the sake of Buddhism, and I dare not stand in the way of your determination. If you wish to stay, then do remain. The government of this land, however, is extremely severe, and, if the officials learn of this, it will entail the crime of disobeying an Imperial order, and you will probably have trouble. You should think it over.[63]

On the nineteenth day of the third moon the Prefect of Ch'u-chou held a farewell wine party for the embassy, though the Ambassador again felt it was beneath his dignity to attend, and three days later the Japanese boarded their ships. They left Ch'u-chou in state, riding on horseback from the inn to the ships, with eight men clearing the road in front of them. Then, after purifying themselves according to the Shintō custom and worshiping the Great God of Sumiyoshi who watches over seafarers from his shrine at the head of the Inland Sea, they embarked. Each ship was under the command of one of the higher officers and had from five to seven Korean sailors on board. Ennin was assigned to the second ship, which was commanded by Nagamine no Takana, who was considered to be the second ranking member of the embassy.

A Chinese military officer accompanied the Japanese down the Huai on a separate vessel, and orders were sent by the Chinese officials to the prefectures and subprefectures along the coast to provide for the embassy. The trip from Ch'u-chou to the sea was a slow one. The wind at times was contrary, and even when it blew from the west the river was so winding that the wind seemed to be constantly shifting. The tide also had to be reckoned with most of the way, and at least once the Korean sailors held up the ships by failing to return on time from shore leave. But finally, on the twenty-ninth, they passed out of the mouth of the Huai and, after running north the better part of a day, anchored in a cove on the hilly coast of what was then a large island east of Hai-chou but is now part of the mainland near the eastern terminus of the Lunghai Railway. Since the accompanying Chinese ship was unable to go beyond the river mouth, a Japanese sailor who was considered to be ritually impure because he had had unnatural relations with another man and was therefore temporarily barred from the Japanese vessels, was transferred from the Chinese ship to a passing vessel bound for Hai-chou, where he was to rejoin the original second ship of the embassy.

ON THE HIGH SEAS

The next day the embassy officers went ashore to make sacrifices to the deities of heaven and earth, and then, as the wind blew up and the ships began to bump each other dangerously in the crowded cove, they held a conference to decide the next step. The Korean sailors obviously favored the less hazardous northern route by way of the Korean coast and argued that, in order to repair the ships, they should first sail one day north to Mt. Ta-chu, which is on the Shantung coast about thirty miles southeast of the modern port of Tsingtao. The Ambassador supported this proposal, but his second in command, Nagamine no Takana, led the opposition, arguing that even if they sailed directly eastward from where they were, there would still be some danger of being blown to the hostile shores of Korea, where a revolution was said to be in progress, and that this danger would increase the farther north they went. Since four of the Ship's Commanders sided with Takana, the Ambassador decided that the ships of these five could cross the sea from where they were while the other four would go to Mt. Ta-chu. However, when he attempted to get the five dissenting Ship's Commanders to sign his letter of decision, the only signature he obtained was that of a Scribe on Takana's ship.

In conformity with the Ambassador's decision, Ennin and his three followers were transferred from the second ship to the eighth, under the command of the former Scholar Tomo no Sugao, who was planning to stay with the Ambassador. But by the time the move had been completed, the Ambassador himself had begun to waver. A steady west wind was blowing toward Japan and, at Takana's insistence, he de-

cided that if the wind had not changed by the next morning,
which would be their fifth day in the cove, all the ships would
set sail directly eastward for Japan. When on the next day
the west wind still prevailed, Ennin entrusted all his baggage to Sugao and, after receiving from the Ambassador
twenty ounces of gold for his support, had his party of four
landed on the desolate shore.

All appeared serene as Ennin watched "the white sails
moving in a row over the sea," but he began to worry about
his compatriots when the wind shifted to the east after a
thunderstorm that night. If he had known more about the
seasonal winds, he would have worried even more. The Japanese had delayed their departure too late in the spring to
have much chance that a west wind would blow long enough
to take them all the way to Japan. The day they set sail was
the fifth of the fourth moon, which corresponded to May 21,
839, in our calendar. A few days later Ennin heard that the
third of the nine ships had been blown back to the Shantung
coast a little east of Tsingtao, had then proceeded to Mt.
Ta-chu, and had started out again across the sea from there;
still later he learned that five of the ships had come ashore
east of Tsingtao and that eventually all nine had been reunited and were at anchor there.[64]

After being put ashore, Ennin and his companions had
their encounter with the Korean boatmen transporting charcoal from Shantung to Ch'u-chou and through their kindness were taken to the nearest village across a range of hills.
There the Japanese claimed to be Korean monks from Ch'u-
chou who had taken passage on a ship bound for Shantung,
but a village elder was familiar enough with Korean to realize
that this was not the language which they were using among
themselves and, having heard that the embassy ships had
anchored nearby, at once surmised that Ennin and his companions were Japanese deserters. Three police officers happened to be in the village, dispatched by Hai-chou, the local
prefecture, very probably to check on the whereabouts of the
embassy ships, and the four Japanese were soon handed over
to these men. Ennin could see that the game was up and now

lamely explained that he had gone ashore because he was
suffering from beri-beri and that he and his companions had
been left behind by accident.

The arrest of the Japanese produced a flurry of activity.
Men were sent to the cove to see if the ships had really departed, and an officer came from the subprefectural town of
Tung-hai-hsien, located on the same island, to question the
fugitives and arrange for their transfer to the original second Japanese ship, which still lay anchored in the harbor of
Hai-chou. Two days later the four were taken across the
island, and the next day they traversed the bay lying between
it and the city of Hai-chou, going right by the Japanese
vessel. On the other side they met some of the officers of the
ship, who were staying in the Hai-lung-wang-miao, the
"Temple of the Dragon-King of the Sea," and then were
conducted to an audience with the Prefect of Hai-chou.

A few days later Ennin boarded the Japanese ship, empty-
handed, as he writes, and sighing over his failure to accom-
plish his "search for the Law." On the eleventh day of the
fourth moon his compatriots hoisted sail, but the ship ran
fast aground before it had cleared the harbor. Not until two
days later was it refloated, and then, after purifying themselves and worshiping the Great God of Sumiyoshi, the Japanese headed eastward into the open sea straight for Japan.

At dawn on the second day at sea the ocean was suspici-
ously white and muddy, and at noon the wind died and shortly
thereafter came up in the south. Northeast by north was the
best that the vessel could do with such a wind. This situation
called for the reciting of scriptures and incantations and the
making of offerings of the five grains to the Dragon-Kings
of the five directions (the fifth being the center). These measures apparently had some temporary efficacy, for that night
the wind swung back to west. But shortly after noon of the
third day, it shifted again to southeast, and the ship was
forced to head north.

A diviner was now called upon to foretell the wind, but he
was cautious enough not to commit himself, although he did
predict that, even though they should be blown to the coasts

of Korea, they need have no fear. The officials then made vows and prayed for a favorable wind, and the monks recited scriptures, renewed their offerings of the five grains, and prayed to the Shintō deities. Again their prayers were answered, but only briefly. By the dawn of the fourth day they were fogbound and had no idea in which direction they were sailing. When the fog lifted temporarily they found themselves going northeast and again later north. The situation was not encouraging, and it was decided to conserve the water supply. Henceforth those who ranked as officers were to receive a little over a quart a day, and the others three-quarters as much. Some of the Japanese were in poor physical condition. A sailor had died the first day at sea and another two days later. On the fourth day Ennin himself was too ill to eat or drink.

On the morning of the fifth day the Japanese found themselves again drifting aimlessly in a dense fog, and, when they discovered that they were in shallow water, they thought it best to anchor. Then the fog lifted a bit to show a rocky coastline, which the diviner first pronounced to be Korea and then China. More reliable information was soon forthcoming when a party sent out on one of the ship's skiffs returned with two Chinese who told them that they were on the south coast of Shantung at a point which was only some fifty or sixty miles short of its eastern extremity. The Chinese were given wine and silk floss and sent back with letters to the local subprefecture and prefecture.

OFF THE COAST OF SHANTUNG

With the comforting knowledge of their whereabouts came the discouraging realization that the whole way still lay ahead of them. On the eighteenth day of the fourth moon, the day after their return to land, the food and water rations were each cut to a little over a pint a day per person. Ennin had the diviner pray to the Shintō deities and himself made offerings of crystals to the Great God of Sumiyoshi and the Dragon-King of the Sea and a razor to the patron deity of ships in order to guarantee the safe return of all to Japan.

These measures were well taken, for the Japanese were to endure three stormy months along the rocky coast of Shantung. On the nineteenth day the ship entered an inlet where it anchored for six days, swinging back and forth with the tides and losing anchor after anchor as the submerged reefs cut through the ropes. Then on the twenty-fifth, the Japanese moved southwestward down the coast a little way, reaching a safer anchorage the next day after having spent a fog-bound night on the open sea.

Before leaving the first anchorage the Japanese had already established contact with an officer representing the local subprefecture, with whom they had exchanged presents of silk floss for wine and cakes. The day they entered the new anchorage they re-established contact with the local officials, and a Secretary went ashore to make a written request for food to a local Guard Officer (*Ya-ya*), who seems to have taken charge of relations with the Japanese. The document stated, "Previously while we were in Tung-hai-hsien, we were given provisions for crossing the sea, but this ship, while crossing the sea, was driven back by contrary winds and drifted ashore here. It would not be right for us to consume our provisions for the ocean crossing while here, so we ask for fresh provisions." Although the Japanese were able to buy some food at a nearby village a few days later, they received no answer to their request for almost three weeks, and even then, in response to a second inquiry, they were merely told that they would receive nothing because no Japanese goods had been presented to the local prefecture and subprefecture.

Meanwhile, the safer anchorage had apparently restored Ennin's spirits, for he had the Korean Interpreter of the ship, the monk Tohyŏn, make inquiries about the possibility of his slipping ashore at this point. The answer was favorable, but before Ennin could make up his mind, the ship was on the move again. Before setting sail the Japanese had this time "worshiped the deities of heaven and earth and made offerings of government and private silks, tie-dye cloth, and

mirrors to the Great God of Sumiyoshi," for whom there was
a small shrine on board the ship. They also moved a seriously
ill sailor ashore. A few days earlier still another man had
died on shipboard, but this one was removed before he could
ritually defile the vessel by his death. The man "asked for
food and water and said that, if he recovered from his illness, he would look for a village." Small wonder that Ennin
records that "there was none on board but did grieve."

Even after all these preparations, however, the ship was
blown back to its starting point within a few hours, and the
next day it was able to move only a mile or two southwestward down the coast. The monks then went ashore to perform the festival of the fifth day of the fifth moon, now
known as the Boys' Festival in Japan, and to bathe and
launder their clothes. While they were still on land a message
came from the young officer in command of the ship, the
Acting Administrative Officer, Yoshimine no Nagamatsu,
ordering the whole company to observe ritual purity and requesting the monks to hold services for three days in order
to obtain a favorable wind for the crossing. This time their
prayers did not have even temporary success. Further services were held for the Chinese deities of heaven and earth,
but still the wind remained unsteady.

While the Japanese were waiting for the wind to change,
the Guard Officer obtained a detailed report on the number
of men on board and a letter from the embassy to the subprefecture, and Ennin renewed his inquiries about staying
in China. Meanwhile the weather grew worse, and on the nineteenth the ship came close to disaster when the wind snapped
the anchor ropes and damaged the superstructure. Two days
later the Japanese again raised sail to cross the sea, only to
have the wind die. The same day the diviner, who had been
ill for a long time, was put ashore, where he died before morning. On the twenty-fifth another start was frustrated when
the wind again died, though a more maneuverable Korean
ship slipped in and out of the anchorage so quickly that the
Japanese could not find out if their compatriots were on
board.

Disaster finally struck at dawn on the twenty-seventh, after a thunderstorm which had lasted all night. The mast was hit by lightning, and several huge splinters were torn off, including one piece "over four inches deep, about six inches wide, and over thirty feet long." This called for more offerings to the gods and divination by the ancient Far Eastern system of "burning a tortoise shell" and observing the cracks produced. The answer was that the unlucky diviner "had been buried in front of the local deity, and consequently we had incurred the anger of the deity, who had brought down this disaster upon us, but if we could purify ourselves, we might then be safe." This, of course, was attended to, but there remained the problem of the weakened mast. After some discussion, it was decided to bind it up as best they could and not to attempt to replace it, for adequate wood was not to be found locally, and it was feared that finding a new mast might delay their departure until the following year.

The next few days witnessed several more false starts, including an effort, which almost ended on the rocks, to row out of the anchorage. On the third day of the sixth moon the ship actually did run onto a reef near the mouth of the anchorage and was carried along by the ebbing tide bumping over the rocks until it floated out onto the open sea. Here the Japanese were caught by another thunderstorm, though this time they managed to fend off the thunderbolts by brandishing spears, axes, and swords and shouting with all their might.

Two days of fitful sailing northeastward up the coast brought the Japanese to Mt. Ch'ih near the eastern extremity of the peninsula, but they were discouraged from entering the anchorage at its foot by unfavorable weather and a black bird which circled the ship three times. They turned back and anchored on the open sea, but another thunderstorm bore down on them. In a frenzy of fear over these signs of the displeasure of the deities, the Japanese made vows, purified themselves, worshiped the Great God of Sumiyoshi and other Japanese deities, the Dragon-King of the Sea, and the gods of the mountains and islands of this part of China. They also "prayed to the god of the thunderbolt on board the ship," which very probably was the scar on the mast sanctified by the lightning bolt of a few days earlier. All this effort saved them from further calamity, but Ennin noted that the movement of the ship "is unbearable, and our spirits have been worn down," and the next day he added, "Never have we been more miserable than this."

On the following day, which was the seventh day of the sixth moon, the ship finally entered the anchorage at the foot of Mt. Ch'ih, and the fortunes of Ennin and his three followers, though not of their compatriots, took a decided turn for the better. The day after entering the anchorage, Ennin and his two disciple novices climbed up to the Mt. Ch'ih Cloister which stood on the mountain above the harbor. This Buddhist establishment was also known as the Korean Cloister, since it had been founded by a Korean and all the resident monks were themselves of Korean origin. The term "cloister," or *yüan*, literally meaning "courtyard," was used for the various architectural and administrative subdivisions of a large monastery or, as in this case, for a small monastery or perhaps one which lacked government recognition.

Ennin had intended to make only a short visit to the Mt. Ch'ih Cloister, but instead he and his companions prolonged their stay day after day. Luckily for them they were not on board the ship when a violent storm struck two weeks later. The anchors dragged, and the ship struck on the rocks three or four times, breaking its rudder and smashing two of its small boats. As a consequence, the men were divided into groups to search for new anchor stones and wood for the rudder.

Ennin, comfortably ensconced in the Mt. Ch'ih Cloister, once again consulted with the Korean Interpreter Tohyŏn about staying in China, and on the fourteenth day of the seventh moon he bade farewell to the other Japanese on shipboard. The next day the ship once more set sail for Japan, ironically only one day before four representatives of the prefectural government arrived with seventy Chinese bushels

(118 of our bushels) of rice as official provisions for the
Japanese. Less than a week later, on the twenty-first, the
Ambassador's nine ships, which Ennin had last seen setting
sail for Japan three and a half months earlier, entered the
Mt. Ch'ih anchorage. Ennin sent his disciple Ishō to make
polite inquiries, and the Ambassador's attendant, Awada no
Ietsugu, and an archer were sent from the ships to return
the call. Two nights later the nine ships in turn departed for
Japan.

THE HOMEWARD VOYAGE

Ennin was to hear no more of the ships and members of
the embassy until almost three years later, when news from
Japan reached him at the Chinese capital.[65] But as the ten
ships passed out of his diary, they sailed back once more into
the Japanese records.

The Ambassador's nine ships took the same northern
course by the shores of Korea which Ennin was to follow
eight years later. On the way two of the ships became separated from the others, and one of these, the sixth, arrived in
northern Kyūshū on the fourteenth day of the eighth moon,
about three weeks after leaving the Mt. Ch'ih anchorage. On
hearing this news, the Japanese court ordered the guards
along the coasts to keep their fires lit and to lay by stores for
the men on the other ships. At the same time orders were sent
to fifteen monasteries to have scriptures read, and offerings
were dispatched to the main shrine of the God of Sumiyoshi
and to another deity enshrined on the northwestern shores of
Honshū, who, according to mythology, was also connected
with foreign intercourse.[66]

Meanwhile seven more of the nine ships had arrived safely
at a small island near Hirado, which lies off the northwestern
tip of Kyūshū. The day after this news reached Kyōto, the
court ordered the envoys to hasten on to the capital by land,
since it would soon be time for the autumn harvest and it was
feared that their presence in the provinces would disrupt the
work of the peasants. The Ambassador and two other high

officers were to lead the first group to the capital, and Nagamine no Takana and nine other officers were each to lead subsequent parties. An Inspector was to have the medicines
which had been brought back from China transported by
land to the capital, and the remainder of the goods and personnel were to be sent by sea or land, depending upon a later
decision. Meanwhile, lookouts were to be maintained for the
missing ship of the nine and also for the original second
vessel, which was even longer overdue.[67]

It was not until a month and a half later that the first of
these two missing ships reached northern Kyūshū, but the
records fail to mention why the vessel fell so far behind the
other eight. Month after month passed, but still no word
came of the original second ship, and in the spring of 840
the court renewed orders to maintain the coastal watch and
fires. Then finally, a month later, Dazaifu reported that survivors from this ship had reached southern Kyūshū, almost
nine months after the vessel had set sail from the Shantung
coast.[68]

The ship, without the benefit of Korean sailors on board,
may have attempted to avoid the Korean coast and sail directly from the Mt. Ch'ih anchorage to Japan. In any case,
it encountered a storm which drove it southward and snapped
the weakened mast. After the unfortunate Japanese had
drifted for some time in weather so cloudy that they lost their
bearings, they floated ashore in the eighth moon on an island
which may have been near Formosa or even further south.
Here they were attacked by the unruly inhabitants. The exhausted travelers were greatly outnumbered, but the Ship's
Master and physician, Sugawara no Kajinari, prayed to the
Buddhas and Shintō deities, and through divine intervention
they won a miraculous victory, though not without losses. A
five-foot lance, a sword with a scabbard covering only one
side, and an arrow from among the trophies captured at this
time were later presented to the court and were found to be
quite different from the weapons of China. After the battle,
Kajinari and the Ship's Commander, Yoshimine no Nagamatsu, supervised the construction of small boats from the

wreck of the ship, and on board these the survivors sailed
northward toward Japan. Kajinari's boat was the first to
arrive, and Nagamatsu's took over two months longer to
reach southern Kyūshū, but, according to the report Ennin
was to receive two years later in China, only thirty-odd men
from the second ship ever got back to Japan.[69]

The court, on hearing of Kajinari's return, ordered that
silks and goods be given the survivors so that they could be
provided with clothing, and, after learning of their miraculous victory and checking the dates, the credit was assigned
to a god of the Province of Dewa in the far north, who was
appropriately promoted from the Senior Fifth Rank Lower
Grade to the Junior Fourth Rank Lower Grade and was
given two families in fief. The Imperial edict, written in the
clumsy Sinicized Japanese used for such documents, stated:

> Of late there has been a ghost at court, which on
> divination proved to be because of the Great God's curse. In
> addition, the men of the second ship of the Embassy to China
> have returned and reported that in the eighth moon of last
> year they floated to the region of the southern brigands and
> that, when they fought them, although the other side was
> numerous and ours few and by no means a match for them in
> strength, unexpectedly we defeated the enemy, which ap-
> parently was because of the Great God's aid. Now in this re-
> gard We remember that last year the Province of Dewa re-
> ported to Us that the sounds of battle were to be heard for ten
> days in the clouds of the Great God and later stone weapons
> rained down. The days and the moon coincide exactly with the
> time of the battle in the south seas. We are both awed and
> gratified that the Great God caused his majestic power to be
> felt afar. Therefore We announce that We respectfully confer
> upon him the Junior Fourth Rank and give him two families
> in fief.

Ennin was to add the final footnote to the story of the embassy's return voyage to Japan. He tells us that he learned
through a letter from a Korean friend in Ch'u-chou, which
he received in Ch'ang-an on the twenty-fifth day of the fifth

moon of 842, that the Korean sailors who had guided the
Ambassador and his party in safety to Japan in 839 had re- ⟋
turned to their homes in China in the autumn of the following
year. The loss of all four of the original Japanese ships and
the safe crossing to Japan of all nine of the Korean vessels
and their apparently successful return to China show clearly
the navigational superiority of the Koreans at this time. The
Japanese certainly were not lacking in daring, but it was not
until several centuries later that their skill as deep sea sailors
began to match their boldness as warriors and enabled them
through sail and sword to win dubious renown for themselves
as the scourge of the East China Sea.

THE WELCOME HOME

While the unfortunate men of the second ship were still on
their southern isle or wandering on the high seas, the Ambassador and his companions were being welcomed back by
the Japanese court and rewarded for accomplishing their
perilous mission. On the sixteenth day of the ninth moon of
839, Tsunetsugu returned his "sword of authority" at the
capital. The next day "the Imperial letter" from China was
presented to the Emperor in the main hall of the palace. The
document was probably an official patent of investiture for
the Japanese ruler, but the Japanese records are perhaps
purposely vague on this point. The Ambassador was then
summoned to the Imperial presence, and the Emperor com-
mended him in person. Tsunetsugu called out "Aye" in response and performed a ceremonial dance. Wine was served,
and the Emperor was given a detailed report of the mission.
At the conclusion of the ceremony the Ambassador was presented an outfit of clothing accompanied by another Imperial
statement of commendation, this time pronounced by a Minister of State, and again in response Tsunetsugu cried out
"Aye" and performed his ceremonial dance. The following
day the document from China was delivered for safekeeping
to Private Secretaries (*Naiki*) of the Ministry of Central
Affairs (*Nakatsukasa-shō*). The man who transmitted it to

them was the high court dignitary, Fujiwara no Yoshifusa, who seventeen years later was to make himself the first of the Fujiwara Regents.

On the twenty-eighth day of the ninth moon, the Emperor bestowed special promotions in rank on all members of the embassy from the Ambassador down to the sailors. The first of the next moon was the day upon which the Emperor traditionally entertained his ministers at a wine feast, and on this occasion Tomo no Sugao, the embassy Scholar and a Ship's Commander on the homeward voyage, and another expert were ordered to play five games of chess in the Imperial presence. On each game four strings of new copper cash were wagered. Like Sugao's chess techniques, these coins may have been new imports from China. The musician and Acting Administrative Officer, Fujiwara no Sadatoshi, was also ordered to play his lute, and all got drunk and were sent home with gifts befitting their various ranks. Five days later the Ministers of State received the officers of the embassy in audience as the final ceremony for the returning envoys.

On the thirteenth of the tenth moon articles brought back from China were presented as offerings to the Great Ise Shrine, and exactly two moons later similar offerings were made to four Imperial tumuli, including those of Kōnin and Kammu, who had dispatched the two preceding embassies to China. Nine days later the court remembered to include the tumulus of Kammu's Fujiwara Empress in the offerings. Meanwhile, a "palace market" had been opened at which the surplus goods from abroad were bartered.[70]

In the promotions made shortly after the Ambassador's return, he was raised two grades from the Senior Fourth Rank Lower Grade to the Junior Third Rank, and the deceased Administrative Officer, Fujiwara no Toyonami, likewise received a double promotion, from the Senior Sixth Rank Upper Grade to the Junior Fifth Rank Upper Grade. Two other Administrative Officers received only single promotions, although one of these, Nagamine no Takana, was given another promotion to the Senior Fifth Rank Lower Grade in the regular New Year's honors list early in 840. Meanwhile reassignments of post were made for some of the officers, but not for the Ambassador himself, who, perhaps suffering from the rigors of the trip, died on the twenty-third day of the fourth moon of 840. The return of the survivors of the second ship necessitated another promotions list, and on the twenty-sixth day of the ninth moon of 840 the court ranks of the 391 men who had completed the trip to China were all finally settled. Most of them received very considerable promotions, but five men, whose misdeeds must have been serious, received no promotions at all.[71]

Not many months after the return of the Ambassador, the Emperor, remembering his old association with Ono no Takamura, who had been his tutor when he was Crown Prince, took pity on the erstwhile Vice-Ambassador languishing in exile on the lonely island of Oki and recalled him to the capital. But it was not until more than a year later that Takamura was restored to court rank, receiving once again the Senior Fourth Rank Lower Grade which he had held at the time of his disgrace. The Imperial edict at the time stated, "Because We are mindful of old times and furthermore love literary talent, We show this clemency and make an exception to restore him to his original rank." Takamura went on to enjoy a distinguished career as a courtier and man of letters, and before his death in 852 he equaled in rank and court posts his former superior officer on the embassy who had caused his temporary eclipse.[72]

The final and also the most important aftermath of the embassy was the introduction of new ideas and religious practices by the monks who had accompanied it. The records tell of such activities by the monk Jōgyō shortly after the embassy's return,[73] but Ennin, of course, was to do far more. In fact, of all the members of the embassy, he was to prove historically the most important and also the most famous. The books on the embassy were not to be officially closed until the entry was made in the Japanese annals on the second day of the tenth moon of 847 that "Ennin, the Tendai Scholar Monk who had been sent to China," had at last returned home.

IV

Ennin and the Chinese Officials

Ennin at least in one respect was a man who could have adapted himself with ease to life in our own times. He was not to be overawed or discouraged by the all-pervading and inflexible authority of government nor by skeins of official red tape. During the year the embassy was in China he learned a great deal about the ponderous and complicated procedures of T'ang officialdom through his own petition to be allowed to go to Mt. T'ien-t'ai and also through the various other contacts of the Japanese with the Chinese bureaucracy. His one attempt while at Yang-chou to solve his own problem by by-passing the embassy and the central government met with no success. He attempted to persuade Li Te-yü, the Regional Commander of Yang-chou, to issue him a document that would do as a permit for travel to Mt. T'ien-t'ai. The courteous but firm reply was that, although a document issued under the authority of the Regional Commander of Yang-chou would enable Ennin to travel at will in the eight prefectures under Li's control, it would be of no use in the Mt. T'ien-t'ai region south of the Yangtse River, which was not under the jurisdiction of Yang-chou.[1]

Ennin's contacts with the authorities of Hai-chou were scarcely more encouraging. He was arrested the very day he set foot ashore in that area, and, although he was well provided for by his captors and was granted a friendly interview with the Prefect himself, he was given another taste of the bureaucratic rigidity of the Chinese officials. At the time of his arrest he was made to write out a full statement of his reasons for being ashore and also a complete list of his possessions. For the latter he jotted down, "The baggage we have brought with us [consists of] robes and clothing, begging bowls and cups, small bronze bells, writings, water bottles, over seven hundred cash, and straw rain hats." In omitting the twenty ounces of gold he had been given by the Ambassador, Ennin falsified his list of possessions as seriously as the reasons for his having been left behind, but the Chinese officials, in typically bureaucratic fashion, were content to have something in writing and made no further effort to ascertain the truth.

INQUIRIES FROM THE SUBPREFECTURE

Another flurry of inquiry was of course inevitable when the local officials in Shantung discovered that Ennin and his companions had been left behind at the Mt. Ch'ih Cloister by the departing embassy. Only thirteen days after the second ship of the embassy had set sail from the Mt. Ch'ih anchorage, an official arrived with a document of inquiry from the subprefectural town of Wen-teng-hsien, located in the middle of the Shantung Peninsula about thirty miles from its tip. This document and several more like it, which Ennin copied into his diary *in toto*, are presumably typical examples of the "gobbledegook" of the petty Chinese officials of that time. In any case, like the writings of the modern bureaucrat, they tend to be long on technical but now obscure clichés and short on content.

The inquiry from Wen-teng-hsien apparently was drafted by one minor official of the subprefecture, approved by another slightly higher officer, and finally signed by the substitute Subprefect himself. It was addressed to Ch'ing-ning-hsiang, the local canton, and was meant for the canton elders and for two men whose respective titles were *Ts'un-pao* ("Village Guarantee [Chief]") and *Pan-t'ou* ("Group Head"). These two probably were officers in the mutual guarantee system through which the government kept the common people in line by making all members of a group responsible for the actions of each individual in it. The document reads:

The subprefecture notifies Ch'ing-ning-hsiang:

We have received a report from the *Pan-t'ou* Tou Wen-chih about the three men abandoned by the Japanese ship.

The dossier on this case reveals that we have received the above-mentioned report from the *Pan-t'ou*, informing us that the ship left on the fifteenth day of this moon and that the three abandoned men are to be found at the Korean Cloister of Mt. Ch'ih. This report is as stated above.

In accordance with our investigation of the said persons, when they were abandoned by the ship, the *Ts'un-pao* and *Pan-t'ou* should have informed us on that very day. Why have they allowed fifteen days to pass before informing us? Furthermore, we do not find the surnames and given names of the abandoned men or what baggage and clothing they have. Also there has been no report at all of your having checked with the Monastery Administrator and Supervisor monks of the Mt. Ch'ih Cloister on their having foreigners living there. The canton elders are hereby notified to investigate the matter. On the very day this notice reaches you, report on the matter in detail. If anything does not tally in your investigation, or if there are any falsifications, you will be called in and held responsible, or if in your eventual report on the investigation you disregard the time limit, or if the investigation is not careful enough, the original investigators will most definitely be judged severely.

Notice of the twenty-fourth day of the seventh moon of the fourth year of K'ai-ch'eng by the Intendant Wang Tso.

Hu Chün-chih, the Superintendent of Registers and the Vice-Chief of Employees.

[Signed] *The substitute Subprefect, Ch'i Hsüan-yüan.*

Although the inquiry was not addressed to either Ennin or the Prior of the cloister, each felt that it called for a full reply from him. In his statement Ennin at last stated his aims with frankness, though he was again cautiously reticent about his funds. He wrote:

The reasons why the Japanese monk, his two disciples, and his servant are staying at the mountain cloister.

The said monk, in order to search for the Law of Buddhism, has come far across the sea. Although he has reached China, he has not yet fulfilled his long-cherished vow. His original intention in leaving his homeland was to travel around the holy land [of China], seeking teachers and studying the Law. Because the tributary embassy returned early, he was unable to accompany it back to his country and in the end came to reside in this mountain cloister. Later he intends to make a pilgrimage to some famous mountains, seeking the Way and performing [Buddhist] practices. His baggage [consists of] one iron alms bowl, two small bronze bells, one bronze jug, more than twenty scrolls of writings, clothes against the cold, and nothing else. Undergoing an investigation by the subprefectural government, he fully presents his reasons as above and gives his statement as above. Respectfully written.

A statement made on the twenty . . . day of the seventh moon of the fourth year of K'ai-ch'eng by the Japanese monk Ennin and humbly presented by the attendant monk Ishō, and the monk Igyō, and the servant Tei Yūman.

In a separate document, Pŏpch'ŏng, the Korean Prior of the cloister, vouched for the accuracy of Ennin's list of possessions and explained that the Japanese "are staying for the time being in this mountain monastery to escape the heat, waiting for it to become cool, after which they will start" on their pilgrimage, and "consequently, they did not obtain their [travel] documents from the subprefectural government."

No reply was forthcoming from the subprefecture until the third day of the ninth moon, when a man arrived with a document dated the thirteenth day of the previous moon, ordering the local Harbor Master (*Hai-k'ou-so-yu*), the *Pan-t'ou*, and the officers of the cloister to keep constant track of the Japanese, as had been requested by the apprehensive officials of the local canton. Ennin was to discover a few months later how stringently these orders were construed when he attempted to move to a small branch establishment of the cloister, in order to escape the daily lectures that were being held at that time in the main cloister. He had hardly reached his new quarters before the officers of the cloister, perhaps reminded by the canton elders, sent a note requesting his immediate return. Ennin replied with a request for "fifteen days leave," which was granted but seems to have been subsequently overruled by a higher authority, for he recorded five days later that, "because the matter was not properly settled, I returned to my original cloister." [2]

Attached to the orders from the subprefecture was a second document explaining the long delay in its transmission. A minor official had lost the original document before it had been delivered, and the loss had not come to light until some time afterward. The second document also revealed that the local prefecture and the Regional Commander in charge of the Shantung area had been informed of the presence of the Japanese.

Ennin took advantage of the arrival of these documents to send the officials another letter, reminding them of his desire to go on a pilgrimage, but, since it was already autumn, he reversed Pŏpch'ŏng's earlier request that the monks be allowed to stay at the cloister through the heat of the summer and wrote of himself and his companions, "Because it is now about to become cold, they have not yet gone anywhere, and they are passing the winter in this mountain cloister, but when spring comes, they will make a pilgrimage to famous mountains and will search out sacred sites."

THE REQUEST FOR TRAVEL CREDENTIALS

Meanwhile Ennin had made his decision to go on a pilgrimage to Mt. Wu-t'ai in the north instead of to Mt. T'ient'ai in the south. Two of the Korean monks of the cloister had been to the former and not only told him of the learned monks and holy wonders of that region but also gave him detailed information about the road there.[3] On the twenty-sixth day of the ninth moon Ennin made out a formal petition for travel credentials, using as a model a travel permit granted the Prior, Pŏpch'ŏng, when the latter had been in the Chinese capital in 807. Pŏpch'ŏng's permit, which Ennin

copied into his diary, had made reference to the successful
petition of an Indian monk the previous year, requesting
that some of his disciples be allowed to travel as mendicants,
and Ennin also referred hopefully to this precedent. His
request, which was typical of many similar documents he
was to make out over the next several months, reads:

*The Japanese monks in search of the Law inform this
monastery:*

A document in which the monk Ennin, his attendant
monks Ishō and Igyō, and his servant Tei Yūman request the
monastery to write the prefecture and subprefecture to give
them official credentials to wander and beg as their destiny
permits.

We monks, having in mind merely our longing for
the Buddhist teachings, have come from afar to this benevolent
land with our hearts set on sacred places and our spirits rejoicing in the pilgrimage. It is said that Mt. [Wu]-t'ai and
some other places are the source of the teaching and the places
where the great saints have manifested themselves. Eminent
monks from India have visited them, crossing their precipitous
slopes, and famous patriarchs of China have there attained enlightenment. We monks have admired these glorious places, and
having chanced to meet with this happy destiny, have by good
fortune come to this holy land. Now we wish to go to these
places to fulfill our long-cherished hopes, but we fear that on
the road [others] will not honor our reasons for traveling. We
have heard that the Learned Doctor Prajñā petitioned for
official credentials on behalf of some mendicant monks, and that
they [were allowed] by Imperial edict to practice [their mendicancy. Thus,] this started of old and has continued until recent
times.

We humbly hope that this monastery, in accordance
with the laws and precedents of the land, will address the prefecture and the subprefecture, asking for official credentials. If
it does so, the . . . glorious fame of the Monastery Administrators will stir foreign lands afar, their encouraging magnanimity will make gloriously manifest the sun-like Buddha,
and we shall be more than indebted to you.

The full statement is as above. The statement of the
matter is as given above. Respectfully written.

The twenty-sixth day of the ninth moon of the fourth year of K'ai-ch'eng.

The Japanese monk in search of the Law from the Enryakuji.

The winter passed quietly for Ennin, but with the advent of the new year, which according to the Far Eastern calendar signaled the coming of spring, he renewed his efforts to obtain a travel permit. On the nineteenth day of the first moon he again presented a formal petition to the officers of the cloister, who drew up a statement the very next day and sent it to a local Korean called Chang Yŏng. The latter's function as a sort of Korean consul can be seen from the various titles Ennin uses for him: "Korean Interpreter Guard Officer," "Military Guard Officer of this prefecture," and "Guard Officer in charge of Korean Embassies." Several years later when Ennin was again to meet Chang, he explicitly described him as being "in charge of the Korean population of the Wen-teng-hsien area," which embraced the whole eastern tip of the Shantung Peninsula.[4] Chang obviously was a man of influence. It was probably through him that Ennin had arranged to stay ashore in the first place, and it was undoubtedly because of Chang's aid that the Japanese were able to approach the authorities, not as fugitives from a departed embassy but in the more acceptable guise of recognized foreign residents of the area.

Naturally Ennin too sent a letter to his benefactor, in which he expressed in fulsome terms his gratitude for past favors and humbly hoped for Chang's "all-embracing compassion" and "gracious protection" in his efforts to obtain permission for the proposed pilgrimage. The next day Chang's reply came, stating that since he was sending a messenger to the subprefecture and a special messenger would speed the latter's reply to the cloister, the monks "should wait for it calmly." Six days later the reply did come by way of the Guard Officer: the subprefecture had notified the prefecture, from which a favorable reply was to be expected in ten days.

Meanwhile Chang, the Korean monks, and also the local villagers had been warning Ennin against leaving on his pilgrimage just then. Their reason was that the Shantung area for the past three or four years had been "suffering from plagues of locusts, which have eaten up all the grain, and because people are starving, there are many bandits and not a little killing and robbing." They advised him to wait until after the autumn harvests, or, if the Japanese insisted on starting at once, to go back to Yang-chou or Ch'u-chou and to proceed north from there. Ennin was somewhat perplexed by the conflicting reports he heard, but he was also anxious to be on his way. Long before the conclusion of the ten-day period mentioned in the subprefectural document, he addressed another and much longer letter to Chang. In this he excused his importunity by explaining that, "although I should be covered with embarrassment, I cannot remain quiet," and he expressed his fear that, despite the subprefecture's promise, the officials would prove dilatory in handling a petition from a mere private individual. Chang replied that he would send another messenger to the subprefecture and expressed the hope that Ennin would not worry. There was, however, a slight note of irritation in his reminder to Ennin that, since the monk "had come under his jurisdiction and stopped here, a number of people had been doing what they could for him all day long."

Ennin's concern did not prove unfounded. Two more weeks passed with no word from the subprefecture, and, when he met the Guard Officer at a Buddhist service on the fifteenth day of the second moon, Chang suggested that, if Ennin was "particularly anxious to hasten matters," he could have the officials in charge take him to the subprefecture. Ennin, after waiting a few more days, decided to take this advice, but before leaving the cloister he wrote some letters which he hoped would facilitate his subsequent return to Japan.

Ennin had heard that the ship of a Korean named Ch'oe, whom he had met at the Mt. Ch'ih Cloister seven months earlier,[5] was anchored nearby. Ch'oe, who also had the title of Guard Officer but was at the same time a trading agent for the powerful Korean merchant prince, Chang Pogo, had promised to provide a ship to take the Japanese back to the Ch'u-chou region on their way to Mt. T'ien-t'ai. Ennin, therefore, wrote to him, explaining the change in plans and also asking for the Korean's assistance when it came time for him and his party to return to Japan, which he thought might be in the autumn of 841. He also enclosed a brief note to a subordinate officer, whom he requested to keep his eye on the matter, and a long and extravagantly respectful letter to Ch'oe's master, Chang Pogo, whom he calls "the Commissioner." In this letter he explained that he had been entrusted with a missive from a Japanese official to the Commissioner but that it had been lost in the shipwreck on the Yangtse mud flats. Ennin also made appropriate reference to the fact that Chang Pogo had founded the Mt. Ch'ih Cloister. This is the meaning of his statement, "By great good fortune to my insignificant self, I have been sojourning in the area blessed by the vow of the Commissioner," and he thanked Chang Pogo for his "benevolence from afar."

Before leaving the cloister, where he could profit from the experience and literary skills of the Korean monks, Ennin also had the foresight to draw up a draft statement of thanks to local Chinese officials which might serve as a model when needed in the future. Finally, on the nineteenth day of the second moon, the Japanese, accompanied by Pŏpch'ŏng, left the cloister for the home of Chang Yŏng. There they discovered that the Guard Officer had just received the awaited document from the subprefecture, authorizing him to issue credentials to the Japanese.

AT THE SUBPREFECTURE

Armed with a document from the Guard Officer, Ennin and his three followers bade farewell the next morning to Pŏpch'ŏng and Chang Yŏng and, accompanied by one of the latter's men, started out for Wen-teng-hsien. One long day's tramp brought them to the subprefectural town, where they lodged in a monastery. In the morning the Japanese moved to another monastery, while Chang's man went to the sub-prefectural offices to present the document from his master and to renew the petition from the monks, for Chang's credentials were apparently designed to take them only this far. The chief magistrate made no decision that day, and the next he declared to be a holiday, but Ennin at least was beginning to learn something about official procedures, for he recorded in his diary, "According to Chinese usage, officials, in governing, hold hearings twice a day, morning and evening. They wait until they hear a roll of drums and then go to their seats and hold hearings. Official or private visitors must wait until the time for hearings to see officials."

On the twenty-third some petty officials came to the monastery to question Ennin in detail, and the next day he received credentials which would take him on the next stage of his pilgrimage. This document reads:

> *Wen-teng-hsien of the Government General of Teng-chou notifies the Japanese traveling monks Ennin and three others.*
>
> The monk Ennin, his disciples Ishō and Igyō, his servant Tei Yūman, and the clothing, alms bowls, etc., which they have with them.
>
> *Notice:* On examination of the dossier, we find the statement of the said monk, [saying that] in the sixth moon of the recent fourth year of K'ai-ch'eng, they came on a Japanese tributary ship to the Korean Cloister of Mt. Ch'ih in Ch'ing-ning-hsiang in Wen-teng-hsien and stayed there and that they are now free to travel and wish to go to various places on a pilgrimage, but that they fear that everywhere in the prefectures and subprefectures, the barriers and fords, the passes and market places, and along the road, their reasons for travel will not be honored, and so they humbly seek to be granted official credentials as evidence and ask for a decision.
>
> In accordance with our examination of the afore-mentioned traveling monks, we find that they still have no written permit and that they ask for something to be done about granting them official credentials. In accordance with the said statement, they are given official credentials as evidence. Respectfully written.

Notice of the twenty-third day of the second moon of the fifth year of K'ai-ch'eng by the Intendant Wang Tso.

Hu Chün-chih, the Superintendent of Registers and the Vice-Chief of Employees.[6]

AT THE PREFECTURE

The following day Ennin paid a farewell call on the chief magistrate of the subprefecture, and then in the early afternoon he and his three companions set out for the local prefecture, which was Teng-chou, the modern P'eng-lai on the north coast of the Shantung Peninsula, about eighty-five miles northwest of Wen-teng-hsien. The Japanese, after several months on shipboard and an inactive autumn and winter at the Mt. Ch'ih Cloister, had yet to develop their walking legs, and the trip to Teng-chou proved to be both slow and painful for them. The second afternoon they were forced to rest because of sore feet, and another day they were happy to spend as the feted guests of a small monastery. Finally, on the second day of the third moon, their seventh day on the road, they reached Teng-chou. With understandable exaggeration, Ennin wrote, "Tramping across mountains and hills, we had worn out our feet and had gone, staff in hand, on our knees." There had been few houses along the way, and the scanty population he had found "starving and using acorns for food."

At Teng-chou the Japanese for a third time lodged in a monastery called the K'ai-yüan-ssu. On the very day of their arrival a minor city official came to the monastery to question them, and Ennin wrote out for him a brief statement of their travels since boarding ship in Japan. The next day they were invited to call on the chief magistrate, who served them tea and wrote out an order bestowing on them "two bushels of rice, two bushels of flour, one *tou* of oil, one *tou* of vinegar, one *tou* of salt, and thirty sticks of firewood" as provisions for their travels. The Chinese bushel of the time was the equivalent of about one and two-thirds of our bushels, and a *tou* one-tenth as much.

The following day the chief magistrate and some of his subordinates went to the K'ai-yüan-ssu for a religious ceremony, after which they summoned the Japanese and served them tea and asked them questions about the customs of Japan. The next day Ennin presented a formal request for further travel credentials, which was similar to the original application he had made through the Mt. Ch'ih Cloister almost six months earlier, but had the more explicit heading: "Requesting official credentials to go to Wu-t'ai and other famous mountains and places in order to make a pilgrimage of holy sites, to seek teachers and to study the Law." The document passed over the reasons why the Japanese happened to be in Shantung in the following rather vague terms:

. . . In the sixth moon of the fourth year of K'ai-ch'eng they reached the Korean Cloister at Mt. Ch'ih in Ch'ing-ning-hsiang in Wen-teng-hsien, separated by the ocean wastes from the land of their birth and forgetting their beloved land on this ocean shore. Fortunately they were free to travel and were able to come to the Magistrate's enlightened territory.[7]

With this request Ennin also presented a letter of thanks to the chief magistrate for his gift of provisions, in which he made good use of the draft letter of thanks he had made out before leaving the Mt. Ch'ih Cloister. The same day he presented the K'ai-yüan-ssu with all of the firewood, which was obviously too heavy to carry with him, half of the flour, a quarter of the rice, and such of the vinegar, salt, and oil as would be needed for a maigre feast,[8] as a banquet for clerics was called. In his document of presentation Ennin explained that he was giving these provisions for a meal for the ten-odd monks of the monastery the following day because he did not dare "to receive alone the gracious benevolence of the Magistrate," but his real reason, of course, was to repay the monastery for lodging his party.

On the eighth day of the third moon Ennin wrote two more letters to the chief magistrate, one merely a polite inquiry and the other a brief reminder that he was waiting to be given his official credentials. The first letter, which is a good example of several similar notes Ennin recorded in his diary, reads:

> The end of spring has turned very warm, and I humbly hope for a myriad blessings for the person and actions of the Magistrate.
> I, Ennin, have received your benevolence, but since the way of a monk has its limitations, I have not been able to come to pay my respects for several days. Unworthy that I am, I am overcome with trepidation and respectfully send my disciple monk Ishō to present this letter. Respectfully written in brief.
> *Presented on the eighth day of the third moon of the fifth year of K'ai-ch'eng by the Japanese monk in search of the Law, Ennin.*
> *To the Magistrate.*

Following the final word "Magistrate" were written in tiny characters two polite formulas which might best be rendered, "His Honor, with humble respect." Ennin was obviously impatient to be on his way again, but the friendly attitude of several of the local Chinese at least helped make the delay more bearable. Four times he was invited out for the forenoon meal, which was the big meal for clerics, since they were not supposed to eat after noon. Two of these invitations came from a certain Military Guard Officer who also gave him a donkey to carry his supplies. During these days Ennin also made an interesting historical discovery. He found in one of the halls of the K'ai-yüan-ssu wall paintings of Buddhist paradises which had been presented by members of a Japanese embassy. No one remembered the date of this embassy, and the names of the donors as recorded in an inscription were all so abbreviated that Ennin could not identify them. However, he carefully copied down all the names and titles. Unfortunately they are as baffling to the modern scholar as they were to him.

Finally, on the eleventh day, Ennin, in response to a previous notice, went to the chief magistrate's office to receive his credentials and took advantage of the opportunity to say his farewells. There were two documents. One was addressed to the Regional Commander of Ch'ing-chou, the modern town of I-tu about 150 miles southwest of Teng-chou, which at this time was the capital of all eastern Shantung. The other was for the Base Officer (*Liu-hou-kuan*), who was the representative of Teng-chou at the regional commandery. The letter to the Regional Commander, which Ennin copied into his diary, included verbatim the greater part of his own original petition to the prefectural government of Teng-chou and also referred to the earlier official reports about the departure of the embassy ships and the remaining of the Japanese monks at the Mt. Ch'ih Cloister. It concluded with the statement that the Teng-chou officials lacked the authority to issue the necessary travel credentials and were, therefore, sending the Japanese on to Ch'ing-chou for a decision by the Regional Commander. Ennin perhaps had hoped for more from these documents, but at least they would take him a long way and one administrative step closer to his goal.

THE IMPERIAL RESCRIPT

While at Teng-chou Ennin had the opportunity to attend a great official ceremony—the formal reception by the local prefectural and subprefectural governments of an Imperial Rescript, which probably announced the accession of the new Emperor, Wu-tsung, of which Ennin had first heard two weeks earlier. Ennin's graphic account of the occasion, which is a unique description of a ceremony of this sort for the T'ang period, is perhaps worth quoting in full:

An Imperial Rescript by the new Emperor has arrived from the capital. Two carpets were spread in the court in front of the gate of the mansion inside the city walls, and above the steps on the north side of the great gate was placed a stand, on which was spread a purple cloth, and on this was placed the Imperial Rescript, written on yellow paper. The Administrative Officers and Secretaries of the prefecture, the Subprefect and the Superintendents of Registers of the subprefecture, the Commissioner of Troops, the military officers, the military officials, the common people, and the monks, nuns, and Taoist priests stood in ranks according to their posts on the east side of the court facing west. The Magistrate came out from within [his mansion], preceded by twenty military officers, ten each leading the way on the left and the right. When the Secretaries, the subprefectural officials, and the others saw the Magistrate come out, they bowed their heads almost to the ground.

The Magistrate called out, "The common people," and they chanted a response all together. The Magistrate stood on one of the carpets and an Administrative Officer stood on the other, both of them facing west. Then a military officer called out the titles of the various officials, and the row of Secretaries and subprefectural officials chanted their response in unison. Next he called out to the row of Military Guard Officers, Generals, and Commissioners of Troops, and the row of military men chanted their response in unison. He also said, "The various guests," and the official guests and clients chanted their response. Next he said, "The common people," and the common people, both old and young, chanted their response together. Then he said, "The monks and Taoist priests," and the monks, nuns, and Taoist priests chanted their response all together.

Next, two military officers brought the stand with the Imperial Rescript and placed it in front of the Magistrate, who bowed once and then picked up the Imperial Rescript in his hand and lowered his head, touching it to his forehead. A military officer knelt and received the Imperial Rescript on his sleeve and, holding it up, went into the court and, standing facing north, chanted, "An Imperial order has arrived." The Magistrate, Administrative Officers, Secretaries, and the military all together bowed again. A military officer called out, "Let the common people bow," and the people bowed again, but the monks, nuns, and Taoist priests did not bow. They had two Assistant Judges spread out the Imperial Rescript. These two men wore green coats. Two other Assistant Judges read it alternating with each other. Their voices were loud, as when government decisions are announced in our country. The Imperial Rescript was some four or five sheets of paper long, and it took quite a long time to read, while no one sat down.

After the Imperial Rescript had been read, the Magistrate and the others bowed again. Next a Secretary and a military officer came out into the court and voiced their thanks to the Magistrate and then hastened back to their original posts and stood there. The Magistrate announced to the officials, "Let each be diligent in his charge," and the Administrative Officers and the others all chanted their response. Next a general representative called out, "The monks and Taoist priests," and the monks, nuns, and Taoist priests chanted their response. Next he said, "The common people," and they chanted their response. Then the Commissioner who had brought the Imperial Rescript walked up in front of the Magistrate and bowed again, whereupon the Magistrate stepped off his carpet and stopped him with his sleeve. Several tens of officials and guests went up in front of the Magistrate and stood with their bodies bowed toward the ground. A military officer called out, "You may leave," and they all chanted their response in unison. The officials, the military, the monks and Taoist priests, and the common people thereupon dispersed.

AT THE REGIONAL COMMANDERY

Ennin and his companions set out from Teng-chou at dawn on the twelfth day of the third moon, the day after receiving their documents, and covered the distance to Ch'ing-chou in ten days of steady walking. They found the inhabitants of the area "rough" and the common people "starving and poor." Ennin recorded in detail the locations of their stopping places along the way and the names of their hosts as well as the varying treatment the Japanese received from each. One night the travelers had trouble finding a place to lodge because of a local epidemic, and another night the somewhat bewildered Ennin wrote in his diary, "The lady of the house reviled us, but her husband explained that she was making a joke." One day they took the wrong road for five *li;* at another point they encountered an embassy returning to the country of P'o-hai in Manchuria.

Perhaps the most interesting aspect of the trip for Ennin was the discovery of two archaeological remains. One was a stele telling of the erection of two pagodas in the year 665 by a Chinese soldier named Wang who apparently had been in the wars of 662–663 in Korea, when T'ang and Silla had fought against Japan and Paekche and had destroyed Paekche. Wang's ship had been sunk and he had been taken as a captive to Japan, but had managed to escape and return home to erect these commemorative pagodas. The other archaeological site was an old walled town, which Ennin reports was about four miles in circumference. The local villagers told him that, although it had been deserted for more than a thousand years, rainstorms still uncovered from the ground "gold, silver, pearls, jade, ancient coins, horse trappings, and the like."

At Ch'ing-chou the Japanese were lodged at a monastery called the Lung-hsing-ssu, and the monastic officers at once made a written report on the travelers for the prefectural government. The next morning Ennin himself went to the prefectural offices for the morning audience and then to the residence of the Regional Commander, but arrived there too late to be received. He therefore went to the Teng-chou Base Office to deliver one of his two letters, and at the evening audience managed to present the other to a representative of the Regional Commander.

Once through these introductory formalities, Ennin found his reception at Ch'ing-chou very warm. After returning to the monastery, he received calls from two high officials, Assistant Regional Commander Chang and a military officer named Hsiao. The latter invited Ennin to his home for breakfast the next morning and proved to be a devout Buddhist who loved theological discussions. The same day the Assistant Regional Commander invited Ennin to his office for a clerical forenoon meal. On the twenty-fourth, their third full day in Ch'ing-chou, the Japanese were shifted, perhaps as a sign of official recognition, to the Korean Cloister, which was probably for the entertainment of Korean embassies, though it seems to have been located within the Lung-hsing-ssu.

The following morning Ennin presented his formal petition for travel credentials to the Regional Commander. At the same time he wrote a letter to his friend, the Assistant Regional Commander, asking for provisions. He explained in his diary that he was forced to do this because of the famine conditions he had found all the way from Wen-teng-hsien to Ch'ing-chou, but in his letter he wrote more elegantly of himself and his request: "He makes his home anywhere and finds his hunger beyond endurance, but, because he speaks a different tongue, he is unable to beg [for food] himself. He humbly hopes that in your compassion you will give the surplus of your food to the poor monk from abroad." The response from the Assistant Regional Commander was immediate, if not very generous. On the same day he gave the monks three *tou* of rice and a like amount of flour and millet. Ennin at once wrote him a letter, stating, "I am overwhelmed with gratitude and find it difficult to express my thanks."

Since there was still no reply to his application for travel credentials, two days later Ennin sent Ishō to the government offices to inquire about this matter. Ishō was told that the credentials were to be issued and would be signed in another two days by the Regional Commander and that a report on the monks was being sent to the throne. On the appointed day Ennin again sent Ishō to the Regional Commander's offices, where he was told that the decision would be made the next day. Ishō, however, succeeded in presenting a letter from Ennin to the Regional Commander, asking for provisions for the monks, because "they have had hard times in their travels" and "go hungry at mealtime." Two days later, on the first of the fourth moon, the Japanese finally received their official credentials at the morning audience and at the same time were given three lengths of cloth and six pounds of tea.

The next morning Ennin went to the government offices to present a letter of thanks to the Regional Commander for his gifts. The latter graciously summoned Ennin into his presence and told him that "what he had given was trifling and did not merit mention" and, after thanking the monk for coming, dismissed him. Next Ennin made a farewell call

on the Assistant Regional Commander, who served him tea
and cakes. In all it was a busy social day for Ennin, for he
also had an engagement for the forenoon meal at the home
of another Chinese and at dusk paid a farewell call on his
friend Hsiao, from whom he had received a final gift of two
tou of grain for himself and his companions and two *tou* of
"small beans" as fodder for the donkey Ennin had been
given in Teng-chou. During the monk's stay in Ch'ing-chou,
Hsiao had invited him for breakfast at least twice and once
for the forenoon meal and, as Ennin states, "daily bestowed
gifts on us and inquired kindly after us all the time." When
the Japanese set out once more on their pilgrimage the next
morning, it was one of Hsiao's men who accompanied them
outside the city gate to see them off.

ON THE ROAD

When Ennin and his companions walked out of the city
gate of Ch'ing-chou, they seemed to have passed suddenly
from a world of officialdom into one inhabited almost exclusively by monks and commoners. Armed with the necessary travel permit, they could virtually ignore the bureaucrats for the next four and a half months of carefree travel
and happy pilgrimage. Even when they crossed the Yellow
River on their ninth day on the road, there seems to have
been no official surveillance. Ennin recorded that "the water
is yellow and muddy in color and flows swift as an arrow,"
and he described the wall-enclosed ferry stations on each
side of the river with their "many boats which are anxious to
carry travelers." He even noted that on the far side of the
river each of the Japanese ate four bowls of porridge and
their astonished host warned them that, if they ate so much
cold stuff, they would not digest it, but there is no mention of
any inspection of their documents.

Only during a two-day rest at the administrative center
of Chü-chou in the middle of the North China Plain in what
is now southern Hopeh did Ennin again come in contact
with officialdom.[9] The Japanese stopped at the K'ai-yüan-

ssu of that city, and the monastery officials immediately made out a report on the foreign travelers for the government. The next morning Ennin himself called on the chief local official, who entertained him and several other monks at a maigre feast, and at the evening audience on the following day Ennin took leave of the magistrate, before proceeding on his way the next morning.

The Japanese met no other representatives of government the rest of the way to Mt. Wu-t'ai. As they were leaving the North China Plain and entering the mountain valleys leading up to the holy site, they passed through another famine area and at one point found the people eating the "small bean" fodder of cattle.[10] They also encountered some monks from Mt. T'ien-t'ai, who told them of a Japanese monk and his disciple and servant who were living at this Buddhist center in South China.[11] These, of course, were Ensai and his party. Once in the holy region of Wu-t'ai, the Japanese might as well have been in a different country for all they saw or heard of Chinese officials. Ennin tells of ceremonies sponsored by the government, legends in which past Emperors figured, and pagodas erected by a devout Empress, but there were no documents to be made out or petitions to be filed.

Even when Ennin had left the mountains and returned to the China of cities and regional commanderies, his contacts remained primarily with his fellow clerics and their disciples. At T'ai-yüan-fu, the Northern Capital of the T'ang and the chief administrative center of what is now Shansi Province, Ennin did go to the prefectural headquarters, but only to see a so-called Dragon Spring.[12] Two days later, when he met a local military officer, it was as the Chinese official's guest for the forenoon meal. At the city of Fen-chou, the modern Fen-yang, southwest of T'ai-yüan-fu, he received at his monastery lodgings a call from a Guard Officer, but the man was merely paying his respects as the disciple of a friend Ennin had made while at Mt. Wu-t'ai. The next day the same officer invited Ennin to his home for early morning tea and also for the forenoon meal, after which the Japanese

resumed their journey. During the remainder of the trip to
Ch'ang-an, Ennin's only contact with the government was at
the occasional barriers along the way, where his papers were
checked. While following the Fen River southwestward
through Shansi, the Japanese passed successive barriers
some seventy-five and eighty miles southwest of T'ai-yüan-fu,
and a third barrier was encountered just before they crossed
the Yellow River near the southwestern corner of Shansi.[13]

Three days earlier the Japanese had had the interesting
but disconcerting experience of finding themselves briefly in
the center of a plague of locusts, such as had ravaged other
famine spots through which they had passed. "Locusts were
swarming over the road," Ennin recorded, "and in the
houses in town there was no place to put your foot down."
After crossing the Yellow River the Japanese passed through
another area of which Ennin wrote, "The grain sprouts have
all been consumed by the locusts, and the people of the
countryside are in great distress."

The crossing of the Yellow River occasioned the travelers
no difficulty, for they passed over it at a point a few miles
above its great bend where it flowed in two separate channels,
the one on the east crossed by a pontoon bridge some two
hundred paces long and the one on the west by a bridge. On
the nineteenth day of the eighth moon the Japanese saw
clear signs that they were approaching the capital when they
encountered the Commissioner for the Imperial Mausoleum
returning to Ch'ang-an after the interment of the Emperor
Wen-tsung whose death Ennin had heard of while still in
Shantung. According to Ennin, "The tomb builders and
soldiers stretched out for five *li*. Soldiers stood facing each
other on either side of the road, but did not interfere with
the people or horses and carts going along the road." Later
the same day the Japanese crossed a long bridge over the
Wei, the principal river of the capital area, finding a military garrison on the northern bank of the river. The next
day they crossed the bridges over two of the Wei's southern
tributaries and that evening finally lodged at a monastery
outside the east wall of Ch'ang-an.

AT THE CAPITAL

Arrival at Ch'ang-an meant for Ennin a return to official red tape, of which he may have had a taste while still outside the city walls. The Japanese apparently had to stay a day and a half outside the city, waiting for the Commissioner for the Imperial Mausoleum, whom they had passed on the road three days earlier, to re-enter the capital. Finally, on the afternoon of the twenty-second they entered one of the city gates and lodged in a monastery within the great walls of Ch'ang-an.

The following day Ennin started the serious business of getting his party officially accepted at the capital. For this purpose he went to an office under the powerful court eunuch and army general, Ch'iu Shih-liang, whose post as Commissioner of Good Works for the Streets of the Left (*Tso-chieh ta-kung-te-shih*) gave him jurisdiction over all Buddhist and Taoist priests of the eastern half of the capital. At this office he presented a document to one of Ch'iu's subordinates, whom he usually calls a Guard Officer or Censor (*Shih-yü-shih*). This document, which was accompanied by his official credentials from Ch'ing-chou, briefly presented his history and requested that he be allowed to "reside in the monasteries of the capital and seek teachers and listen to their instruction."

The Guard Officer Censor had the Japanese placed for the night in the Tzu-sheng-ssu, a monastery in the northeastern part of the city, and the next day he dispatched a man to take them to Ch'iu's own offices in the Ta-ming Palace grounds, which were outside the north wall of the city. Ennin described the route there through gate after gate, and he included in his diary the long document relating his travels which he presented on this occasion, but the expedition came to nought, for Ch'iu failed to appear at his office that day. A subordinate took the Japanese back within the city and lodged them in a monastery inside the Imperial City, the wall-enclosed area devoted to government offices in the north central part of Ch'ang-an, directly south of the Imperial Palace.

The following day the Japanese were conducted once more to Ch'iu's offices, where they were given a document provisionally assigning them to the Tzu-sheng-ssu. The officials then took them back to this monastery where they had spent their second night in the city. After one night in temporary quarters, the Japanese were assigned to more permanent quarters in a part of the establishment known as the Paradise Cloister (Ching-t'u-yüan), where they were to reside for more than a year before transferring to the West Cloister of the same monastery.[14]

Ennin and his party had not found a permanent home any too soon. On the day they moved into the Paradise Cloister the rains of early autumn started and did not let up for two whole weeks, or "for some tens of days," as Ennin wrote with pardonable exaggeration in a letter to a friend. But he was now free to remain quietly indoors and to start making inquiries about suitable religious teachers, without further thought about officialdom or visits to government offices. However, before he immersed himself in his studies, he had a final exchange of letters with the Guard Officer Censor. Ennin wrote this friendly official an extravagantly phrased letter of thanks. The latter sent an oral message with his reply, suggesting that the Japanese might wish to move to a monastery where they could be served proper Buddhist fare from the monastery kitchen and expressing a willingness to transmit such a request to Ch'iu. Ennin, however, decided to leave well enough alone, writing that he did not wish to cause any further trouble and would be content if he were allowed to stay in the Tzu-sheng-ssu and to go from there by day to seek teachers in other monasteries. The Censor's oral reply left the matter up to the monk and assured him that he would be happy to do anything further that might be desired.[15]

Ennin's contacts with the officials of the capital ended for the time being on this happy note, while he gave himself over with enthusiasm to his studies. But, of course, this was not to be the last of documents and visits to government offices for Ennin. Some years later he was to learn, to his sorrow, a great deal more about official obfuscation and arbitrariness, but this was after Wu-tsung's anti-Buddhist bias had drastically changed the relationship between monks and officials and, therefore, belongs to a different chapter of Ennin's life.

V

Life in T'ang China

Ennin, despite his zeal as a pilgrim, was a prototype of the universal tourist. His eyes and ears were open for what was new and strange to him, and during his early years in China he confided to his diary many stray bits of personal observation and hearsay information about the customs and ways of the great land of T'ang. Typical of such items are the passages quoted at the beginning of this volume, telling of New Year's Eve in 838 in Yang-chou and the arrest of Chen-shun, the unlucky commercial agent of the K'ai-yüan-ssu of that city.

POPULAR FESTIVALS

One could almost reconstruct the calendar of festivals of T'ang China from Ennin's scattered references to them. The coming of the new year, then as now, was one of the most important of the annual events. After telling of the burning of paper money and the exploding of bamboo in Yang-chou on New Year's Eve, Ennin noted that, unlike Japan, where lamps were lit everywhere on New Year's Eve, in China they lit only the usual lamps, and he concluded with the following description of the ceremonies that night in the K'ai-yüan-ssu where he was staying:

> After midnight they struck the bell in the monastery, and the congregation of monks gathered in the dining hall to pay reverence to the Buddha. At the moment for worshiping the Buddha, the whole congregation descended from their benches and, spreading out their mats on the ground, wor-

shiped the Buddha, after which they climbed back onto the benches. Then the Monastery Steward and Controller monks read out in front of the assembly the various account books for the year for the assembly to hear. Before dawn came, they dined on gruel in front of the lamps, after which they scattered to their rooms.

Ennin's later descriptions of New Year's Eve celebrations are not as detailed as his first, but they make clear that the ceremonies observed in the K'ai-yüan-ssu of Yang-chou that night were not unlike those of the other monasteries of the land. The next year at the Mt. Ch'ih Cloister in Shantung Ennin described the occasion as follows:

In the evening they lighted lamps as offerings at the Buddha Hall and Scripture Storehouse of this Korean Cloister, but they did not light lamps elsewhere. They burned bamboo leaves and grass in the stoves in each of the cells, and smoke poured from their chimneys. At dusk, before midnight, after midnight, and before dawn they worshiped Buddha, and after midnight the novices and disciples went around to the various cells with congratulatory words on the new year, in the Chinese manner.

Ennin's third New Year's Eve in China, spent at the Tzu-sheng-ssu in the capital, was even more like his first:

Since we were once again entering a new year, the congregation of monks went to the hall and ate gruel, dumplings, and mixed fruits. While the congregation of monks was eating gruel, the Monastery Administrator, Controller, and Manager read before the assembly the books of the uses of money and goods for the monastery's estates, its trade, its provisions for guests, and various expenses.

On New Year's Day itself a year later Ennin recorded, "All the households erected bamboo poles and hung banners from them and made New Year's prayers for long life. The various monasteries held lectures for laymen." The first day of the first moon was the start of a three-day holiday for officials and commoners, and the monasteries traditionally held maigre feasts during this period. In 839 Ennin noted that Li Te-yü, the Regional Commander of Yang-chou, himself came to the K'ai-yüan-ssu to worship on New Year's Day, and twice he states that the monks attended religious services that morning before exchanging greetings with one another.[1]

The new year always brought the need for a new calendar. In 838 Ennin recorded buying his a few days early, on the twentieth day of the twelfth moon, but the next year at the Mt. Ch'ih Cloister, which was near no large town, he was not able to obtain his copy until the fifteenth day of the first moon. This time, however, he took the trouble to copy the whole of it into his diary, thus giving us one of our earliest examples of a detailed Chinese calendar as used by the common citizenry. It gave the length of each moon, the order of the first day of each moon according to the traditional sixty-day cycle, the day on which each of the twenty-four sub-seasons of the Chinese year commenced, certain other festival days, and a good bit of astrological and magical information that is not entirely understood today.

Ennin did not note many of the subseasons in his diary. The "clear and bright" festival of mid-spring, the beginning of summer, and the beginning of autumn, for instance, he mentioned only once each, but the winter solstice must have been one of the most important of the seasonal festivals, for he mentions it in each of his first four years in China.[2] In 838, when it fell on the twenty-seventh day of the eleventh moon, he recorded that "no one sleeps" the night before, as on New Year's Eve in Japan. On the day of the winter solstice itself he wrote:

. . . Monks and laymen all offer congratulations. Those who are laymen pay their respects to the officials and congratulate them on the festival of the winter solstice. . . . Officials of high and low rank and the common people all offer one another congratulations when they meet. Clerics offer each other congratulations when they meet, uttering phrases about the winter solstice and making obeisance to one another. Laymen on enter-

ing the monastery also show the same courtesy. . . . All use
congratulatory phrases on the season, conforming to the tastes
of the men of former times.

The three-day festival of the winter solstice was marked
by feasting and, according to Ennin, was "exactly the same
as New Year's Day in Japan." Ennin even recorded some
of the set greetings used on this occasion. Thus he tells us
that to Li Te-yü, or the Minister of State as he is usually
called in the diary, one should say: "Moving by degrees, the
sun has reached its southern extremity. We humbly hope for
a myriad of blessings for the Minister of State's honored
self." The Chinese monks greeted their Japanese colleagues
with the words, "Today is the festival of the winter solstice.
May you have a myriad of blessings; may the propagation
of the lamp [of the Law] be without end; and may you
return soon to your own land and long be National Teachers." In 840 at the capital Ennin recorded the following
observation on the ceremonies accompanying the winter
solstice:

. . . The monks exchanged felicitations, saying, "I humbly
hope that you will long be in the world and will be in harmony
with all creatures." The ordained and the novices in speaking
to the Superior observed exactly the regulations of the written
codes of conduct. The novices touched their right knees to the
ground in front of the monks and spoke words of congratulation on the festival. When we ate our gruel,* they served us
dumplings and fruit.

"Spring begins" also appears to have been one of the
more important of the fortnightly seasonal festivals, and
Ennin mentions it twice, on the fourteenth day of the first
moon of 839 and the sixth day of the same moon in 841. In
the latter year at the capital he recorded, "Hempseed cakes
were given by the Emperor, and at the time for gruel, the
monastery served the hempseed cakes. All the lay households

---

* Meaning "breakfast."

did likewise." In Yang-chou two years earlier Ennin noted that on this day "the townsmen made orioles and sold them, and people bought them and played with them." The next three days that year were given over to a great illumination festival, which may have been part of the observance of the coming of spring. On the first of these days Ennin recorded:

At night they burned lamps in the private homes along the streets to the east and west. It was not unlike New Year's Eve in Japan. In the monastery they burned lamps and offered them to the Buddha. They also paid reverence to the pictures of their teachers. Laymen did likewise.

In this monastery they erected a lamp tower in front of the Buddha Hall. Below the steps, in the courtyard, and along the sides of the galleries they burned oil. The lamp cups were quite beyond count. In the streets men and women did not fear the late hour, but entered the monastery and looked around, and in accordance with their lot cast coppers before the lamps which had been offered. After looking around, they went on to other monasteries and looked around and worshiped and cast their coppers.

The halls of the various monasteries and the various cloisters all vie with one another in the burning of lamps. Those who come always give coppers before departing.

Ennin then gave a description of a "spoon-and-bamboo lamp" erected by one of the local monasteries. It apparently was a marvelous tree-like structure some seven or eight feet high with, according to Ennin's estimate, a thousand metal or pottery spoons tied to the ends of the bamboo branches. When the oil in all these spoons was lighted, the resultant Christmas-tree effect must indeed have been a wonderful sight.

Ennin continued his description of the illumination celebration on the last of the three days by telling of a display of the treasures of the K'ai-yüan-ssu, which included all sorts of rare colored silks and forty-two distinctive portraits of Buddhist sages and saints, as well as other paintings. That night the lamps were again lit, and an all-night service noon meal at the Mt. Ch'ih Cloister was an oblique reference to this festival. The next year he was at T'ai-yüan-fu in the modern province of Shansi on this day. At this time he noted that the celebration lasted for three days and that the various Buddhist cloisters had all arranged displays of great beauty and wonder, which were respectfully viewed by the whole populace of the city, though in the evening the people "carried on wantonly." Ennin did not bother to record the All Souls' Festival as it was observed in Ch'ang-an until the year 844, when he described it briefly in connection with indications of the Emperor's hatred of Buddhism. He wrote:

On the fifteenth day of the seventh moon the various monasteries of the city made offerings. The monasteries made flowery candles, flowery cakes, artificial flowers, fruit trees, and the like, vying with one another in their rarities. Customarily they spread them all out as offerings in front of the Buddha halls, and [people of] the whole city go around to the monasteries and perform adoration. It is a most flourishing festival.

NATIONAL OBSERVANCES

In addition to the popular festivals, there were many official holidays, such as anniversaries for former Emperors, which were observed by the government and were often marked by special religious services in the monasteries of the land. Ennin, while in Yang chou, described on the eighth day of the twelfth moon of 838 the service held in memory of the Emperor Ching-tsung, who had been assassinated on that day in 826. The Minister of State he mentioned on this occasion was of course Li Te-yü, and the General presumably was the eunuch Yang Ch'in-i, who, as a Military Inspector (*Chien-chün*), was a direct representative of the Emperor, with the duty of keeping his eye on the Regional Commander. Ennin's detailed account of the occasion, which is a unique description of such a ceremony, runs as follows:

Today was a national anniversary day, and accordingly fifty strings of cash were given to the K'ai-yüan-ssu to arrange a maigre feast for five hundred monks. Early in the

was held before the forty-two portraits, a cup lamp being placed in front of each one. At dawn more offerings were made. Crowds of onlookers gathered during the morning, and subsequently a maigre feast was held for the monks. This day also saw the start of another annual practice which was secular rather than religious in its significance, though it too may have been connected with the celebration of the coming of spring. This interesting custom Ennin described in detail as follows:

The great officials, the military, and the monks in the monasteries on this day all pick over the hulled rice. The number of days [for this work] is not limited. They bring the rice from the prefectural government and divide it among the monasteries according to the size of the congregation [of monks]. The number of bushels is not fixed, being either ten or twenty bushels [per monastery]. The monastery storehouse receives it and then apportions it out to the monks, either one *tou* or one *tou* and five *sheng* apiece.* The monks on receiving the rice select the good from the bad [grains]. The broken ones are bad and the unbroken good. If one receives one *tou* of rice and divides it into the two types, the good will amount to only six *sheng*. The good and the bad are put into different bags and returned to the government. All the monasteries also follow this same practice, each selecting the good from the bad, and returning both to the government, which, on receiving the two types, presents the good to the Emperor as Imperial rice and retains the bad in the [local] government.

[The work of picking] is assigned to the civil and military [officials], including monks among the civil [officials], but not to the common people. When they pick over millet in the prefecture, it is harder to do. The rice selected in Yangchou is extremely black in color, but they reject unhulled and damaged grains, taking only the perfect ones. The other prefectures differ from this. I hear that the Minister of State picks over five bushels, the Military Inspector's Office the same, the Senior Secretaries two bushels, the Deputy Secretaries one

* There were ten *sheng* in a *tou*, just as there were ten *tou* in a Chinese bushel.

bushel, and the military and monks one *tou* and five *sheng* or one *tou*.

Ennin also mentioned various other popular celebrations, though not always in great detail. The twenty-third day of the ninth moon of 838, he tells us, was "the great festival" of Yang-chou, but he merely noted that about two hundred horsemen and six hundred foot soldiers took part and compared it to the "Target-Shooting" Festival of the fifth day of the fifth moon in Japan, which is now known as the Boys' Festival. At Ch'ing-chou a year and a half later he mentioned that the twenty-fourth day of the third moon was the day for the "Springtime Triumph Song" and that a banquet was held in the "ball field" inside the prefectural offices. This occasion may have been in commemoration of an early T'ang victory.

In the second moon of 839 Ennin also made note in Yang-chou of the annual festival which is sometimes called the Chinese Lent. The fourteenth, fifteenth, and sixteenth days, he recorded, were "cold" days when "no smoke is produced throughout the empire and only cold food is eaten." The next year in Shantung he reported that the Cold Food Festival started on the twenty-third day of the second moon and that for three days no fires were allowed to be lit. Two years later at the capital he noted that the Cold Food Festival lasted from the sixteenth to the eighteenth of the second moon. On this occasion he remarked that "all the households paid reverence to the [family] graves," and three years later he implied that it was customary for government laborers to receive a seven-day vacation at this time.[3]

On the fifteenth day of the seventh moon came the annual All Souls' Festival, or *Urabon* as it is called in Japan. Though a purely Buddhist festival, it appealed to the Chinese because of their traditional veneration for their ancestors and in Ennin's time had already become the great popular celebration it has remained ever since in the Far East. Perhaps Ennin's remark on the fifteenth day of the seventh moon of 839 that they ate new millet for the fore-

morning the monastic congregations gathered in this monastery and seated themselves in rows in the flanking buildings on the east, north, and west. At 8 A.M. the Minister of State and the General entered the monastery by the great gate. The Minister of State and the General walked in slowly side by side. Soldiers in ranks guarded them on all sides, and all the officials of the prefecture and of the regional commandery followed behind. They came as far as the foot of the steps in front of the lecture hall, and then the Minister of State and the General parted, the Minister of State going to the east and entering behind a curtain on the east side [of the courtyard], and the General going to the west and entering behind a curtain on the west side. They quickly changed their slippers, washed their hands, and came out again. In front of the hall were two bridges. The Minister of State mounted the eastern bridge and the General the western bridge, and thus the two of them circled around from the east and west and met at the center door of the hall. They took their seats and worshiped the Buddha.

After that, several tens of monks lined up in rows at both the east and west doors of the hall. Each one held artificial lotus flowers and green banners. A monk struck a stone triangle and chanted, "All be worshipful and reverence the three eternal treasures." * After that the Minister of State and the General arose and took censers, and the prefectural officials all followed after them, taking incense cups. They divided, going to the east and west, with the Minister of State going toward the east. The monks who were carrying flowered banners preceded him, chanting in unison a two-line hymn in Sanskrit, "The wonderful body of the *Nyorai*," † etc. A venerable monk followed first [behind the Minister of State] and then the soldiers guarding him. They went along the gallery under the eaves. After all the monks had burned incense, they returned toward the hall by this route, chanting Sanskrit hymns without cease. The General went to the west and burned incense, performing the same rite as [that performed by the Minister of State] in the east, and [the two of them] came [back] simultaneously and met in their original place [before the central door of the hall].

---

* The Buddha, the Law, and the Church, or more strictly the "monastic community."
† A term for the Buddha.

During this time, there was beautiful responsive chanting of Sanskrit hymns by [the groups of monks] on the east and west. The leader of the chants, standing alone and motionless, struck a stone triangle, and the Sanskrit [chanting] stopped. Then they again recited, "Honor the three eternal treasures." The Minister of State and the General sat down together in their original seats. When they burned incense, the incense burners in which their incense was placed stood side by side. A venerable monk, Yüan-ch'eng Ho-shang, read a prayer, after which the leader of the chants intoned hymns in behalf of the eight classes of demi-gods. The purport of the wording was to glorify the spirit of the [late] Emperor. At the end of each verse he recited, "Honor the three eternal treasures." The Minister of State and the officials rose to their feet together and did reverence to the Buddha, chanting three or four times. Then all [were free] to do as they wished.

The Minister of State and the others, taking the soldiers [with them], went into the great hall behind the [lecture] hall and dined. The congregation of five hundred monks dined in the galleries.

Ennin noted this same memorial day again in 840 and 841, when he was in Ch'ang-an, though he showed that he was completely confused about whose memorial day was being celebrated. In 840 Li Te-yü, who was once more actually occupying the post of Minister of State, happened to be one of the two high dignitaries who came to burn incense at the monastery where Ennin was residing. The next year Ennin recorded that after the maigre feast, "the various monasteries in the city arranged baths." This apparently was an annual custom for the seldom-bathed monks of China. On the same day in 838 Ennin had recorded that the Regional Commander of Yang-chou "gave out cash and sent managers to two monasteries to have water heated and the congregations of monks of the various monasteries bathed." The annual clerical ablution apparently was not a simple undertaking, for Ennin added, "This is to be done for three days."

While at Teng-chou in 840 Ennin recorded that all the higher prefectural officials came to the local K'ai-yüan-ssu

to burn incense on the occasion of another national anniversary on the fourth day of the third moon, and in 841 in
Ch'ang-an he noted that a thousand monks were invited on
the fourth day of the first moon to one of the capital monasteries for an incense-burning ceremony in memory of Wen-
tsung, the Emperor who had died on that day the year before. At the time of the latter's death, Ennin had recorded
that three days of mourning had been decreed throughout
the empire, though in 846 he noted that there were several
months of official mourning throughout the provinces, prefectures, and subprefectures of the land when Wu-tsung
died.[4]

The national holiday Ennin mentioned most frequently
was the birthday of this same Wu-tsung, which appears in
his diary on the eleventh day of the sixth moon of each year
between 840 and 843. On the first of these occasions Ennin
was at Mt. Wu-t'ai, where he recorded, "On Imperial order
to the several monasteries of Wu-t'ai, birthday maigre feasts
were arranged. The various monasteries simultaneously rang
their bells, and five or six eminent monks in the highest seats
rose from their places and burned incense." The next three
years in the capital Ennin noted that on this day a maigre
feast and religious ceremony were held in the Palace and the
Emperor invited prominent Buddhist monks and Taoist
priests to debate the merits of their respective faiths in his
presence.

At the capital Ennin either had no opportunity to witness
any great official celebrations or else was by then too in-
different to bother to record them in detail. When Wu-tsung
changed the name of the year period from K'ai-ch'eng
to Hui-ch'ang on the ninth day of the first moon of 841, his
first full year on the throne, Ennin recorded in his diary
merely an outline of the ceremonies performed. Two days
earlier, perhaps in preparation for this important occasion,
the Emperor participated in a Taoistic maigre feast at the
official temple to Lao-tzu, the reputed founder of the religion. Early the next morning he went to the Altar of
Heaven, which in ancient Ch'ang-an, as in contemporary

Peking, was located in the southern suburb of the city. He
was accompanied by 200,000 guards and soldiers, Ennin
recorded, but then disappointingly concluded his entry with,
"The many wonders [of the occasion] were quite beyond
count." After completing his worship at the Altar of Heaven
before dawn on the ninth, the Emperor returned to the city
and announced the change of year period from the tower
above the central gate leading from the city into the Ta-ming
Palace north of the main walls.

It was in this same tower, we learn from other sources,[5]
that the Emperor received a long honorary title from his
ministers on the twenty-third day of the fourth moon of 842.
Ennin, who possibly was there for the occasion, merely noted
in his diary: "The troops of the various armies were drawn
up in front of the tower, and the many officials, monks, and
Taoist priests were in ordered ranks."

TABOOS, MYTHS, AND PORTENTS

Ennin naturally picked up a great deal of information
about various myths, natural portents, and popular taboos.
It did not take him long, for example, to discover that it was
best to avoid in letters and documents the use of characters
which were the personal names of T'ang Emperors or of the
chief local officials and their immediate ancestors. Even certain characters which had the same pronunciation as these
names could not be used. Ennin had only been in Yang-chou
a month when a Chinese official tipped him off on the common characters to be avoided in writing to Li Te-yü, and a
few months later Ennin took pains to record, though with
some errors, the personal taboo names of ten T'ang ancestors
and rulers together with characters which could conveniently
be substituted for some of the tabooed ones.[6] Later in Shantung he similarly inquired about the taboo characters of the
two chief officials of Wen-teng-hsien, the Prefect of Teng-
chou, and the Regional Commander of Ch'ing-chou.[7] The
latter, fortunately, had none to worry about, but the Prefect
had three, including the common character *ming*, which made

it necessary for people in that area to substitute the term *lai-jih* for *ming-jih*, the usual word for "tomorrow."

Ennin also showed an interest in Chinese myths and historical legends, recording several in his diary.[8] Some of these differ quite substantially from the now standard forms of the myths or legends, but it is hard to say whether these variations represented locally accepted forms of these traditions or were merely the result of misunderstandings on Ennin's part, growing out of his imperfect command of spoken Chinese.

Ennin was a man of his times in his interest in astrology, portents, and other natural phenomena. He not only recorded with care the various phases of the weather which meant so much to him on shipboard, but also the major snow- and rainstorms throughout much of his stay in China, and he carefully noted three eclipses of the moon and one partial eclipse of the sun, in which he estimated that all but a tenth of its surface was obscured.[9] One of the lunar eclipses occurred while he was at the Mt. Ch'ih Cloister, where the Korean monks "all went out and cried out and struck boards," in a manner reminiscent of the actions of the Japanese on board the second embassy ship when they sought to fend off thunderbolts.

Ennin also noted on one occasion that "the moon and Venus were in conjunction," and twice he wrote of comets.[10] He saw one of these comets in Ch'ang-an in 841, at which time the government ordered the various monasteries to read scriptures as a precautionary measure. The other comet he saw in 838 in Yang-chou. Coming as it did shortly after the close approach to the earth by Halley's comet in the spring of 837, the comet of 838 was identified by the Chinese as a reappearance of that spectacular heavenly body and occasioned considerable excitement. Ennin spent one whole night looking at it, and the local Chinese claimed that it resembled a "shining sword." Li Te-yü ordered each of several local monasteries to have seven monks read scriptures for seven days, and one of Ennin's Chinese friends gave him the following account of the significance of the phenomenon:

. . . When comets appear, the nation greatly declines and meets with military disturbances. The Lords of the East Sea, the leviathan and the whale, these two fishes, have died. The auguries are very alarming. Blood will flow, forming torrents. Military revolutions will break out all over and will lay low the empire. If it be not Yang-chou, then [this augury] will apply to the capital.

This same man also told Ennin of a previous case in T'ang history when a comet presaged a revolt, though Ennin obviously was confused by what he heard and appended to his misdated and faulty account the statement, "Although the matter is not clear to us monks, I have recorded it for later reference." Ennin was also told that the previous year when Halley's comet had appeared, the Emperor had been "alarmed and would not stay in his palace but placed himself apart in a lowly seat and clothed himself in thin garments," and that there had been "prolonged fasts and an amnesty."

Long periods of rain or drought apparently called for some of the same measures which were effective in the case of comets. Ennin recorded that during a prolonged rainy spell seven monks in each of the seven official monasteries of Yang-chou were called upon to read scriptures for seven days, with such completely successful results that a few months later it was necessary to carry out the same measures once again, but for the reverse effect. This time the response was even more sudden and spectacular. The day after the prayers commenced the rains started and did not let up for a solid week.[11] Later, at Ch'ang-an, Ennin indicated that when droughts occurred there both the Taoist temples and Buddhist monasteries of the capital were called upon to read their respective scriptures, but at Ch'ing-chou in Shantung he noted that the high officials prayed for rain at the various local shrines.[12] One of these, on a hill a few miles northeast of the city, was the Shrine of King Yao, that is, the mythical Emperor Yao, and Ennin heard that whenever prayers were made at this shrine, rain would fall in response.

In Yang-chou Ennin had learned something about the general theory of rain and drought making, which was but one aspect of the popular concept of *yin* and *yang*, the dual but complementary forces of Chinese cosmology. Since *yin* represented both rain and the north, it could be excluded by closing the northern gates of the city wall, or "the north ends of the roads," as Ennin describes them. The reverse was of course true of *yang*, which represented sunshine and the south. Ennin's account of this belief runs as follows:

. . . The custom in China is that when seeking good weather they close the north end of the roads, and when seeking rain they close the south end of the roads. The tradition says, "When, seeking good weather, you block the north, *yin* is obstructed, and *yang* then pervades, and the skies should clear. When, asking for rain, you block the south, *yang* is obstructed, and *yin* then pervades, and rain should fall."

THE TRAVELER IN T'ANG CHINA

Much of Ennin's stay in China was devoted to travel—by coastal ships, by river and canal boats, and particularly by foot on the highways and byways of the land. Though, of course, it never occurred to him to compose an essay on travel conditions in China, the hundreds of small comments on his own wanderings which he noted in his diary add up to a fairly detailed picture of land and sea travel in the T'ang Empire.

Perhaps the most surprising aspect of this composite picture is something that is missing from it entirely. Not once during his months of wandering between the major cities of the land and through remote and sparsely populated mountain and coastal areas was Ennin in danger from bandits or brigands of any type, and only twice is there any mention in his diary of the possibility of such danger. Once was when he encountered along a deserted part of the coast the Korean charcoal boatmen whom he feared might prove to be pirates. The other time was when friends in Shantung warned him against traveling in that area because famine conditions had given rise to considerable banditry. Despite such warnings

Ennin and his companions did traverse at least three different areas suffering from famine conditions, but each time in complete safety and apparently without trepidation. One can only conclude that T'ang China, even in its days of political decline and disruption, was a far safer land to travel in than the China of recent decades.

The traveler in T'ang China was also safer from the banditry of officialdom than has been his counterpart in more modern times. Ennin found that he could travel only with official documents, which were checked at barriers along the way and had to be inspected or renewed at the major administrative cities through which he passed, but not once did the officials at these places take advantage of the defenseless Japanese wayfarers to extort bribes or presents from them. Instead, the more devout among the officials loaded presents on the foreign clerics.

During his first stay in Yang-chou, Ennin tried to give presents to Li Te-yü to add weight to his original request to be allowed to go to Mt. T'ien-t'ai, but the Regional Commander returned everything except for a conch shell and then himself gave the monk a princely gift of two bolts of silk and two bolts of silk damask.[13] By the time Ennin came into contact with the officials in Shantung, he knew enough not to offer them presents and accepted without surprise the various gifts they pressed upon him. Similarly at the capital friendly officials apparently showered him with presents, which must have defrayed a large part of his total living expenses.

Even when Ennin was deported from Ch'ang-an at the height of the persecution of Buddhism, several of his patrons among the local officials gave him substantial farewell gifts. One, for example, presented him with ten bolts of damask and other costly presents.[14] On his way from Ch'ang-an to the coast Ennin called on certain officials in the cities along the way to whom he had letters of introduction from one of his Ch'ang-an friends, and, despite the cloud of persecution under which he traveled, even these officials treated him courteously and in some cases gave him presents.[15] One of these

men, the Prefect of Cheng-chou in the northern part of the
modern province of Honan, entertained Ennin at a meal and
also bestowed on him two bolts of silk, which was a very generous gift, since this harried official happened to be stationed
on the main route between the capital district and the coast
and consequently found his generosity sorely taxed by the
hordes of travelers passing through the city. As Ennin wrote
in his diary:

. . . People all told us that, since this was the great road from
the two capitals, there were floods of those asking for [the
Prefect's] hospitality, and he could not [always] do the proper
thing for them. If it were not a great official but an ordinary
official or client who came, when he was being very courteous to
them, they would receive one or two bolts [of cloth]. That I
received two bolts showed the great depth of his kindness.

In view of the rampant bribery of modern China, the almost total absence of references to bribery in Ennin's diary
is noteworthy. Only after the start of the Buddhist persecution while he was at Ch'ang-an and subsequently when he was
being sent from the capital to the coast, a defrocked, alien
monk marked for deportation, did he find any need to resort
to monetary arguments, and even then not very often or with
much success. At the capital he tried bribery in a fruitless
effort to obtain permission to return to Japan. Later in
Yang-chou, when he was on his way to deportation, he was
more successful in bribing the officials to let him go to Ch'u-
chou on his way back to Japan. Since his deportation orders
apparently did not specify the exact route he was to follow,
the officials, with proper inducements, could find this request
within their discretionary powers to grant. At Ch'u-chou one
of Ennin's Korean friends was unsuccessful in his attempt to
bribe the officials to allow Ennin to remain in the city awaiting a ship bound for Japan, but he did succeed, at the cost
of 300 copper cash, in persuading some government hirelings to delay Ennin's departure three days in order to allow
him and his companions to rest a little before resuming their
journcy.[16]

These are Ennin's only references to bribery. And this at a time of obvious administrative decline and in dealings with a wandering foreigner who, as a defrocked monk condemned to deportation by the court, had no possible recourse to higher official protection. Obviously the standards of official honesty in T'ang China would not compare unfavorably with those of many modern governments which are more self-conscious and also self-righteous in their claims to incorruptibility.

Ennin and his companions, in their wanderings in China, were never inconvenienced by any lack of information on routes and distances. Ennin sometimes recorded these in advance,[17] and the roads which he and his party took not only led them directly to the bridges and ferries across the rivers in their paths but also, when plotted on a modern map, prove to be as direct and well chosen as if these travelers of more than a millennium ago had had the benefit of the best of modern cartographic knowledge.

The Japanese were good walkers and, while on the road, covered an average of about sixty *li* a day and once as much as ninety-five *li*.[18] The Chinese *li* is a little over one-third of an English mile. However, as Ennin himself recorded, "the people's [use of the] word *li* is not consistent." [19] From those distances he recorded that can be checked on modern maps, we see that he, like most fallible humans, tended to overestimate a trifle his walking accomplishments. Thus, sixty of Ennin's *li* probably equaled a little less than twenty of our miles, and his record day's hike of ninety-five *li* must have been about thirty miles—not a bad day's walk for a scholarly monk in his forties.

After an early breakfast of gruel, the Japanese would trudge for as much as thirty *li* before pausing for their midday rest, at which time they would eat their clerical forenoon meal. Then, resuming their trip, they would walk until late in the afternoon before stopping for the night. Sometimes they would break the afternoon stint with a short stop for tea. Tea, however, was not necessarily a five-o'clock affair. It was drunk on almost any occasion and at any time of the day, as it still is in the Far East—during formal calls, after the regular meal, or during a friendly pause for conversation along the way.[20]

T'ang China was a great centralized empire which required a good network of roads and waterways, with the most important being those radiating outward from the capital to the far ends of the land. Ennin's diary indicates that these waterways and roads were in reasonably good repair even in the middle of the ninth century, when T'ang was long past its prime. Only once, in the remote delta region north of the mouth of the Yangtse, did he come upon an obstacle in a waterway. In contrast to this one adverse comment on a waterway, stand his many indications of their excellence and his constant wonder at the quantity of traffic they bore. This was especially true around Yang-chou and also around the far inland city of Pien-chou, the modern K'ai-feng in northern Honan, which at this time was at the head of the Pien River system connecting the Yellow River with the Huai. Ennin also described the Huai itself as a great "crossway" leading to the "East Sea." That the Japanese embassy could obtain nine seagoing vessels at Ch'u-chou, where the Grand Canal met the Huai River, indicates something of the Huai's place among the major waterways of the time.[21]

Although Ennin complained of the rough trails he traversed on the edges of the Shantung Peninsula, never once did he complain of the many hundreds of miles of main roads he followed. The bridges he came to were all passable and the ferries operating efficiently. During most of his land travels he transported his baggage on one or more donkeys, but the one time he used a wagon for this purpose was along an admittedly inferior coastal road in Shantung.[22] If wagons could negotiate such a road, they obviously were even more usable on the highways leading to the capital. Only once did Ennin record losing his way while traveling on a main road, and that time he discovered his mistake before he had gone two miles.[23] Clearly these were well-established thoroughfares, and Ennin indicates that they were also well marked. The very first day he spent on such a route was the day he left Wen-teng-hsien at the far end of the Shantung Peninsula on the road leading westward toward the capital, and, impressed by the "mileposts" he found along this road, he recorded that night:

> In China at a distance of five *li* they erect a lookout and at a distance of ten *li* they erect another lookout. They construct them as square mounds of earth pointed at the top and broader below, varying from four to five or six feet in height, and they call them *li* posts.[24]

FOOD AND LODGING ON THE ROAD

Even the recent traveler in rural China has often found lodging and food difficult to obtain, and, since the modern network of inns and hostels is thought to date back no further than the Sung dynasty at the earliest, one naturally wonders how Ennin and his companions fared in this respect during their wanderings. Actually they had little trouble. Food and lodging were always to be had, no matter where they went. The bigger cities and major routes frequented by state officials naturally had the best accommodations for travelers. While at the capital, the Japanese embassy, of course, stayed in the special accommodations for foreign embassies, but at Yang-chou and Ch'u-chou it lodged in inns. There were at least three of these in Yang-chou, and one of these inns Ennin specifically described as an "official" establishment.[25] These inns presumably were open to all official travelers of sufficient importance, but in the city of Teng-chou, where embassies from Korea and the Manchurian state of P'o-hai were likely to land and embark on their way to and from the Chinese capital, there were a Korean Inn (Silla Inn) and a P'o-hai Inn, presumably devoted primarily to the entertainment of embassies from these two countries.[26]

Between the major cities and along the main routes radiating out from the capital were post stations for the benefit of official travelers. Ennin gives us some inkling of the system when he tells us of his overland trip in 845 from Hsü-i-hsien, at this time a port on the Huai River, to Yang-chou. Ennin wrote, "From Hsü-i-hsien to Yang-chou there are nine post

stations with no water route, and at each post station we
hired donkeys for our hampers of writings." [27] Ten days
earlier while traveling down the Pien River system from the
Pien-chou area to the Huai River, he had given indication
of a similar post station system on this waterway when he
recorded that "along the way we ourselves had to hire a
[new] boat at each subprefecture."

At the post stations and perhaps at other points along
the main routes there seem to have been official inns and
hostels of one sort or another. Ennin mentioned such an inn,
where the chief officers of the Japanese embassy spent a
night, at a place called I-ling-kuan, on the waterway about
twenty miles northeast of Yang-chou, describing it as "a
place which provided for official travelers going back and
forth." [28] The final element in the place name, I-ling-kuan,
means "inn," indicating that the town, which still exists,
probably grew up originally around this official hostel. Ennin
later mentioned another inn by name on the Grand Canal
between Yang-chou and Ch'u-chou, and while traveling along
the main highway on the Shantung Peninsula he twice stayed
in inns at two other places with names ending in *kuan*.[29] Both
times he commented on the innkeepers, noting that they lived
in their inns but that, while the first made "a very cordial
host," the other was "neither particularly good nor particularly bad." Ennin also mentioned at least five other places
along the same road in Shantung with names ending in *kuan*,
but he did not say whether inns still existed there when he
passed through, and at two he noted that he stopped for his
forenoon meal in private homes rather than in inns.[30]

Another word that turns up at least nine times in Ennin's
diary as the final component of place names along the major
highways he traversed is the word *i*, meaning "post station." [31] Most of these places were along the great northeast
to southwest road through the modern province of Shansi,
which Ennin followed on his way from Mt. Wu-t'ai to the
capital. Unfortunately he did not describe the accommodations in any of these places, except to say that he stayed in
private homes in some of them.

Another word that occurs even more often as the last element in place names along the great roads Ennin traveled is *tien*, which I have usually translated in its commonest modern sense as "store" in order to distinguish it from the word *kuan*, but which like the latter also meant "inn." Ennin mentioned at least sixteen place names ending in *tien*, most of them between T'ai-yüan-fu and Ch'ang-an.[32] Some of these were at bridges or barriers. In one case Ennin expressly states that the "store" or "inn" was located at a post station, while two of the place names he mentions included the combination *i-tien*, implying the same thing. Some indication of what the *tien* originally were may be gathered from Ennin's use of the word not as a place name. The "official inn" at Yang-chou at which the main officers of the embassy stayed was actually an "official *tien*," and, while traveling in North China in 840, Ennin once recorded taking his midday rest at a *tien* in a prefectural town. In 845 he mentioned spending a night at a *tien* a short distance outside Ch'ang-an and stopping a few days later at a wayside *tien* to drink tea and talk with a friend.[33]

One need not assume that there were official accommodations for persons traveling on government business at each place with a name ending in *kuan, i,* or *tien,* but it is perhaps safe to conclude that most of these places had grown up around installations of this sort which had existed at one time or another and that, whether or not an official inn still existed, there were private shops and homes where a traveler could find food and lodging. In fact, Ennin's diary implies that, whatever the origin of the towns and villages along the major highways, lodging was usually easy to find. Though he commented several times on niggardly or surly hosts, only twice did he and his companions find difficulty in obtaining a night's lodging. Once in Shantung, as has been noted, they came to a village suffering from an epidemic and were turned away. Some months later, near the capital, Ennin recorded, "We passed about thirty houses, looking for a place to stay, but found none, and so we forced our way into the house of [a man called] Chao and spent the night." [34]

Most of Ennin's overland travels in China were on main roads leading toward or away from the capital. But during his twenty-two day hike across the North China Plain from a point about fifty miles west of Ch'ing-chou to the Wu-t'ai region in northeastern Shansi, he was not following such roads but was cutting across them transversely. Over this whole distance Ennin, significantly enough, recorded only one place name ending in *kuan*, *i*, or *tien*, thus suggesting an almost total absence of officially established inns and post stations for government travelers. This, however, was clearly a well-traveled road, and the party encountered no lack of accommodations. In fact, one gathers the impression from Ennin's diary that, while the radial routes leading outward from the capital were provided with post stations and official inns for government travelers, along all the major roads of China at this time there were many private homes and stores catering to travelers or at least prepared to take them in or feed them on demand.

The official traveler in T'ang China, if bearing the proper credentials, could expect to be provided free with food, lodging, and means of transportation along the way. When Ennin was being deported from China in 845 and was traveling from Ch'ang-an toward the east coast, he commented that, "since our documents from the capital said nothing about our provisions on the way; we had to bring our own food on the journey." But he seems to have felt that the government at least should have provided him with boats for the trip down the Pien River system. It was probably for this reason that, after his statement, "Along the way we ourselves had to hire a [new] boat at each subprefecture," he added bitterly, "The people along the banks of the river from Pien-chou on are evil at heart and not good. One could compare them to the swift and turbid waters of the Pien River, which they drink." [35]

During his first land travel in Shantung in the spring of 840, Ennin also apparently had felt that food and lodging should be provided him free not only at the inns but also at what he describes as private homes along the way. The implication is that the latter either had some sort of official status or else were actually inns which Ennin merely chose to identify by the personal names of the innkeepers. Ennin probably had a double claim to the hospitality of these men. One perhaps was the fact that he bore credentials from the chief local officials, though no specific authorization for free travel accommodations. The other was his clerical status.

The chief evidence that Ennin expected and at least part of the time received free food and lodging while traveling in Shantung is the fact that he occasionally commented with indignation upon the necessity of paying for these services. Once he wrote, "Our host was a rough and unpleasant man and did not perform the courtesies. We asked our host for vegetables, soy sauce, vinegar, and salt, but did not get any. Finally we paid a pound of tea and bought soy sauce and vegetables, but they were not fit to eat." A few days later Ennin and his companions had bad luck both at their mid-day and evening stops. Ennin recorded of their first host that he "was extremely niggardly and would not give us a single pinch of salt or spoonful of soy sauce or vinegar without payment," and of the other that he "was avaricious and took lodging charges for putting up guests." [36]

Such comments give added meaning to Ennin's other references to travel accommodations in which no mention is made of charges for food or bed. Thus, when Ennin wrote, "Our host was extremely niggardly, and we had to ask for a dish of vegetables several times before he would give it to us," or again, "Our host on first seeing us was unwilling [to take us in], and we had trouble getting anything, but finally he gave us pickled vegetables in great abundance," we can assume that the food was given without charge, even if with reluctance. When Ennin merely remarked on the friendliness or courtesy of their host or when he commented more specifically, "Our host was very cordial, [providing] vegetables for our forenoon meal without being stingy," it would appear that the travelers were received both willingly and gratis.[37] On the other hand, when Ennin found one household too poor to have any food and another which had no soy sauce, vinegar, or pickled vegetables, he may have encountered men who were not necessarily destitute but were merely sly as well as niggardly.[38]

Once out of the Shantung area Ennin seems to have relied exclusively on his position as a man of religion for what free food and lodging he received. Only once, while crossing the North China Plain, did he remark unfavorably on a host who he said "had the heart of a bandit and cheated people," but the implication this time was not that Ennin had expected free lodging but rather a more modest price. Certainly while traveling in the Shansi area, he depended largely on the generosity of devout Buddhists, and most of his comments upon his hosts on his trip across the North China Plain have to do with whether or not they were religious men, with the strong implication that if they were they would give the clerical travelers free food and lodging, but otherwise would charge them.[39] For instance, Ennin tells us of one man who "had become a believer some time ago and had long been preparing maigre meals which he offered to [passing] monks, regardless of their number." One exception, however, was a man who, although he "did not understand Buddhism, of his own accord served us maigre food at our midday rest." [40]

Ennin tells us nothing of the arrangement or appearance of the inns and homes at which he stayed. He does mention, however, that his first night on land in Yang-chou he and Ensai had separate rooms in the official inn, and he complained of a monk at a small wayside monastery on the North China Plain because the latter "did not attend at all to fixing up the rooms and beds," implying that the Japanese usually expected one or more separate rooms for themselves.[41]

Ennin's remarks on the food supplied him in his travels suggest that travelers commonly brought their own rice or noodles but expected to be provided with vegetables, soy sauce, vinegar, and salt at the inns and homes where they stopped. He made little comment on the quality of the food he received until after his long stay at the capital, by which time he must have developed a sophisticated palate for Chinese food. When in 845 he returned to Shantung he complained of the saltiness and coldness of the food served him there.[42] That a Japanese could ever have complained of the coldness of Chinese cooking seems strange today in view of the piping hotness of almost all Chinese dishes and the frigidity of most Japanese fare, but saltiness is still considered to be the outstanding characteristic of Shantung cooking.

MONASTERIES, CLOISTERS, AND THE TRAVELER

Inns and private homes were not the only places where travelers could eat or sleep in T'ang China. Twice Ennin mentioned stopping for a meal or the night at agricultural estates, one the property of a monastery, the other at the grave site of a former great official.[43] An even more frequent haven for the traveler were the monasteries and cloisters in the towns and also in the rural areas of China. As a cleric, Ennin naturally stopped in these wherever they were to be found, which was in every one of the prefectural cities and subprefectural towns through which he passed and a fair number of smaller places as well. In the monasteries where he stayed the longest, he sometimes paid for his keep by providing a maigre feast for the monks of the institution. Twice while at the K'ai-yüan-ssu of Yang-chou he and Ensai paid for maigre feasts for the monks of that monastery, and at the K'ai-yüan-ssu of Teng-chou in Shantung Ennin devoted part of the supplies given him by the Prefect to a maigre feast for the monks living there.[44]

Most of the time, however, Ennin apparently was not expected to pay for food and lodging at a monastery or cloister and made no effort to do so. It is small wonder, then, that he and his companions found scant welcome in some of the smaller and poorer religious institutions at which they stopped. In Shansi they came upon a Prior of a cloister who "did not understand the proper courtesy between host and guest" and another who "was not happy to see guests." A few days later the Abbot of a city cloister was not pleased to see them but, being a learned man in secular matters, soon warmed up to his scholarly Japanese guest.[45] In a city on the North China Plain the travelers received an even less friendly welcome from two fellow monks who, "on seeing us guests, railed at us and drove us off several times, but we forced our way into the cloister and prepared our food, and our hosts had a change of heart and themselves made noodles for us guest monks." [46]

Monastic accommodations were apparently not reserved for clerical travelers but were open to all who needed them. Thus, for instance, the senior officers of the Japanese embassy, while in the delta region north of the mouth of the Yangtse, were the first to go to a nearby monastery to reside, leaving Ennin and the ailing Ensai to join them there later, and on the canal trip to Yang-chou it was again the officers rather than the monks who alighted from the boats at the subprefectural town of Hai-ling-hsien to spend the night in a local monastery.[47] Similarly at Hai-chou Ennin found some of the officers of the original second ship of the embassy residing, not in a Buddhist monastery, but in the Hai-lung-wang-miao, the Taoistic "Temple of the Dragon-King of the Sea." [48] In Shantung on the route from Teng-chou to the capital Ennin also came across two large monasteries which had Korean Cloisters, presumably for the use of embassies from Korea on their way to and from Ch'ang-an. One was in Ch'ing-chou; the other was the Li-ch'üan-ssu on Mt. Ch'ang, about fifty miles west of Ch'ang-chou. In each case Ennin was himself lodged in the Korean Cloister, either because he was a foreigner from the east or simply because it was used for the regular guest accommodations of the monastery.[49]

These clearly were not isolated examples of the use of monasteries by lay travelers. In fact, some monasteries were so much used for such purposes that they were as much official hostels as they were religious institutions. Even in Teng-chou, which Ennin tells us was provided with a Korean Inn and a P'o-hai Inn, the local K'ai-yüan-ssu too was used as an official hostel, and Ennin, who lodged there himself, recorded with some indignation: "The K'ai-yüan-ssu has

quite a few cells for monks, but they are all occupied by
official travelers, and none are vacant. When monks come,
they have nowhere to put them." It seems probable that the
K'ai-yüan-ssu had been used as an official inn for many years
before Ennin visited Teng-chou. The unidentified Japanese
embassy which commissioned the wall paintings and inscrip-
tions Ennin discovered on the walls of the monastery very
probably had been lodged there on its way to or from the
Chinese capital.[50]

The K'ai-yüan-ssu of Teng-chou was by no means a unique
combination of hostel and monastery. At a subprefectural
town between Wen-teng-hsien and Teng-chou Ennin had
come upon another monastery with only five resident monks,
of which he wrote: "The Buddha halls were dilapidated, and
the monks' living quarters were all occupied by laymen and
had been converted into ordinary living quarters." [51] Some
days later, beyond Teng-chou Ennin spent the night at a
former monastery, called the Fa-yün-ssu, which had definitely crossed the line between monastery and inn and was
now usually known as the T'ai Inn, named for the village of
T'ai-ts'un in which it was located. Though two pagodas still
stood in front of the inn, it was operated, not by monks, but
by an innkeeper, who, according to Ennin, "performed his
function well." [52]

In addition to the monastic inns which Ennin found along
the main roads of China, he also discovered a well-organized
system of religious hostels on the routes leading to the great
holy center of Mt. Wu-t'ai, which would normally be used
by few but clerics or pilgrims. The first time Ennin came to
one of these hostels, which were called common cloisters (*p'u-
t'ung-yüan*), he explained its name and function in the following terms: "For a long time there has been rice and gruel
there, and, when men come there, regardless of whether they
are clerics or laymen, they are lodged and, if there is any
food, it is given to them, and if there is none, none is given.
Since neither clerics nor laymen are prevented from coming
and lodging there, it is called a common cloister." Ennin
then added a less consequential comment on this particular

hostel: "At the cloister there are two monks, one of whom is pleasant of disposition and the other dour. There is [also] a yellow-haired dog. When it sees a layman, it growls and snaps, with no fear of blows from a stick, but when it sees a monk, whether he be its master or a guest, it wags its tail very submissively." [53]

This first common cloister was on the edge of the mountains just before the pilgrim trail entered the sparsely populated valleys leading up to Mt. Wu-t'ai. During the six days Ennin and his companions followed this mountain trail before coming to the great monasteries of the holy mountain itself, they came upon eleven more common cloisters, conveniently spaced from about three to ten miles apart, where the pilgrim could find shelter and usually food as well. At least two of these cloisters, however, were out of provisions because of local famine conditions, and the resident monks had left one of them, at least temporarily. Others, however, must have been both large and bustling. At one "a party of more than a hundred monks, nuns, women, and men on a pilgrimage to Mt. Wu-t'ai" lodged with the Japanese, and at another they were invited to take part in a maigre feast being held for one hundred clerics.

Ennin found at least one more common cloister along the pilgrim trails around the five summits of Mt. Wu-t'ai, and, coming down from the mountains on his way to the capital, he encountered another series of cloisters leading all the way to T'ai-yüan-fu. The eleven places at which the Japanese stopped for the midday rest or the night between Mt. Wu-t'ai and T'ai-yüan-fu were spaced from about six to eleven miles apart, and eight of these were common cloisters, two others were monasteries which were probably part of the same chain of pilgrim hostels, and only one had no religious institution.[54] Even south of T'ai-yüan-fu Ennin mentioned three other scattered common cloisters along the road, but, since one of these was in a subprefectural town, another in a prefectural city, and the Prior of the third showed the travelers scant welcome, it seems probable that these three cloisters were not part of any organized chain of pilgrim hostels.[55]

ECONOMIC AND GEOGRAPHIC OBSERVATIONS

Ennin's mention of paying a pound of tea for some soy sauce and vegetables while traveling in Shantung is his only comment on the cost of food or lodging for the wayfarer. However, he frequently jotted other prices down in his diary, and these together with other casual statements on economic matters, such as his remarks on the prohibition of the purchase or sale of iron and copper in Yang-chou, do give some idea of certain aspects of the economic life of the time.

Ennin made several chance references to commodities produced in various parts of China. His mention of a "salt bureau" in the delta region north of the mouth of the Yangtse and his description of long trains of salt barges on the canal leading to Yang-chou indicate that this swampy coastal area was a major salt-producing region. Even as far north as the coastal area east of Hai-chou he found himself "wading through places where salt is gathered." Ennin also commented on the large scale on which water fowl were raised in the delta region, with flocks of up to two thousand birds.[56]

The day after Ennin first reached the Shantung coast, he recorded in his diary a comment which could have applied equally well to the whole of North China: "It is said that this prefecture grows millet, and rice is very expensive." [57] A more interesting revelation of his diary is the fact that at least parts of Shantung were wooded at the time and exported charcoal to other areas in China. The Korean mariners he encountered in the spring of 839 on the deserted shore east of Hai-chou were engaged in transporting charcoal from the southern coast of the Shantung Peninsula to Ch'u-chou on the treeless alluvial plains of North Kiangsu, and eight years later he actually traveled from the south coast of Shantung to Ch'u-chou on another charcoal-carrying ship.[58] The Korean sailors with the returning Japanese embassy also implied the presence of forests in Shantung when they argued that the ships should proceed to the Mt. Ta-chu area on the southern coast of Shantung for repairs before crossing to Japan. But when the mast of the ship on which Ennin was embarked was damaged along this same coast, the Japanese complained of the unavailability of good lumber to replace it, thus suggesting that the coastal woods of Shantung were no forests primeval.[59]

Ennin's diary also makes it quite clear that the hills of Shantung and the whole coastal area of North China were very lightly populated in T'ang times in comparison with today. It was only with difficulty that the members of the Japanese embassy established contact with the natives when they first came ashore in the Yangtse delta region, and the canal trip to Yang-chou took them through long stretches empty of human habitation. Later, along the hilly coast east of Hai-chou, the embassy ships anchored in a deserted cove, and when Ennin and his companions struck inland from this point, they had to walk some six or seven miles across a range of hills before they came to a village. Ennin himself gave a dismal picture of the sparsely populated wastes of Shantung when he described his overland trip from Hai-chou to Teng-chou in 845 in the following terms:

The road from Hai-chou up to Teng-chou is impassable. There are broad waste lands, the paths are narrow, and the grass and trees close in over them. Every few steps we got into mud, and we constantly lost our way. If we had not had someone who knew the way to guide us, we could not have gone a step. We went from waste lands into mountains, and from mountains into waste lands. The slopes are steep, the streams deep and icy, hurting us to the bone when we forded them. In the mountains, we would cross a hundred mountains and ford a hundred streams in a single day. In the waste lands, the trees were dense and the grass was thick, and if someone went a little ahead, it was difficult to see him. Only when one saw the movement of the grass did one know there was a man walking there. The mosquitoes and horseflies were like rain, and we did not have enough strength to swat them. The mire beneath the grass came to our knees or to our waists.

The prefectural and subprefectural towns along the way were like single mounds in the wilderness. . . . We went north for 1,300 *li* at one stretch, going all the way through mountains and waste lands. Although we had been close to the seashore, we had not seen the sea and only did so when we reached Teng-chou.[60]

Naturally the rugged area around Mt. Wu-t'ai also was sparsely inhabited at this time, and we learn from Ennin that these now barren mountains were then covered with a dense growth of virgin timber. Ennin described the view from the central of the five "terraces" of Mt. Wu-t'ai as follows:

. . . the five terraces are high and stand out above the mass of ridges. The five terraces are five hundred *li* in circumference, and out beyond them there are high peaks, one after the other, rising high above the intervening valleys. They are in the form of a wall around the five terraces. These peaks vary [in height], but they are densely wooded, and only the five summits are quite bare of trees from halfway up to the top.

Of the trees themselves, Ennin wrote: "The groves of pines on the peaks and the trees in the valleys grow straight and tall; groves of bamboos and fields of flax are not comparable to them [in straightness]." [61]

The whole area not only looked very different from the way it does today, but it must have had a somewhat damper climate. According to Ennin, icy cold water bubbled up out of the ground on the flat summits of some of the terraces. In the deeper valleys there were even some small glaciers that may have been the scattered and fast-dying remnants of the last ice age. Ennin saw two such masses of ice, one of which he described in the following terms:

. . . We saw far off to the northeast a whitish silver color covering an area of several tens of *chō*,* deep at the bottom of a valley. People said that this is snow which does not melt year after year and remains frozen for a thousand years and piles up in a frozen mass. The valley is deep and shaded, and the rays of the sun are cut off by the cliff in front, so that they

---

*A *chō* in Japan today is a distance of 119 yards.

never shine on [the snow]. As a result, ever since antiquity
there has never been a time when the snow melted at all.[62]

The scant population of this mountainous area, so close
to the border between agricultural China and nomadic
Mongolia, may have been largely pastoral. In the eastern
foothills of Mt. Wu-t'ai, near the North China Plain, Ennin
encountered a shepherd driving some five hundred sheep.
The day before he had met some monks from one of the Wu-
t'ai monasteries returning with "fifty donkeys loaded with
hempseed oil" which had been obtained at a city out in the
plain.[63] No doubt the large monastic communities of the holy
mountain depended for much of their supplies on the agricultural population in the valleys to the southwest and on
the great plain to the east of their isolated retreat.

Ennin's other references to economic production are few
and scattered. He spent one night at the home of a metal-
worker in a part of western Shantung still known for its
iron deposits. His mention of a visit to a water-powered
mill on a monastery estate a few miles north of T'ai-yüan-fu
suggests that such mills were unusual, at least in that part of
China. A few days later he visited a hill a mile or two east of
the city where coal was dug—coal which was to be such a
surprise to Marco Polo more than four centuries later.
Ennin's casual comment was: "There is coal all over the
mountain, and all the people from prefectures near and far
come and get it to burn. For cooking meals it has a great
amount of heat." Unconvinced by the naturalistic explanation of the phenomenon suggested by the local Chinese, he
attributed it to divine grace, writing: "We saw where the
rocks of the cliff had been scorched to coal, and people told
us that it had been burned by lightning, but I thought to
myself that it was not necessarily so and that this had been
brought about as a reward to sentient beings." [64]

GOLD FOR THE MONKS

One point of economic interest is how Ennin supported
himself and his three attendants during his more than nine
years in China. At first his funds obviously came from the

Japanese government, which not only provided for him as a
member of the embassy but also seems to have given him a
considerable amount of gold dust for his special religious expenses during the year he had originally planned to be in
China. Early in his stay, for instance, we find him twice
dispensing an ounce or so from this supply. Later, when he
decided to prolong his stay on the continent, the Ambassador
gave him twenty more ounces of gold. Similarly Ensai, when
he set out from Ch'u-chou for Mt. T'ien-t'ai, received from
the Japanese officials twenty-five ounces of gold and in addition thirty-five bolts of silk and seventy-five pads and packages of silk floss.[65] The more generous treatment of Ensai
may have been because, as a Student Monk, he had been expected to remain in China beyond the departure of the
embassy, and therefore more ample funds had been reserved
for his use.

The Japanese government made at least two later attempts to supply Ennin with funds when his stay in China
became still further protracted. In the latter part of 847, not
long before Ennin returned to Japan, Shōkai, who had been
sent out to find him, brought him some gold from the
Japanese Emperor, but an earlier attempt to supply him
with gold from Japan proved less successful. In the summer
of 842 Ennin learned through Yu Sinŏn, his Korean friend
in Ch'u-chou, that twenty-four ounces of gold had been sent
him from home. The bearer had apparently departed from
Japan either in the second half of 840 or else in 841, but,
unfortunately for Ennin, the gold went no further than
Ch'u-chou. Ishō, whom Ennin sent to get it, returned in the
late autumn with the disconcerting news that Yu had spent
it on Ensai's instructions.[66]

Although Ennin made no other mention of funds sent to
him from home, it is possible that more were sent, since it
was common practice for the Japanese government to attempt to send gold through intermediaries to Japanese monks
studying in China. For example, the Japanese histories tell
us that in 842 the court in Kyōto was still worrying about
one hundred ounces of gold it had sent through a P'o-hai

embassy to Reisen, a monk who had gone to China with the embassy of 804 and who was reported to have died before the funds reached him.[67]

Ennin incidentally found several traces of this man in the Wu-t'ai region. One was an inscription Reisen himself had written on the walls of a common cloister in 820 recording his arrival in the holy region. Another was a strip of skin from Reisen's arm, four inches long and three wide, on which the devout Japanese pilgrim had drawn a picture of the Buddha and which, placed in a small gilt bronze pagoda, was still treasured as a holy relic by one of the major Wu-t'ai monasteries.[68] But the most interesting reminder of Reisen was a long inscription with a partially unintelligible poem dedicated to him, which had been written on a board at a deserted monastery where Reisen had once lived. The man who had composed the poem and written the inscription was a monk from P'o-hai who had been Reisen's disciple.

According to the inscription, the P'o-hai cleric had gone to Ch'ang-an in 825 to pick up a hundred ounces of gold from Japan, had been subsequently dispatched to Japan by Reisen with a return gift of relics to the Japanese Emperor, and had returned from there in 828 with another hundred ounces of gold from the Japanese court, only to find his master dead. Although this inscription gave a fuller accounting of the funds sent Reisen than is to be found in the Japanese histories, Ennin discovered that there was more mystery surrounding the man than merely the missing gold. According to some resident monks of the monastery where Reisen met his end, the Japanese priest "was poisoned by someone and died, and they did not know where his disciples had buried him." [69]

The sums of gold sent Reisen were probably not as great as they first appear to be, for the Japanese court seems to have still been using old-fashioned "small ounces," a trifle less than one-third the weight of the newer "large ounces," which have remained the standard measure since T'ang times. Thus, while Ennin specified that the sums of gold given him and Ensai by the embassy in China were in large ounces, he noted that the twenty-four ounces sent him from Japan in 842 were small ounces. Moreover, his first disbursement of gold in China, when he and Ensai together provided for a maigre feast for the monks of the K'ai-yüan-ssu of Yang-chou, was in the form of small ounces. On this occasion the four small ounces they gave were found to equal one and one-quarter of the large ounces. When Ennin later changed some gold dust into copper cash, he found that one and three-quarters large ounces were worth 9,400 cash, making one large ounce worth about 5,371 cash and a small ounce only about 1,700 cash.[70]

ENNIN'S EXPENSES

It is hard to say how long the twenty large ounces of gold given Ennin by the departing Ambassador lasted him and his followers, but it could not have carried them very long. A single category of Ennin's expenses during his stay at the capital was greater than the whole of this sum. This was his tuition for instruction in Buddhism from one of his principal teachers, the monk Yüan-cheng. According to Ennin, he made payments to this man totaling twenty-five ounces of gold plus other things. Perhaps most of this sum was paid in the form of small periodic presents. For instance, we have two letters of presentation for such gifts from Ennin to I-chen, another of his clerical teachers at the capital, one for three bolts of silk and the other for ten strings of cash, that is, for 10,000 cash.[71] Clearly to cover costs of these proportions in addition to the normal living expenses of himself and his party, Ennin must have depended heavily on the generosity of monastic institutions and devout private households as well as on gifts from his many Chinese patrons.

In addition to tuition for religious instruction, Ennin must have dispensed large sums for the hundreds of Buddhist scriptures and religious paintings which he eventually took back to Japan with him and which were the basis of so much of the esoteric lore he introduced into Japanese Buddhism. The only book price he noted in his diary was 450 cash for a commentary in four scrolls on a Buddhist scripture which he acquired in Yang-chou.[72] Later, in Ch'ang-an, he mentioned the prices he paid when he commissioned a painter named Wang Hui to make five copies each of the *Kongōkai Mandara* and the *Taizōkai Mandara*, two huge schematic portrayals of the Buddhist pantheon, so arranged that between them they represented the metaphysical principles underlying Esoteric Buddhism. Unfortunately, the prices, as they now appear in the diary, do not tally, for Ennin claims to have given fifty strings of cash for the first five paintings, or 10,000 cash apiece, and only sixty or else 6,000 cash for the other five, exclusive of the cost of the silk on which they were painted. The second figures probably should be corrected to "sixty strings," though this seems a little high if the silk were not included, or else to 6,000 cash apiece.[73]

In any case, we can be sure that these paintings constituted for Ennin major outlays of funds, which weighed heavily on his mind. While he was negotiating over the price with Wang Hui, Ennin twice dreamed that patrons sent him substantial funds with which to defray these costs, and when a lay disciple of his master, I-chen, gave him forty-six feet of silk for the *Kongōkai Mandara*, he wrote in a letter of thanks to I-chen that he was "overwhelmed with gratitude." Remaining *mandara* of the time show them to have been huge paintings by Far Eastern standards, being sometimes ten feet square or more in size. Because of the scores of different deities portrayed in these *mandara*, each with his many attributes, these paintings demanded much detailed work of scrupulous iconographic accuracy. Wang Hui, no doubt, had an atelier full of assistants, but even so such works took a long time to complete. Earlier, Wang had taken forty-six days to draw four other *Kongōkai Mandara* at Ennin's request.[74]

Another religious expense Ennin recorded in his diary was a tailor's charge for some of the accoutrements of his two disciples, Ishō and Igyō. While in Yang-chou Ennin ordered for them "sitting-mats," which also served as sleeping

mats, and three Buddhist scarves apiece. The latter were
made up of strips of cloth, originally signifying the rags
and patched clothing which impoverished monks were supposed to wear. The simplest scarf was traditionally made up
of five strips, the next of seven, and the most complicated of
nine or more, in this particular case twenty-five strips. The
five-strip scarf took twenty-eight and a half feet of silk, the
seven-strip scarf forty-seven and a half feet, and the twenty-
five-strip scarf forty feet. The tailor's charges, no doubt
exclusive of the cost of the silk, were 300, 400, and 1,000
cash respectively. These charges compare well with the
tailor's bill of 250 cash for each of the "sitting-mats." These
were made out of twenty-one feet of coarse silk each, eight
feet four inches for the top surface, a similar piece of cloth
for the bottom surface, and four feet two inches for the
border, and were probably a slightly easier tailoring job
than even the five-strip scarf.[75]

How much the silk cost for the scarves and mats can be
estimated from the fact that Ennin paid 2,000 cash for two
bolts of white silk of almost forty feet each, out of which he
had a five-strip and seven-strip scarf made, apparently for
himself. This price corresponds well with the more than six
strings of cash brought in by the sale of four bolts of silk and
three of silk damask, which were donated by Ennin and
Ensai for a maigre feast at the K'ai-yüan-ssu.[76]

This last transaction gives an indication of the cost of
maigre feasts as well as of bolts of silk. The sum of more
than 6,000 cash provided for more than sixty monks. This
checks reasonably well with the other costs of maigre feasts
Ennin mentions. He and Ensai had previously given the
K'ai-yüan-ssu one and a quarter large ounces of gold, probably the equivalent of something less than 7,000 cash, for a
maigre feast originally intended for one hundred monks.
Another member of the embassy paid out 5,600 cash for a
feast for more than sixty monks, and in Ch'u-chou the
Japanese Ambassador provided 7,500 cash for a maigre
feast and alms for the same number of monks.[77] These figures
indicate that the cost of a maigre feast at this time averaged

close to 100 cash per participant. Obviously this was the basis of estimation for the assignment of fifty strings of cash for the five hundred monks who took part in the great maigre feast in Yang-chou on the anniversary of the death of a former Emperor on the eighth day of the twelfth moon of 838.

Among other miscellaneous prices noted by Ennin were charges of from 20 to 50 cash for the use of a donkey for twenty *li*, say about six miles, in the Hai-chou region, a fare of five cash per person and fifteen per donkey on a ferry-boat across the Yellow River on the North China Plain, a fare of five bolts of silk, perhaps the equivalent of 5,000 cash, for a boat trip from the southern coast of Shantung to Ch'u-chou, and finally a stiffer charge of seventeen lengths of cloth for the hire of a wagon to make the trip from the tip of the Shantung Peninsula to Ch'u-chou.[78]

Ennin tells somewhat more about the prices of grain in various parts of Shantung and the North China Plain. He noted prices in four places between Teng-chou and Ch'ing-chou, giving the costs in terms of one *tou* of grain, which was one-tenth of a Chinese bushel and the equivalent of a little more than a half quart in our system of measures. In this part of Shantung, which was suffering from famine conditions, he found that millet was selling for from 30 to 80 cash per *tou* and rice from 60 to 100 cash. The one price he gave for "small beans," which were sometimes used for cattle fodder, was the relatively high figure of 35 cash per *tou*. On the North China Plain he noted prices in only one town, where "small beans" were only 15 cash per *tou*, millet 45, rice 100, and flour from 70 to 80 cash.[79]

It is interesting to note that the early T'ang system of prices, in which the major units of cash, gold, cloth, and rice were all of approximately equivalent value, was still at least in part effective. Thus, a bolt of silk was still worth about one string of cash, and the highest rice prices Ennin quoted of 100 cash per *tou* would have made a Chinese bushel of rice also the monetary equivalent of a string of cash. Only the gold was now out of line with the other prices, for even a small ounce was worth close to 1,700 cash instead of the standard string of 1,000 cash.

The most unusual costs mentioned in Ennin's diary were those for the reconstruction of a building in the K'ai-yüan-ssu in Yang-chou, a balcony, possibly above a gateway, housing some images. The total cost was estimated at 10,000 strings of cash, in other words 10,000,000 copper coins, of which at least 500 strings were spent for lumber. Li Te-yü himself contributed 1,000 strings. The rest was to be raised through a series of religious fund-raising meetings. Even members of the foreign merchant community in Yang-chou were expected to contribute, possibly at Li Te-yü's pointed suggestion. Some Persians and some citizens of the state of Champa in what is now Southern Indochina, contributed 1,000 strings and 200 strings respectively. The Regional Commander requested only fifty strings from the Japanese embassy, which Ennin felt to be a modest figure, though he failed to tell us whether the Japanese actually paid up.[80]

On this as on other economic matters, Ennin's comments are more intriguing than conclusive. But, for a man of religion, little concerned with such mundane affairs, he was not a bad economic reporter. In particular, when compared with most of his more worldly contemporaries, he deserves credit for the breadth of interest which led him to include even this sketchy but still very valuable information on what must have seemed to him an extremely inconsequential subject.

VI

Popular Buddhism

After these lengthy discursions into Japanese embassies and Chinese governmental practices, popular customs, and travel conditions, it is well to remind ourselves that Ennin's diary, which has led us down these various worldly paths, is after all a "Record of a Pilgrimage to China in Search of the Law." For him and for those who piously preserved the document through the centuries, it was a religious text, recounting the glories of Buddhism and the joys as well as tribulations of the devoted pilgrim. The many comments that Ennin makes on the secular world are merely the crumbs from a repast of more spiritual fare.

But not many of Ennin's readers today can hope to partake in full of these main dishes. Buddhism as a philosophy and religion is as rich as the meatless Buddhist diet is simple. One of the most diverse and complex of all religions, its texts, its rites, and its theological and philosophical variations and subtleties seem almost limitless. Ennin lived after Buddhism had evolved and proliferated for more than a millennium over the whole eastern half of the civilized world, and he combined as his major interests the eclectic and all-inclusive philosophy of the Tendai Sect with the highly involved, esoteric practices of Shingon. Thus, he represents Buddhism in perhaps its most complicated phase, before declining intellectual interest in China and the growth of a simpler faith in Japan cut living Buddhism down again to more comprehensible proportions.

The scattered references in Ennin's diary to his studies, to the Buddhist ceremonies in which he participated, and to the texts and paintings he acquired no doubt would give a

164

good idea of the philosophy and beliefs of this important figure in the history of Buddhism, and the picture could be rounded out by the full list of texts he brought back from China, the record of his religious innovations in Japan, and his later writings. But it would take a lifetime of intense research to enable the writer to make such a study, and a volume of background explanation to prepare the reader to understand it. With the reader's indulgence, I shall leave these richest dishes to those better able to savor them. I do this with a clear conscience, since, for all their richness, they are the commonest of all Buddhist literary fare. Hundreds if not thousands of other texts provide as much or more information on Buddhist scriptures and thought. Ennin's diary, however, is our only detailed picture of Buddhism at the height of its glory in China as a dynamic, living religion, occupying a large place in the daily lives of the people, and it is to this simpler side of the story that I shall confine myself.

MONASTIC ESTABLISHMENTS

Buddhism was so all-pervasive in T'ang China that it has necessarily been encountered already many times in the preceding pages—in popular festivals, national observances, and along the highways and byways of Ennin's travels. The presence of monastic establishments in all the towns and cities that Ennin visited as well as in many remote places throughout the countryside has already been noted. Ennin from time to time even gives indications of the total number of monasteries and monks in certain areas. Thus, he informs us that the prefectural city of Teng-chou in Shantung had only three monasteries, one of which had so declined that it housed only about ten monks.[1] On the other hand, Yang-chou, which at the time was one of the largest cities in China, had more than forty monasteries, of which seven were classified as official monasteries where ceremonies in behalf of the state were held on government order. This represented a sizable clerical population, because the K'ai-yüan-ssu alone had at least one hundred monks.[2] Ennin notes that on one occasion five hundred Yang-chou monks were assembled on a selective basis, with no more than thirty coming from any one monastery.

Since there were so many monasteries in the Yang-chou area, one can well believe Ennin's report that there were three hundred "Buddha halls," as he calls them, within the city of Ch'ang-an itself, as well as thirty-three small monasteries and an unspecified number of large ones. All of these seem to have been outstanding in quality as well as in quantity, for Ennin claims that their buildings and the images they contained were all magnificent and the works of famous artisans. A single cloister or "Buddha hall" in the capital, he states, would "rival a great monastery in the provinces." However, he only hinted at the clerical population of the capital, which must have been tremendous. The Tzu-sheng-ssu, where Ennin resided, was not one of the most famous of the capital monasteries, nor was it probably one of the largest. Nevertheless, it may have had about one hundred resident monks or even more, for Ennin records that thirty-seven Tzu-sheng-ssu monks were defrocked in the initial stage of the great Buddhist persecution and thirty-nine more a year and a half later in one of several subsequent purges. Another indication of the great number of monks in Ch'ang-an is Ennin's statement that more than 3,400 monks and nuns who were resident in the capital were defrocked merely in the opening phase of the great Buddhist persecution.[3]

Ennin also gives some indication of the size of the monastic communities in such great mountain strongholds of the faith as Mt. T'ien-t'ai and Mt. Wu-t'ai. While he was in Yang-chou, a monk from the former informed him that the great Kuo-ch'ing-ssu of T'ien-t'ai normally had 150 monks in residence, but said that during the summer period of retirement the number rose to 300 or more, while the smaller Ch'an-lin-ssu usually had forty monks in residence, but more than seventy would stay there during the summer.[4] The three-months-long period of summer retirement had originally grown up in India where monks had found it best to give up their mendicant rounds and stay in the monasteries and study during the rainy season. Ennin himself, however, seems to have paid no particular heed to this tradition while in China.

Ennin naturally learned something of the size of the Wu-t'ai establishments from his stay there. Twelve of these were classified as "the twelve great monasteries," but there were of course any number of lesser establishments, such as the common cloisters. The great monastery where Ennin stayed longest was the Ta-hua-yen-ssu. Although he never tells us how many monks lived there, he does give an indication of its size by informing us that the monastery had twelve (or, as he once says, fifteen) cloisters, that is, twelve or fifteen separate architectural units, which also may have been separate administrative units for the resident monks. Even twelve cloisters made the Ta-hua-yen-ssu a large monastery. The Chu-lin-ssu, which was in the Wu-t'ai area but was not under the administration of the Wu-t'ai monastic community, had six cloisters and about forty resident monks. The total clerical population of the Wu-t'ai region must have been considerable, at least during the summer months of pilgrimage, for Ennin records on one occasion that a maigre feast was held for one thousand monks.[5]

While many of the monasteries of China were in part dependent on government subsidies and all expected donations from believers, some had independent support from the lands they owned. Ennin visited one such monastic estate near T'ai-yüan-fu in Shansi, and, when he passed by the Li-ch'üan-ssu west of Ch'ing-chou in Shantung, he came upon its "fruit gardens" about a mile east of the monastery and one of its estates about five miles north of it. He also learned that the Li-ch'üan-ssu in more prosperous days had owned no less than fifteen estates. Earlier, at the Korean Cloister at Mt. Ch'ih on the tip of the Shantung Peninsula, he had discovered that this institution, which housed twenty-four monks and novices, three nuns, and two old women, was supported by an estate provided by its founder, which annually brought in five hundred Chinese bushels of rice.[6]

The nomenclature and functions of the various monastic officers were so diverse and complicated that I should prefer to leave this subject to the Buddhist encyclopedists. Ennin's references to the many different administrative titles he found in the various monasteries are sufficient warning of the complexity of the subject. However, it is perhaps worth noting that in listing the monks of the Mt. Ch'ih Cloister Ennin indicated that the posts of this establishment rotated, perhaps annually, and that the titles themselves may even have changed. He also tells us that one of the posts was actually assigned to a novice. This was possibly in keeping with the egalitarian spirit of this cloister, for Ennin also tells us that even the Superior joined the others in working in the kitchen garden and adds, "When the monastic living quarters are out of firewood, all the monks in the cloister, regardless of whether they are old or young, go out and carry firewood." [7]

Ennin also tells us about the honorary titles given clerics, such as Reverence (*Daitoku*) and the sometimes functional title, Abbot (*Zasu*). He says that those who were particularly strong in the observance of the *Vinaya*, that is, the monastic rules, would be called "Reverences of the *Vinaya*," while a monk noted for his preaching on the *Vinaya* would be called an "Abbot of the *Vinaya*." Monks with titles of this type are encountered throughout his diary, but Ennin does not mention meeting anyone actually bearing the more curious title he reports for evangelistic preachers, which was "Ecclesiastic Who Converts Laymen." [8]

THE NATIONAL CHURCH

Ennin also learned something about the national organization of the Buddhist church. Early in 839 Li Te-yü brought a new Bishop (*Seng-cheng*) to Yang-chou, where he was to "look after the monasteries and also the monks" of the region. The man came from a monastery on the southern side of the Yangtse River, which was outside of Li's area of jurisdiction. Ennin not only met the new Bishop, who happened to have

the title of Reverence of the *Vinaya,* but also learned that in
theory there were three categories of Buddhist officials: Archbishops (*Seng-lu*), who "control the monasteries of the whole
land and regulate Buddhism," Bishops, who "are only for
the area of jurisdiction of a single Government General,"
and the officers of the individual monasteries.[9] But, whatever
the theory may have been, Archbishops and Bishops actually
exerted little control over the Buddhist church, at least at
this time. Ennin's diary shows no trace of such control,
though he twice mentioned by name an Archbishop of the
Streets of the Left at the capital. On the other hand, he
makes it amply clear that it was the local civil officials who
controlled the provincial monasteries and clergy, while at
the capital it was the two Commissioners of Good Works who
had absolute control over all the religious establishments of
Ch'ang-an and their inmates.

This situation is not surprising in a country where there
has never been any concept of the separation of church and
state and the tendency has been to look on religion as an
instrument of government and not as standing in its own
sovereign rights. Official monasteries, such as the seven of
Yang-chou, were, in a sense, hardly to be distinguished from
official bureaus and offices. They had the somewhat specialized
function of supervising the government's relations with the
spiritual world, holding ceremonies for the souls of deceased
or even living Emperors, reciting the necessary prayers to
produce rains or to keep them within bounds, and performing a number of other spiritual services for which the ordinary government offices were not adequately staffed. This
semiofficial status of the clergy is well illustrated by what
Ennin tells us of the annual rice-picking bee of Yang-chou,
in which monks were included among the civil officials and
were assigned the same amounts of rice to pick over as the
soldiers of the military bureaucracy.

At the capital, the integration of church and state was
still more obvious. Ennin found within the Imperial City,
which was the government headquarters in Ch'ang-an, a
monastery where two sets of seven monks were constantly

in attendance, performing ceremonial readings of the scriptures as a standing precaution against any spiritual mishap to the administration. Similarly he reports that Buddhist images and scriptures had since early times been placed in one of the halls of an Imperial palace at a hot springs resort in the hills a few miles east of the city and that "three sets of seven monks versed in devotions were drawn from the monasteries of the two halves of the city and assigned in rotation to perform devotions there each day without cease, both day and night." [10] The Emperor bestowed titles and honors on favored Buddhist priests, much as if they were court officials. To some he "granted the purple," which was the color reserved for courtiers of the fifth rank. He also had a group of officially appointed Court Priests (*Nei-kung-feng*), whom he could dismiss at will and did. The monasteries and monks were obviously at the beck and call of the Emperor, and he repeatedly issued peremptory orders to them to hold religious ceremonies, such as lecture meetings for laymen.[11]

The strict control of the government over the Buddhist church is well illustrated by the regulations on clerical ordinations that Ennin encountered. He had two attendant novices, Ishō and Igyō, and he naturally was interested not only in their proper religious training but also in their eventual ordination as full-fledged members of the monastic community. While at Yang-chou Ennin had Igyō's head shaved, for, unlike Ishō, he was apparently still unshorn, and then applied through the officers of the Japanese embassy for permission to have both the novices ordained. He made this official petition since he had learned that, "because there had been many secret ordinations," orders had been issued annually since 828 "forbidding the people to shave their heads and become monks" and that only at Mt. Wu-t'ai and one other place were there officially recognized platforms where ordinations could be performed.[12]

The close check on ordinations was the result of the government's unwillingness to see large numbers of able-bodied men enter the nontaxpaying profession of the clergy. A certain number of monasteries and monks, it was felt, was neces-

sary for the spiritual safety of the temporal rulers, but, if
there were too many tax-free monastic estates and too many
monks, the finances of the government would suffer. As a result, the authorities sought to control the number of men
ordained, thus keeping the proper balance between the
spiritual and mundane needs of the state.

The ban on private ordinations seems to have been rigor-
ously enforced. The first request the Japanese officials made
on behalf of the two novices was apparently so embarrassing
to the Commissioner in Charge of the Japanese Embassy,
who was their official contact man with Li Te-yü, that he conveniently lost the document. But Ennin was not the sort of
person to be put off by such a subterfuge. The request was
repeated a couple of months later, and this time it got
through to the Regional Commander, who replied that it
could not be granted without specific Imperial permission.[13]

Ennin later discovered that special dispensations were
sometimes given for local ordination ceremonies. While
traveling across the North China Plain, he and his party
arrived at the city of Chü-chou just one day after ordination
ceremonies had closed there. Ennin learned that the local
Prefect had notified the Regional Commander and had
"posted notices on the streets and at the crossroads so that
people would learn about it. There were over four hundred
monks who came from various prefectures to receive ordination. Yesterday the platform was closed, and the newly ordained monks all scattered." Ennin went to see the ordination platform and described it as follows:

. . . It has two levels of brick paving, the lower one twenty-five
feet square and the upper fifteen feet square. The lower level is
two and one-half feet high and the upper two and one-half feet
[above the lower]. The platform is blue-green in color. The
people nowadays speak of it as standing for a lapis lazuli
color.[14]

Four days after the closing of the ordination ceremonies
for new monks, similar ceremonies were commenced in Chü-
chou for new nuns, though in a different Buddhist establish-

ment, which was probably a convent. Ennin left the city too soon to witness the procedures, but he described the so-called platform as follows: "Banners had been hung in the hall and seating mats spread around. The ground was marked off with ropes, and they had not erected a platform. The level ground had been laid out as an ordination platform."

Although Ishō and Igyō missed their chance to be ordained in Chü-chou by only one day, they finally achieved the status of full monks at Mt. Wu-t'ai, where, with several dozen novices who had assembled from afar weeks in advance, they were consecrated in a night service on the white jade ordination platform of the Chu-lin-ssu. Ennin tells us that this was officially known as the "Myriad Saints Ordination Platform," and it was watched over by a venerable monk who, being a hundred years old, was of understandably "unusual" visage. Ennin gives the following description of the platform: "It is made entirely of white jade and is three feet high and octagonal. The base of the platform is filled in with plaster [made from powdered] incense, and on the platform is spread a silk carpet of five colors, also octagonal and made to fit the platform exactly." [15]

Government control did not stop with ordination. The officials obviously felt free to interfere with monks and monasteries whenever they chose. As we have seen, the somewhat baffled Japanese found themselves barred from a Yang-chou monastery early in their stay in China on the grounds that "the regulations did not allow foreigners to enter monastery buildings at will." At Ch'u-chou two Chinese monks who had followed Ennin there from Yang-chou were each in turn denied lodging at the K'ai-yüan-ssu, presumably because of the presence there of the Japanese, and were forced to seek lodging at other monastic establishments. The strictness of the government controls over monks is perhaps best illustrated by the incident Ennin tells us about a South Indian monk, known as the Learned Doctor Ratnacandra. This scholarly foreign cleric rashly presented a petition to the Emperor asking to be allowed to return to his homeland without first consulting Ch'iu Shih-liang, who, as the Com-

missioner of Good Works of the Streets of the Left, had
direct supervision over him. The unfortunate Indian monk
"was detained by the military for five days and charged with
the crime of going over the heads of the officials. As a result,
Ratnacandra's three disciples were each sentenced to seven
strokes of the rod, and his interpreter monk was sentenced
to ten strokes of the rod, but the Learned Doctor was not
beaten, nor was he allowed to return to his homeland." [16]

SECTARIAN DIVISIONS

The Buddhist church of China, in so far as the government exercised a uniform control over it, was a single national organization, but there were at the same time vague
sectarian divisions within it. In Japan, where the emphasis
at first was on outward forms more than doctrinal content,
these divisions soon became strictly separate and sometimes
in later years mutually warring sects. In China, the sects
represented philosophic shadings rather than definite or-
ganizational subdivisions. Even in Ennin's day, when sectarian divisions were stronger than in most other periods of
Chinese history, they obviously were not sects in the Japanese
or Western sense. While Ennin carefully identified the Japanese clerics who accompanied him to China by their sectarian
affiliations, he rarely attached sectarian labels to the Chinese
monks he met. And the only two sectarian divisions he mentions in connection with Chinese monks are Tendai and Zen
(Ch'an in Chinese), which were in some ways the two philosophic extremes within Buddhism. Tendai emphasized a
strictly graded order of texts and a highly organized, eclectic philosophy; Zen was antitextual and, in a sense, anti-
philosophic and placed its emphasis on personal character
and sudden enlightenment.

The rough and forthright ways of the monks of the Zen
tradition must have struck Ennin as very strange. This perhaps explains his characterization of a group of Zen monks
he encountered in a town on the North China Plain as "extremely unruly men at heart." Four of the Korean monks

at the Mt. Ch'ih Cloister he also identified as belonging to
the Zen Sect, though he had no special comment on them. In
Yang-chou he received a courteous call from twelve Zen
monks who, in the company of one Tendai colleague, were
on their way to Mt. T'ien-t'ai, and at the Ta-hua-yen-ssu of
Mt. Wu-t'ai he noted that a group of more than fifty Zen
monks, all equipped with "woolen robes and priestly staves,"
were lodging in one of the cloisters of the monastery while on
a pilgrimage around the holy mountain.[17]

Mt. T'ien-t'ai, as the fountainhead of the Tendai teachings, was naturally the greatest center of Ennin's own sect,
though he was never able to visit it. He did find, however,
that the Mt. Ch'ih Cloister and a Yang-chou monastery
known as the Lung-hsing-ssu both showed some leanings toward Tendai. At Mt. Ch'ih the Tendai influence could be
seen primarily in the lectures held in winter on the *Lotus
Sutra*, a scripture on which the sect put particular emphasis,
and also in the alternate name of the institution, which was
the Lotus Cloister (Fa-hua-yüan). At the Lung-hsing-ssu
there were several indications of Tendai influence. There was,
for instance, a Lotus Cloister where Ennin found a mural of
T'ien-t'ai Ta-shih ("Great Teacher of T'ien-t'ai"), the posthumous name of Chih-i, the founder of the sect. In this
cloister there was also a building known as the "Lotus Place
of Ritual" for use in one of the special religious observances
of the Tendai Sect, and on the walls of one of its galleries
was painted a mural of the "Reciting of the *Lotus Sutra*." [18]

The only great Tendai center that Ennin visited was the
Ta-hua-yen-ssu of Mt. Wu-t'ai. Here he found two monks,
one of whom had recently come from Ch'ang-an, lecturing on
the *Lotus Sutra*, the various works of Chih-i, and other
Tendai scriptures, sometimes to congregations of as many as
forty Tendai monks, all members of this monastery. One of
the scholar clerics of the monastery, Abbot Wen-chien, when
introduced to Ennin, remarked, "This monastery holds two
lectures to propagate Tendai teachings. I had a feeling that
we should see monks from distant lands coming here to seek
Tendai teachings, and there has indeed been a great fulfill-

ment of my premonitions." Ennin, impressed with all he had
seen and heard, commented enthusiastically in his diary,
"One can truly speak of the Ta-hua-yen-ssu of Mt. Wu-t'ai
as in the Tendai tradition." [19]

The strong Tendai influence of the Ta-hua-yen-ssu was
probably due in large part to Wen-chien and another cleric
called Chih-yüan, who was regarded by everyone in the monastery as "the master" and was much revered throughout the
Wu-t'ai region. Ennin recorded of this devout man that he
"receives no alms and eats but once a day; his observance of
the rules is pure and noble; he never once misses the six times
for worship and repentance." Even at the Mt. Ch'ih Cloister
in Shantung Ennin had heard of these two Tendai scholars,
who were said to have come originally from Mt. T'ien-t'ai.
Chih-yüan subsequently confirmed this report by telling
Ennin that he himself had seen Saichō come from Japan to
Mt. T'ien-t'ai in the year 804. Ennin found the cloisters
where Chih-yüan and Wen-chien resided "full of writings of
the Tendai teachings," and he spent more than a month
"copying Tendai writings which are not yet to be found in
Japan." When he was finished, he made a catalogue of the
texts copied and, presenting it to Chih-yüan, "had him write
his Buddhist name on it." [20]

Ennin, however, gives no indication that the close spiritual
relationship between Mt. T'ien-t'ai and the Ta-hua-yen-ssu
was accompanied by any administrative supervision. The
latter seems to have had administrative affiliations only with
the other Wu-t'ai monasteries. At the same time, the Ta-hua-
yen-ssu was in contact with Mt. T'ien-t'ai on doctrinal matters. Thus, when Ennin asked Chih-yüan to resolve the
doctrinal questions he had brought with him from the Enryakuji, his home monastery in Japan, the latter refused,
saying that, "since he had been told that Mt. T'ien-t'ai had
already resolved these doubts, it would not be proper to resolve them again." Ennin the following day saw the document from the Kuo-ch'ing-ssu of Mt. T'ien-t'ai giving this
information. It will be remembered that Ennin, while in
Ch'u-chou, had given these questions to Ensai to take to

Mt. T'ien-t'ai. Since the monks at Mt. T'ien-t'ai had no way of knowing that the Japanese would go to Mt. Wu-t'ai, we can only assume that these doctrinal decisions had been circulated to branch monasteries like the Ta-hua-yen-ssu as a routine procedure or, as Ennin says, "to spread the virtues of Tendai." Interestingly enough, the authenticity of the communication had been attested to by a statement penned by the Prefect of the T'ien-t'ai area and by his official seal, specifically requested by the clerical authors of the document.[21]

Ennin's account of his studies at the capital illustrates the essential weakness of sectarian divisions in Chinese Buddhism. He made careful inquiries regarding possible teachers and checked on the scholarship of those recommended to him, but all that seems to have concerned him was their mastery of some branch of Buddhist learning, not their sectarian affiliations, which he never mentions.

Only two weeks after reaching Ch'ang-an and after some preliminary inquiries and prayer, Ennin learned from a Chinese monk the names of the leading local authorities on the subjects he wished to study, which were Sanskrit, the original language of most of the Mahayana Buddhist scriptures, and the detailed theological and magical lore surrounding the two great schematic representations of Buddhist philosophy and cosmology, the *Kongōkai* and *Taizōkai Mandara*. Ennin's informant recommended eight Ch'ang-an clerics in four separate monasteries. Two of these scholars, however, were from the Western Lands, meaning that they were either Indians or Central Asians, and consequently did not know enough Chinese to be of much use as teachers. Ennin sent his informant together with his own disciple Ishō to check further on the remaining six possible teachers. They reported back that one of these six "was seventy-three years old and was palsied and senile," while another seemed inferior to his colleagues.

Ennin must have been satisfied with this report, for he eventually studied with all four of the remaining men and at once set about borrowing texts from one of them, Yüan-cheng. Then some days later he called on Yüan-cheng and arranged to commence his studies of the *Kongōkai* under the latter's supervision. Ennin started his course of instruction with various ceremonies, including baptism, and, when he completed his work with Yüan-cheng three and a half months later, he had another round of ceremonies. Among these was "Baptism as a Transmitter of the Law"—a ceremony in which Ennin, though not immersed, had five bottles of water poured over his head. It was perhaps in celebration of the completion of this course of study that Ennin on this same day also climbed a high pagoda originally built by the great Hsüan-tsang, which then stood in the southeastern part of the city but today, known as the Great Wild Goose Pagoda (Ta-yen-t'a), stands about two miles south of the walls of the greatly shrunken city of Sian.[22]

With the *Kongōkai* mastered, Ennin started his studies of the *Taizōkai* under I-chen and subsequently received further instruction on it from the third of the recommended teachers. He also reviewed with the fourth "the rules of the Sanskrit letters." Ennin's last comment on his formal studies comes close to two years after he reached the capital, when he was studying with the Indian, Ratnacandra (who had so disastrously tried to bypass Ch'iu Shih-liang) and "personally learned from his mouth the correct sounds" of the Sanskrit letters.[23]

MAIGRE FEASTS

Ennin, while making many oblique references in his diary to the organization of the Buddhist church, was more interested in describing the ceremonials of the faith as he saw them observed in China. Prominent among these were maigre feasts, which were banquets for clerics and sometimes laymen as well, held before or around noon and limited to the meatless fare prescribed by Buddhist eating regulations. The feast itself was always preceded and sometimes followed by a religious service of worship.

As we have seen, Ennin himself on occasion sponsored
maigre feasts as partial payment for the food and lodging
he was receiving at a monastery. It was perhaps for the same
reason that an envoy from the land of P'o-hai held a maigre
feast for about fifty monks, including Ennin, in the city of
Ch'ing-chou in Shantung. Ennin also tells us of one of his
Japanese colleagues who accompanied the Japanese embassy
to the capital and studied there for fifteen days with Ennin's
later master, I-chen, and in payment for this instruction arranged a maigre feast for one hundred monks.[24]

We also find members of the Japanese embassy sponsor-
ing maigre feasts after having had religious pictures painted.
Since such paintings were normally copied from existing
icons in some monastery, these feasts too can be regarded in
a way as payments for services rendered. Thus, the Japanese
Ambassador held a maigre feast for more than sixty monks
in the K'ai-yüan-ssu of Ch'u-chou in return for the use of
the paintings of that monastery as models. The Administrative Officer, Fujiwara no Sadatoshi, while seriously ill in
Yang-chou, similarly vowed to have religious paintings made,
and, after these had been drawn at the K'ai-yüan-ssu of Yang-
chou, he too held a maigre feast in that monastery for more
than sixty monks.[25]

Maigre feasts, we have seen, were held as part of the religious ceremonies on the birthday of the reigning Emperor
or on the anniversary of the death of one of his predecessors.
Ennin also mentions that one of the maigre feasts he sponsored was timed to fall on the anniversary of the death of
Chih-i, the founder of the Tendai Sect, and while at Ch'ing-
chou he noted that the local Regional Commander held a
"long life" maigre feast on the birthday of his son.[26]

Maigre feasts were sometimes held, as dinners would be
today, as simple ceremonies of welcome or farewell. Thus, a
maigre feast, a "maigre tea," and a concert were held to welcome the Bishop whom Li Te-yü brought to Yang-chou, and
later, when Ennin was leaving the Ta-hua-yen-ssu of Mt.
Wu-t'ai, his Chinese colleagues there held a farewell maigre
feast for him. Ennin was similarly entertained at a small

monastery in the territory under the jurisdiction of Teng-chou in Shantung at a maigre feast sponsored by the Prefect of Teng-chou and attended by the two officers of the monastery and the three Japanese clerics. On this occasion Ennin recorded that "more than twenty villagers, in accordance with their respective abilities, prepared the food in their own houses and brought it to us" and then themselves joined in eating it. This sort of lay participation apparently was not unusual, for Ennin mentions it in connection with the maigre feasts held at Mt. Wu-t'ai and also notes that the porters, artisans, and archers of one of the original Japanese embassy ships went to the K'ai-yüan-ssu of Yang-chou for a maigre feast and to hear scriptures recited. Ennin also attended a maigre feast at the Mt. Ch'ih cloister which was held "without any limit of the number participating," which probably meant that it was open to all comers, including laymen.[27]

Maigre feasts seem at times to have been sponsored by the government or private patrons simply as meritorious acts of faith without any particular commemorative significance or any thought of repayment for specific services rendered. Ennin tells of an Imperial emissary who annually came with gifts to the twelve great monasteries of Wu-t'ai and to hold great maigre feasts, some of which were attended by as many as a thousand monks. Ennin also mentions other great maigre feasts at Wu-t'ai paid for by private individuals. One of these, for 750 participants at the Chu-lin-ssu, was sponsored by a man from distant Shantung. Ennin described this particular ceremony as follows:

At noon they struck a bell, and the congregation of monks entered the hall. After the full monks, novices, laymen, children, and women had been seated in rows according to their ranks, the Leader in Worship struck a mallet and chanted, "Let all be worshipful and pay reverence to the three eternal treasures; let all be widely reflective." Then two junior monks of the monastery, holding golden lotus flowers in their hands, struck gourd-[shaped] cymbals, and three or four men chanted together in Sanskrit. The patron burned incense, and everyone, regardless of whether he was a cleric or layman, man or woman, took his turn at burning incense. After that the Leader in Worship first read the text of offering by the patron and then offered praises [to the Buddha]. Then he chanted, "Let all be widely reflective," and the full monks chanted together, "*Maka-hannya-haramitsu*." * 28

This was followed by a responsive chanting of the names of Buddhist deities between the Leader in Worship and the congregation, which concluded with the latter chanting,

. . . "on behalf of the lasting prosperity of the holy reign [of the dynasty], we pay reverence to the three eternal treasures; on behalf of the manifold grandeur of today's patron, we pay reverence to the three eternal treasures; on behalf of the monks and our fathers and mothers and all sentient beings of the universe of the Law, we pay reverence to the three eternal treasures."
      [The Leader in Worship then] struck a mallet and chanted, "Let the prayer for the presentation of food be said," and a monk in a raised seat said the prayer, after which they served the food. The noble and humble, the old and young, clerics and laymen, men and women, all were provided for equally.
      After the congregation of monks had eaten the maigre feast, they purified themselves ritually with water, rinsing out their mouths. Then a mallet was struck, and they called on the names of the Buddhas. The Leader in Worship struck the mallet and said, "On behalf of the grandeur of today's patron and the sentient beings of the universe of the Law, we call on the *Maka-hannya-haramitta*."

This started another series of responsive chants, calling on the names of Buddhas. Then the mallet was struck a final time, and "the congregation dispersed at will."
At Yang-chou Ennin also recorded in detail the procedures of the maigre feast he and Ensai sponsored for more

* The name of a famous Buddhist scripture, known as the *Mahā-prajñā-pāramitā-sūtra* in Sanskrit. *Maka-hannya-haramitta* is a variant of this same name.

than sixty monks on the twenty-fourth day of the eleventh
moon, the anniversary of the death of Chih-i:

. . . The assembly of monks entered the hall together and sat
down in order, and a man performed [the rite of] purification
by water. We patron monks stood in front of the hall. One of
the assembly of monks beat a wooden mallet, and another
monk chanted a Sanskrit [hymn]. The Sanskrit hymn was,
"How through this scripture is one eventually to reach the
other shore? We desire the Buddha to open to us the subtle
mystery and to explain it in detail for all creatures." It
sounded most beautiful.

During the chanting of the Sanskrit a man was passing out scriptures. After the Sanskrit, the assembly together
recited scriptures, about two pages of each. Then a wooden
mallet was struck, and the reading of scriptures came to an
end. Next, a monk chanted, "Reverence the three eternal treasures," and the assembled monks all got down from their
benches and stood. Then the first master of Sanskrit chanted
in Sanskrit a one-line text, "The body of the *Nyorai* is without exhaustion," etc.

Ennin and Ensai then entered the hall and burned incense
on the left side of the image of the Buddha and were followed in this rite by each of the monks present.

After that, they then gave praise to the Buddha. This
did not differ in wording from the praise of the Buddha at the
beginning of a prayer in our country. After giving praise to
the Buddha, they made known the document in which we patrons
had first requested that a maigre feast be arranged. Then they
read the maigre-feast essay in praise [of Buddha]. After reading the maigre-feast essay, they chanted, "The Buddha, Shakamuni," * the great assembly calling out the Buddha's name in
unison. After that they chanted praises . . . while standing,
and then all together climbed onto their benches and seated
themselves.

This concluded the religious part of the ceremony, after
which ten of the principal participants, including Ennin,

---

* The historical Buddha, known as Sākyamuni in Sanskrit.

Ensai, the monk who had read the maigre-feast essay, and some of the officers of the monastery, had their feast in the living quarters of the institution, while the rest went to the dining hall. The final act of the ceremony was the handing out of some of the money provided for the occasion to each of the participants. This custom, which must have been a major source of cash income for Chinese monks, is described by Ennin as follows:

. . . The custom in China is that, each time a maigre feast is held, in addition to [purchasing] food, they set aside some of the money provided, and when the maigre feast is about to end, they divide it equally among the monks in accordance with how many cash there are and the number of the assembled monks. For the monk who has made the maigre-feast essay, however, they especially augment the number of cash. If they give thirty cash to each of the monks, they give four hundred cash to the one who has made the maigre-feast essay. Both are called alms cash, which I believe is the same as what is called "charity" in Japan.

Ennin on this occasion also learned that, when a breakfast of gruel was being provided the monks by a patron, a notice was sent out at sunset the day before, but for a noon maigre feast the notice was not circulated until the morning of the day. He also learned of a system of rotation of invitations to maigre feasts among the monks of the more than forty monasteries of Yang-chou. Apparently each monastery kept a list of all the monks of each of the other monasteries and, when large maigre feasts were held to which nonresident monks were to be invited, the outside monks were selected from this list in sequence. This meant that all the clerics of Yang-chou would share equally in invitations to the great maigre feasts and in the alms dispensed at them.

This rotation, however, was not an invariable rule of procedure. When five hundred monks were invited to attend a maigre feast organized by the government at the K'ai-yüan-ssu of Yang-chou on the anniversary of the death of a former Emperor, the monasteries of the city were represented by numbers of monks proportionate to their size. Ennin tells us:

. . . The large monasteries had thirty, the middle-sized monasteries twenty-five, and the small monasteries twenty. All were seated together as groups in long rows, and managers were dispatched from each monastery to attend to the serving of their respective groups. The managers from the various places themselves did the serving. The maigre feast was not served in a single place, but was served and eaten at the same time [in all places], and then [the monks] arose and dispersed, each one going to his own monastery.[29]

RELIGIOUS LECTURES

Next to maigre feasts, the religious observances most frequently mentioned by Ennin in his diary were individual lecture services, or more commonly series of lectures on one specific Buddhist text. Ennin often identified prominent clerics by the scripture or commentaries on a scripture in which they were versed and on which they lectured from time to time. This specialization on one text and within that text on one tradition of interpretation is very reminiscent of the Chinese scholars and philosophers of the pre-Buddhist age, and it seems likely that this custom of textual specialization among Buddhist clerics was influenced, if not wholly derived, from the secular scholastic tradition of China.

While at the Korean Cloister at Mt. Ch'ih, Ennin described what he called "The Korean Rite of a Single-Day Lecture," which apparently was a memorial service, sponsored and paid for, no doubt, by a relative of the deceased:

At 8 A.M. a bell was struck. After prolonged ringing, the lecturer and the leader entered the hall. The congregation had entered previously and was seated in rows. When the lecturer and the reader entered, the congregation together called on the Buddha's name, dragging it out. The lecturer mounted to a seat on the north and the leader to one on the south, whereupon the praising of Buddha stopped. Then a monk in a seat below them chanted in Sanskrit a one-line hymn, "How through this scripture," etc. After the Sanskrit chanting had ended, the one seated to the south chanted the headings of the scripture. This so-called chanting of the scripture was drawn out, and his voice quavered a great deal. While the scripture was being intoned, the congregation scattered flowers * three times. Each time flowers were scattered a different hymn was sung. After the intoning of the scripture, the headings were chanted in short syllables. The lecturer expounded the scripture headings, dividing them into three parts and presenting the general meaning of the scripture. After the scripture headings had been explained, the *Ina* † read out the reasons for holding the affair. In this document were stated the principle of the impermanency [of life], the merits of the deceased person, and the date of his death. [30]

This is the only single-day lecture Ennin describes in his diary, but he has many references to series of lectures. For example, there were the lectures for laymen which the Emperor sponsored at the capital. These, Ennin tells us, had been suspended in 835 but were revived by the new Emperor, Wu-tsung. Ennin mentions four such periods of lectures for laymen during the years 841 and 842. The first, which seems to have been held in celebration of the change of year period early in 841, continued for a period of one full month and was held in seven Ch'ang-an monasteries. Ennin happened to mention the texts used by four of the lecturers, which in two cases were the popular *Lotus Sutra*. On two other occasions ten Buddhist monasteries were involved in the lectures, and twice Ennin mentions that two Taoist monasteries were ordered to hold similar lectures on Taoist scriptures, one of which was the early philosophical text of Chuang-tzu.[31]

While such Imperially sponsored lectures may have been limited to the capital, monasteries throughout China on their own initiative held periodic series of lectures which often lasted for a month or possibly even longer. Ennin tells us

---

* A standard Buddhist rite of worship.
† One of the monastic officers.

that the Mt. Ch'ih Cloister regularly held lectures on the *Lotus Sutra* in winter and on another scripture in summer, and the winter lectures lasted from the sixteenth day of the twelfth moon * to the fifteenth day of the first moon of the next year. When Ennin arrived at the Ta-hua-yen-ssu of Mt. Wu-t'ai, he discovered that at least one of two series of lectures in progress there had begun about a month earlier, though the other may have started more recently, for the lecturer on the day Ennin heard him was completing his discourse on only the fourth scroll of the work under consideration.

Each series of lectures at the Ta-hua-yen-ssu was being attended by some forty monks. Clerics also made up the audience of thirty-eight which Ennin, while in Yang-chou, heard was following a course of lectures by a septuagenarian monk in a nearby monastery. At the Mt. Ch'ih Cloister, however, laymen joined the churchmen for the lecture services, and the audience, which numbered about forty at the start, increased on the last two days to 250 and 200 respectively, before the ceremonies broke up with a concluding benediction and the administering of the so-called Rules of the Bodhisattva, the monastic precepts which Ennin himself was later to administer to the Japanese Emperor.[32]

The month-long lecture service at the Mt. Ch'ih Cloister consisted of "lectures in the daytime and worshiping and repenting and listening to scriptures and the order [of worship] at night." With the exception of "the worship and repentance at dusk and before dawn," which were held in the Chinese manner, all the services were in the Korean language and "in accordance with the customs of Korea," for the audience, with the exception of Ennin and his party, was made up exclusively of clerics and laymen from the land of Silla. Ennin described the lecture sessions themselves as follows:

---

* Or possibly the eleventh moon, for Ennin at this point failed to specify the moon clearly.

At 8 A.M. they struck the bell for the scripture lecturing, apprising the group, after which the congregation spent quite a little time entering the hall. At the moment the bell sounded for the congregation to settle down, the lecturer entered the hall and mounted to a high seat, while the congregation in unison called on the name of the Buddha. Their intonation was wholly Korean and did not resemble the Chinese sounds. After the lecturer had mounted to his seat, the invocation of the name of the Buddha stopped. A monk seated below him chanted in Sanskrit, entirely in the Chinese manner, the one-line hymn, "How through this scripture," etc. When he reached the phrase, "We desire the Buddha to open to us the subtle mystery," the crowd chanted together, "The fragrance of the rules, the fragrance of meditation, the fragrance of deliverance," etc. After the singing of the Sanskrit hymn had ended, the lecturer chanted the headings of the scripture and, dividing them into the three parts, explained the headings. After that the *Ina* came forth in front of the high seat and read out the reasons for holding the meeting and the separate names of the patrons and the things they had donated, after which he passed this document to the lecturer, who, grasping his chowry,* read the patrons' names one by one and made supplications for each individually. After that the debaters argued the principles, raising questions. While they were raising a question, the lecturer would hold up his chowry, and when a questioner had finished asking his question, he would lower it and then raise it again, thank [the questioner] for his question, and then answer it. They recorded both the questions and the answers. It was the same as in Japan, except that the rite of [pointing out doctrinal] difficulties was somewhat different. After lowering his hand at his side three times and before making any explanation, [a debater] would suddenly proclaim the difficulty, shouting with all his might like a man enraged, and the lecturer would accept the problem and would reply without raising problems in return.

After the debate, he took up the text and read the scripture. At the end of the lecture, the congregation chanted

---

* A duster-like symbol, thought to represent either leadership (the tail of the leader deer) or a brush to sweep away the impurities of the world.

praises together in drawn-out syllables. Among these praises were words of blessing. The lecturer descended from his seat while a monk chanted the hymn, "Being in this world is like [living] in emptiness." It sounded very much the way it does in Japan. The lecturer mounted the worship platform [in front of the deities], while a monk chanted the three praises. Then the lecturer and the congregation, singing together, left the hall and returned to their rooms.

There was also a repeat lecturer seated below and to the south of the high seat, who discussed the text the lecturer had expounded the day before. When he came to phrases explaining the meaning, the lecturer had written out the explanations, and the repeat lecturer read these. After he had read the whole of the text expounded the day before, the lecturer then read the next text. Thus it went each day.

SERVICES AND FESTIVALS

Ennin also made mention of some other Buddhist services and ceremonies. He tells us of two capital monasteries which held Baptism Rituals "on behalf of the nation," each apparently for a period of twenty-three days, for one seems to have lasted from the fifteenth day of the third moon to the eighth day of the fourth, the traditional birthday of the Buddha, and the other from the first to the twenty-third day of the fourth moon. While Ennin was staying at the Tzu-sheng-ssu in the capital, he also mentioned that a certain priest stayed there for three days, transmitting the "*Nembutsu* Teachings of the Pure Land of Amida." This clearly was the doctrine of easy salvation into the Pure Land, or Paradise, of the Buddha Amida, the compassionate savior, by some outward sign of faith, such as *nembutsu*, the simple repetition of the Buddha's name—a doctrine which, though but a minor aspect of Buddhism in Ennin's day, was to sweep Japan in the great religious awakening of the twelfth and thirteenth centuries. Ennin learned that this Amidist teacher went on Imperial command from monastery to monastery "without stopping month after month," teaching at each for a period of three days.[33]

While at the Tzu-sheng-ssu Ennin had occasion to participate in a funeral, though the attendant ceremonials may
have been somewhat simplified because of the Buddhist persecution then under way. After an eight-month illness, Igyō
the older of Ennin's two disciples, died late at night on the
twenty-fourth day of the seventh moon of 843. The next day
Ennin made out the necessary documents, one giving the
hour of his death, another stating that "Igyō, aside from his
personal clothing, had no money, cloth, or grain in his room"
and requesting punishment for Ennin and Ishō if this statement were subsequently found to be false, and the last asking
the monastery officers to give the Japanese a burial plot for
their dead companion. A space was given them in the monastery's brick-kiln grounds outside the city walls, and, after
temporary interment there on the twenty-seventh, Igyō was
permanently laid away two days later. Ennin asked Ishō and
the six Chinese monks who had been in the funeral procession to call on the name of the Buddha ten times and to recite
incantations. Twenty-one days after Igyō's death the "three-
sevens day" maigre feast was held for him. At fourteen-day
intervals after that came the "five-sevens day" and the
"seven-sevens day" maigre feasts. Fifty-one days later came
the "hundred-day" maigre feast, and that is the last we hear
of Igyō in Ennin's diary.[34]

While at the Chu-lin-ssu of Mt. Wu-t'ai, Ennin was invited to a ceremony held to honor and make offerings to
seventy-two sages and saints. His account of the occasion
runs as follows:

. . . In response to the invitation we went to the ritual place
and saw the religious arrangements for worship. Along the
walls inside the hall were placed in order the portraits of the
seventy-two sages and saints. Valuable banners and jewels in
all the beautiful colors of the world were spread out and displayed, and carpets of varied colors covered the whole floor.
Flowers, lamps, fine incense, tea, medicines, and food had been
placed in offering to the saints.

After dusk the full monks assembled, and one of them, mounting to the seat of worship, first struck a gourd-[shaped] cymbal and then explained the exalted reasons for [holding] this service. One by one he chanted the names of the patrons and the nature of the things they had given, and he called on the names of the Buddhas and Bodhisattvas on behalf of the patrons. Then he supplicated the seventy-two sages and saints, pronouncing the name of each one. Each time, after he had pronounced one of their names, [the monks] would all chant the words, "We merely pray that you be benevolent and pity us and descend to our place of ritual and receive our offerings." After they had stood in worship seventy-two times, he then left his seat for the first time.

Then another monk mounted to the seat [of worship] and offered praises and called on the names of the Buddhas. He supplicated the various Buddhas and Bodhisattvas, saying, "With our whole heart we supplicate the Great Teacher, the Buddha Shakamuni; with our whole heart we supplicate the Buddha Miroku * who is to descend and be born [in the world], the Lapis Lazuli Shining Buddha Yakushi † of the Twelve Noble Vows, His Holiness the Bodhisattva Monjushiri, ‡ His Holiness the Bodhisattva Fugen, § and the myriad Bodhisattvas." At the beginning of all [of the supplications] he said, "With our whole heart we supplicate." They then chanted in unison the text for scattering flowers in offering. There were several tunes.

Next a nun also offered praises exactly as the monk had. Then a monk chanted praises together with the other monks. Then they struck a gourd-[shaped] cymbal and chanted together, "We call on the name of the Buddha Amida." Then they stopped, and next the group of nuns, in place of the monks, did the same thing. Alternating in this manner, they gave praise to the Buddhas. Just at midnight they stopped, and together they left the place of ritual and dispersed.[35]

---

* *Maitreya* in Sanskrit, the Buddha of the Future.
† The Buddha of Healing.
‡ A longer name for Monju.
§ A deity who, with Monju, is often portrayed as a flanking figure of the historical Buddha, Shakamuni.

In earlier chapters we have already heard something of
popular Buddhist festivals in the great illumination ceremony of Yang-chou following the coming of spring and the
All Souls' Festival of the fifteenth day of the seventh moon. A
somewhat similar occasion was the annual festival for the
four teeth of the historical Buddha, Shakamuni, that were
treasured in as many Ch'ang-an monasteries. Ennin's diary
contains contradictory statements regarding the time of this
festival, though it seems to have been held, at least princi-
pally, from the eighth to the fifteenth days of the third moon.
He was much more precise in telling how the various teeth
had reached China, one from the Central Asian state of
Khotan, another from Tibet, a third from India under divine
protection but hidden in the flesh of a man's thigh, and the
fourth more conveniently from heaven. Two successive years
Ennin went to perform adoration before two of these teeth,
and he tells how he reverently held one and worshiped it. The
first year, after informing us that the Archbishop of the
Streets of the Left "served as the head of the festival," Ennin
continued:

. . . The various monasteries took part, each arranging fine
offerings. All sorts of medicines and foods, rare fruits and
flowers, and many kinds of incense were carefully prepared and
offered to the Buddha's tooth. They were spread out beyond
count in the gallery around the storied offering hall. The
Buddha's tooth was . . . in the storied hall. All the Reverences
of the city were in the storied hall adoring it and making
praises. The whole city came to worship and make offerings.
One man donated one hundred bushels of non-glutinous rice and
twenty bushels of millet. Another man provided biscuits plenti-
fully and without restrictions. Another man donated enough
cash for the miscellaneous needs of the meals without restrictions. Another man provided thin cakes without restrictions,
and another donated enough for the meals of the Reverences
and venerable monks of the various monasteries. In this way
each one made his vows and offered his alms, making a glorious
festival of the Buddha's tooth. People tossed cash like rain
toward the storied hall of the Buddha's tooth.[36]

MYTHS AND MIRACLES

Ennin in his wanderings learned much about the legends and wonders of the various monasteries he visited. At the Li-ch'üan-ssu west of Ch'ing-chou he saw the Lapis Lazuli Hall, where even the doorjambs and steps were made of this blue-green stone. Here he saw the image of a fifth-century Chinese monk who was said to have been a manifestation of the Eleven-Faced Kannon and whose soul after his death was believed to have descended to this monastery. He also visited the dried-up spring from which the institution had received its name, Li-ch'üan-ssu, or "Monastery of the Spring of Pure Water." Ennin learned that the water once had "bubbled up fragrant and sweet of taste" and that "those who drank of it avoided illness and prolonged their lives." He also saw a nearby peak called the Dragon Terrace, where, his map informed him, a dragon had once been seen dancing, an incident which, when reported to the Emperor, induced the latter to change the name of the monastery for a while to the Lung-t'ai-ssu, "Dragon-Terrace Monastery." [37]

In the Lung-hsing-ssu of Yang-chou Ennin had seen a stele inscription telling somewhat fancifully of the trip to Japan almost a century earlier of the great Chinese missionary, Chien-chen, or Ganjin, as he is known in Japan. Under the heading, "the monk who crossed the sea," it recorded in part: "In crossing the sea, the monk encountered evil winds. First he came to a sea of serpents, which were several tens of feet long. After proceeding a whole day, he came to the end of it and then reached a black sea, where the color of the sea was like India ink." [38]

In the same diary entry Ennin recorded the miraculous story involving the Bodhisattva Fugen, which accounted for the name of a building in the Lung-hsing-ssu known as the "Hall of Fugen's Counter-Wind." The legend ran that in olden times a fire had destroyed the monastery, but, when it reached the cloister where this building stood, a monk recited the *Lotus Sutra* inside the hall, "whereupon a great wind suddenly arose, blowing from within this cloister, and drove back the fire so that the hall was not consumed."

Near the Mt. Ch'ih Cloister Ennin came into still closer contact with a religious wonder. He visited a place where seven stone images and an iron box containing the Buddha's bones had recently been dug from the ground after a marvelous occurrence. The images were of Fugen, Monju, Kannon, Miroku, and some other lesser deities. The story, as Ennin tells it, ran as follows:

. . . there is a Korean here . . . who dreamed one night that a monk came and said to him, "I am Monjushiri. An ancient Buddha hall has fallen to ruin, and for years no one has repaired it. Its Buddhas and Bodhisattvas are buried in the ground. I have observed your faith and, consequently, have come to tell you about it. If you wish to know the truth, dig around the pagoda southeast of your house and you will see." On awakening, he was awe-struck and told his dream to monks and laymen. Then, going to the ancient pagoda, he dug up the earth with a hoe. When he had reached a depth up to his chest, he discovered the images of the Buddhas and Bodhisattvas.

It is small wonder that Ennin concluded his story with the comment, "When all of us saw this, we marveled not a little. At night we worshiped the Buddha, and monks and laymen gathered and made donations all night long." [39]

Ennin reported a somewhat similar though decidedly more tradition-encrusted occurrence at a monastery near T'ai-yüan-fu in Shansi, known as the T'ung-tzu-ssu, or the "Monastery of the Children." Ennin copied a stele inscription which told the following story about a pious monk, who once resided at this spot:

. . . He suddenly saw a cloud, shining in five colors, rise into the air from the ground and cast its light over all. In this shining cloud were four children seated on green lotus seats and playing. The sound shook the earth, and cliffs crumbled and fell. An image of the Buddha Amida appeared where a bank had fallen away. People came to worship from all over . . . and there were many wonders.

The Monastery of the Children was itself erected in commemoration of this miracle, and a majestic, seated statue of
Amida, 170 feet high and 100 feet wide, and flanking figures
of the Bodhisattvas Kannon and Taiseishi, 120 feet high,
were carved, presumably from the face of the cliff. The
images, however, may not actually have been as tall as Ennin
reported, for it was customary to speak of a seated figure as
having the height it would theoretically attain if it were
standing.[40]

On the same day that Ennin recorded the story of this
earlier wonder, he observed at first hand excited throngs
crowding around the scene of a recent miracle, which had
taken place in a small monastery near by. As Ennin tells
us:

. . . there was a monk who for many years had been reciting
the *Lotus Sutra*. Recently some Buddhist relics were revealed
to him, and everybody in the whole city came to make offerings.
The monastery was overflowing with monks and laymen. I don't
know how many there were.

      The origin of the discovery of the relics [was as
follows]: The scripture-reciting monk was sitting in his room
at night, reciting the scriptures, when three beams of light
shone in and illumined the whole room and lighted up the whole
monastery. Seeking the source of the light, [he discovered that]
it came from the foot of the . . . cliff west of the monastery.
Each night it lighted up the room and the monastery. After
several days the monk followed the light to the cliff and dug
down into the ground for over ten feet and came upon three
jars of relics of the Buddha. In a blue lapis lazuli jar were
seven grains of relics, in a white lapis lazuli jar five grains of
relics, and in a golden jar three grains of relics. He brought
them back and placed them in the Buddha hall and made offerings to them. The noble and lowly, and the men and women of
T'ai-yüan city and the various villages, and the officials, both
high and low, all came and paid reverence and made offerings.
Everyone said, "This has been revealed because of the wondrous
strength of the Priest in his devotion to the *Lotus Sutra*." The
people coming from the city to the mountain filled the roads
and in great crowds worshiped and marveled.

WU-T'AI AND THE CULT OF MONJU

Ennin's "Record of a Pilgrimage" naturally concerns the whole of his trip to China, but the real pilgrimage within this broader journey was to Mt. Wu-t'ai, the holy "Five Terraces" in the northeastern corner of the modern Shansi. This was not only an important monastic center but also the scene of a great esoteric cult centering around the Bodhisattva Monju or Monjushiri. The origins of this cult and cult spot are little known, but the myths Ennin repeats about Mt. Wu-t'ai perhaps give an indication of its early history and in any case convey some of the pious awe which the devout pilgrim felt in this holy region. Ennin at his first glimpse of one of the sacred peaks bowed to the ground and worshiped it, while his "tears flowed involuntarily" at this sight of the "gold-colored world . . . where Monjushiri manifested himself for our benefit." [41]

Among the natural beauties of the region, Ennin was particularly impressed by the alpine flowers covering the slopes and summits of the terraces, "spread out in bloom like a brocade" and with "incense" so fragrant that it "perfumes men's clothing." Such fragrance was surprising, for the five terraces were also covered with leeks, which good Buddhists traditionally avoided in their diet because of their strong smell. But the unusual fragrance of the flowers was no mere natural phenomenon. Ennin learned that the flowers and leeks alike were part of the story of the founding of Wu-t'ai as a Buddhist center in the time of the Emperor Hsiao-wen of the barbarian Northern Wei dynasty, who reigned from 471 to 499. According to Ennin, the legend ran as follows:

. . . Of old the Emperor Hsiao-wen lived at Wu-t'ai, wandering and admiring [the beauty]. The Bodhisattva Monju changed himself into the guise of a monk and asked the Emperor for the land [covered by] one sitting-mat. The Emperor granted it to him. When the monk had been granted this, he spread out a single mat and covered 500 *li* of land. The Emperor, surprised, said, "I merely gave him the land [covered by] a single mat, but this monk has spread a single mat over all the five terraces. This is most wonderful, but I do not want him to live here." Accordingly, he scattered leeks over the five terraces and then left the mountains. The monk, remaining behind, scattered orchid-like flowers over the leeks, causing them to lose their odor. At present leeks grow all over each of the terraces, but they have no odor at all, and orchid-like flowers grow luxuriantly all over the terraces, and their fragrance is heavy. It is said that the 500 *li* of Wu-t'ai is the land on which a single mat was spread out.[42]

Another phenomenon of Wu-t'ai was its cold and stormy weather. This too had a marvelous origin, for it was to be attributed to the five hundred Poisonous Dragons who inhabited the region, one hundred to each of the five terraces. Because of the affinity of dragons for water, they constantly spewed forth winds and clouds so that the traveler never saw "a long stretch of clearness." The five hundred Poisonous Dragons were the subjects of a Dragon King, but he and "his people were subjugated by Monju and, being converted, do not dare to do evil."

Another important incident in the development of the Monju cult at Wu-t'ai seems to have been the visit of a monk called Buddhapāla or Buddhapāli, who in 676 was attracted to this mountain from far-off India by its rising fame. The Indian, who had come empty handed, was met at the southern approaches to Mt. Wu-t'ai by Monju in the guise of an old man, who instructed him to return to India to obtain a certain text of Esoteric Buddhism. Ennin saw an inscription commemorating this famous incident on the spot where it occurred about four miles inside the towered gates marking the southern limits of the holy region. Earlier, at the Chu-lin-ssu, he had seen a picture depicting this confrontation of Saint and Bodhisattva in disguise. Ennin also visited a grotto, deep in one of the valleys of Wu-t'ai, where Buddhapāla had been conducted by Monju when the former had returned from India with the desired scripture. According to Ennin, after the Indian had entered the cave, "the entrance of the grotto closed of itself, and it has not opened to this day." Actually all that Ennin saw of this historic grotto was a hard, yellow-tinged cliff against which a high tower had been erected "where the mouth of the grotto would be."

The tower contained a hexagonal revolving repository for the Buddhist canon, which, thanks to Ennin, is one of the first revolving bookcases known to have existed in the world. In Esoteric Buddhism the idea was developing at this time that one turn of such a bookcase endowed the mover with as much merit as if he had read the whole of the voluminous canon it contained. But the revolving repository was as nothing compared to the wonders concealed within the miraculously sealed grotto. According to the records of the place, which Ennin did see, Monju had here assembled a veritable treasure-trove of relics from various deities and saints of the Buddhist pantheon. There were "three thousand kinds of musical instruments" made out of the "seven treasures" by one saint; "a bell which could hold 120 bushels" and which when tolled brought various degrees of enlightenment to those who heard it; a silver harp of "84,000 notes," each of which "cured one of the worldly passions"; a pagoda of 1,300 stories prepared for the body of one of the Buddhas of the future; and finally "a billion forms of writing of the four continents," which far out-classed the number of languages into which the Bible has been translated, though hardly its geographic spread.[43]

In a region crowded with such glorious though sometimes invisible wonders, it is not surprising that Ennin, carried away by the spirit of the place, recorded in his diary, "When one enters this region of His Holiness [Monju], if one sees a very lowly man, one does not dare to feel contemptuous, and if one meets a donkey, one wonders if it might be a manifestation of Monju. Everything before one's eyes raises thoughts of the manifestations of Monju. The holy land makes one have a spontaneous feeling of respect for the region." Later Ennin again wrote in his diary about the "spirit of equality" engendered by the holy area and illustrated the point with the following comments on the maigre-feast practices of Wu-t'ai:

. . . When maigre feasts are arranged in these mountains, whether one be cleric or layman, man or woman, great or small, food is offered to all equally. Regardless of rank or position, here all persons make one think of Monju. Long ago, the Ta-hua-yen-ssu held a great maigre feast, and commoners, both men and women, and beggars and the destitute all came to receive food, but the patron was displeased and said, "My intention in coming here far up the mountain slopes and holding a maigre feast was merely to provide for the monks of the mountain, and it was not my intention that these worldly laymen and beggars should all come and receive my food. If such beggars are to be provided for, then maigre feasts can be arranged in their native places. Why should I come all the way to this mountain [to feed them]?" The monks persuaded him to have food given to all. Among the beggars was a pregnant woman, heavy with child, and, when at her seat she received her full portion, she demanded a portion for the child in her womb. The patron cursed her and would not give it to her. The pregnant woman said several times, "Although the child in my womb has not yet been born, he counts as a person, so why don't you give him his food?" The patron said, "You are a fool. Even though the child in your belly should count as one, he does not come out to ask for it. If he gets the food, to whom should we give it to eat?" The woman replied, "If the child in my belly does not get food, then I too should not eat," and, rising, she left the dining hall. Just as she went out of the door of the hall, she was transformed into Monjushiri, emitting light which filled the hall with dazzling brightness. With his bright jade-[like] countenance and seated on a lion with golden hair and surrounded by a myriad of Bodhisattvas, he soared up into the sky. The whole assembly of several thousand persons rushed out together and fell dumbfounded and insensible to the ground. They raised their voices in repentance and wept bitterly, raining down tears, and called out together, "His Holiness Monjushiri," until their voices gave way and their throats were dry, but he never deigned to turn around and grew indistinct and then disappeared. The whole assembly had no appetite for the food, and each one of them made vows. Thenceforth, when offerings were sent and maigre feasts arranged, all were provided for equally, regardless of whether they were clerics or laymen, men or women, great or small, noble or lowly, poor or rich. Accordingly, the custom of the mountain is to have a system of equality. There have been many other miracles of divine manifestation besides this one, of which the whole empire knows.

At present at maigre-feast gatherings they have in the dining hall a row of men, a row of women, some of them holding babies who also receive a portion, a row of children, a row of novices, a row of full monks, and a row of nuns, and all receive their offering [of food] on their benches. The patron gives out the food equally. When people demand more than their share, they do not blame them but give them all [they ask for], whatever it may be.[44]

THE MONASTERIES OF WU-T'AI

Ennin spent his first fifteen days in the Wu-t'ai region at the Chu-lin-ssu, where the novices Ishō and Igyō were ordained and the Japanese took part in a great maigre feast for 750 monks and witnessed the service performed before the portraits of the seventy-two sages and saints. Then they moved on to the Ta-hua-yen-ssu, where they spent the next month and a half, with the exception of a four-day trip around four of the five terraces. At the Ta-hua-yen-ssu Ennin not only found two series of lectures on Tendai texts in progress but also saw wondrous relics and glorious works of Buddhist art.

One of these works of art was a sixteen-foot figure of the historical Buddha dying and in this act attaining Nirvana, which appropriately was placed in a building known as the Nirvana Place of Ritual. The sixteen-foot figure of the Buddha was "lying on his right side beneath a pair of trees," his mother was "swooning to the ground in anguish," and around them stood a crowd of saints and lesser deities, "some holding up their hands and weeping bitterly, some with their eyes closed in an attitude of contemplation. Everything that was described in the scriptures was completely portrayed in these figures." [45]

Another work of art Ennin mentions was a picture of Ta-hsieh Ho-shang, a name meaning "Priest Big Shoes."

This monk "made fifty pilgrimages around the five terraces and lived on the summit of the central terrace for three years, both winter and summer, without descending." Finally, with the aid of Monju, he put on the huge pair of shoes from which he derived his name and which Ennin saw placed in front of his picture. These may have been seven-league boots, for, apparently with their aid, Ta-hsieh bustled around performing great deeds, such as making 15,000 robes for monks and arranging for 75,000 meals for his fellow clerics.

Among the other treasures of the monastery were three copies of the *Lotus Sutra*, one in Indian format and therefore obviously from the original home of Buddhism, another in golden characters, and a third in small characters. There was also a two-storied octagonal pagoda, under which was said to be buried one of 84,000 miniature pagodas reputedly made by King Aśoka, the Indian champion of Buddhism of the third century B.C. Another treasure was a lapis lazuli jar containing bones of the Buddha, and there was also the upper part of the skull of a minor Buddha which "had been brought by a monk from the Western Lands" some time between 627 and 650. This rather gruesome relic was "roughly as large as a bowl of [a capacity of] two large *sheng*," and it was "white and black in color and in appearance resembled Japanese pumice stone." On top of it "white hair was growing about five inches long, apparently grown out since it had been shaved."

The most impressive of the artistic treasures of the Ta-hua-yen-ssu was a "solemn and majestic" image of Monju, riding, as he traditionally did, on a lion and filling the whole of a five-bay hall. Ennin described the lion as "supernatural" and added, "It seems to be walking, and vapors come from its mouth. We looked at it for quite a while, and it looked just as if it were moving." The following miraculous story of the casting of the image was told to Ennin by a venerable monk of seventy years, who "at first glance could be around forty" and was so "hale and hearty" because he had "the power of 'devotion.'"

. . . when they first made the Bodhisattva, they would make it and it would crack. Six times they cast it, and six times it cracked to pieces. The master was disappointed and said, "Being of the highest skill, I am known throughout the empire, and all admit my unique ability. My whole life I have cast Buddhist images, and never before have I had them crack. When making the image this time, I observed religious abstinence with my whole heart and used all the finesse of my craft, wishing to have the people of the empire behold and worship it and be specially moved to believe, but now I have made it six times, and six times it has completely cracked to pieces. Clearly it does not meet the desire of His Holiness [Monju]. If this be correct, I humbly pray that His Holiness the Bodhisattva Monju show his true appearance to me in person. If I gaze directly on his golden countenance, then I shall copy it to make [the image]." When he had finished making this prayer, he opened his eyes and saw the Bodhisattva Monju riding on a gold-colored lion right before him. After a little while [Monju] mounted on a cloud of five colors and flew away up into space. The master, having been able to gaze on [Monju's] true appearance, rejoiced, [but also] wept bitterly, knowing then that what he had made had been incorrect. Then, changing the original appearance [of the image], he elongated or shortened, enlarged or diminished it [as necessary], so that in appearance it exactly resembled what he had seen, and the seventh time he cast the image it did not crack and everything was easy to do, and all that he desired was fulfilled. After he had made this image, he placed it in the hall, and with tears welling up in his dewy eyes, he said, "Marvelous! What has never been seen before, I have now been able to see. I pray always to be the disciple of Monjushiri, generation after generation and rebirth after rebirth." And so saying, he died.

Later this image emitted light from time to time and continually manifested auspicious signs. Each time there was a sign, it was recorded in detail and reported to the throne, and on Imperial command Buddhist scarves were bestowed. The one which is at present seen draped on the body of the Bodhisattva is one of these. Because of this, each year an Imperial Commissioner sends one hundred Buddhist scarves, which are bestowed on the monks of the monastery, and each year the Imperial Commissioner on separate Imperial command sends incense, flowers, precious baldachins, pearl-[decorated] banners and baldachins, jades, jewels, precious crowns of the "seven treasures," engraved golden incense burners, large and small mirrors, flowered carpets, white cotton cloth, marvelous imitation flowers and fruits, and the like. A great many of these have already accumulated and are displayed in the hall. But this is not all, the remainder being in the storehouse, put away for the present. The things sent yearly by various other official or private patrons from the provinces, prefectures, or regional commanderies are quite beyond count. When the monasteries of Wu-t'ai now make images of the Bodhisattva Monju, they always [make them] resembling this holy image, but they all are no more than one-hundredth [as grand].

Ennin learned that his Japanese predecessor, Reisen, had had a vision of "a myriad Bodhisattvas" from a pavilion of the Ta-hua-yen-ssu overlooking "a thousand-fathom precipice," and it is not surprising that one of Ennin's three modest miracles occurred at this monastery. But he was to find at another Wu-t'ai monastery a more tangible memento of his countryman. This was the drawing of the Buddha on a strip of skin from Reisen's own arm, which was one of the treasures of the Chin-ko-ssu, the "Monastery of the Golden Balcony," where Ennin stopped overnight during a final round of pilgrimages before he set out on the highway to Ch'ang-an.

The strip of Reisen's skin was kept in a small gilt bronze pagoda on the ground floor of the Golden Balcony for which the Chin-ko-ssu was named. This was a towering structure, which at this time was something of an architectural innovation in China. Ennin described it as nine bays wide and three stories tall, rising "over a hundred feet high" and standing out "alone and majestic above the cryptomeria grove," with "the white clouds rolling below it." Ennin found it "very impressive" both inside and out, for there was "no place without paintings on the walls, eaves, beams, or pillars." [46]

On the ground floor of the Golden Balcony, Reisen's dermal icon shared honors with the tooth of a minor Buddha and other similar relics as well as an image of Monju "riding

on a lion with blue-green fur," placed under a baldachin of
the "seven treasures," which had been presented by an
Emperor. The second story was given over to images of five
Buddhas, each with two flanking Bodhisattvas. These had
been made by or, more probably, under the direction of
Amoghavajra, a great eighth-century Ceylonese missionary
and the reputed introducer of Esoteric Buddhism to China.
The figures had been fashioned in imitation of a similar
galaxy of deities in the famous Nālanda Monastery of North
India. The third story of the Golden Balcony was occupied
by a similar group of images of five Buddhas and attendant
Bodhisattvas, again made by Amoghavajra. These two sets
of Buddhas and Bodhisattvas represented the deities of two
different esoteric texts, and therefore Ennin found that all
of the Buddhas and Bodhisattvas displayed distinctive
countenances and mudras, or symbolic hand positions. Although the Golden Balcony must have been erected before
Amoghavajra's death in 774, Ennin noted that the colors
had not been completely filled in on the *mandara* which the
Ceylonese had drawn on the whitewashed inner walls of the
third story of the structure.

The Chin-ko-ssu also had other wonders besides the Golden
Balcony and its contents. One was a small platform "three
elbow-lengths" long, where a Chinese disciple of Amoghavajra on Imperial command had performed rituals in behalf of
the ruling house of T'ang. The platform was "covered with
white sandalwood sap mixed with mud," and Ennin reports
that "each time the wind blows, its fragrance can be detected
at a distance." He also saw a picture of an impression of the
Buddha's foot with its thousand-spoked wheel, one of the
thirty-two stigmata of the historical Buddha and now the
central symbol of the Indian national flag. Ennin recorded
in his diary the sign under this painting, telling how it had
been copied from a rubbing made of the original footprint
in India and brought back to Ch'ang-an by a Chinese envoy
in 649. Another treasure was a copy of the Buddhist canon
in "more than six thousand scrolls, all in gold and silver
characters on dark blue paper with rollers of white sandal-

wood, jade, and ivory," which had been made by a man from
Ch'ang-an who, while on a pilgrimage to Wu-t'ai in 779,
saw a vision of Monju and "the Myriad Bodhisattvas." And
finally there was a Fugen Hall which contained, among
other wonders, some pictures of Buddhas made of strings of
pearls "embroidered onto silk cloth with marvelous results."
There was also a remarkable image of Fugen in this building. Normally Fugen was portrayed mounted on an elephant, but this image was unusual in that the Bodhisattva
was seated on three of the beasts standing side by side.

Ennin visited several other Wu-t'ai monasteries on his
way out of the mountains.[47] One of these was the Ling-ching-
ssu where Reisen had met his mysterious fate. Here he found
a small grotto under a mountain elm where from time to time
was to be heard the tolling of a bell which made "the mountain summits quiver." On either side of the main gate of this
monastery stood the image of a fierce Guardian Deity. There
was nothing unusual about this, for Guardian Deities flanking the gate of a monastery are still a common sight in the
Far East, but these particular figures had a marvelous story
connected with them, which Ennin copied from a stele inscription. It seems that in earlier times Guardian Deities
suddenly appeared in three different regional commanderies
and, after identifying themselves as manifestations of a certain Buddha "in the form of local deities to guard the Buddhist Law," related:

". . . We were buried in the ground and over the years crumbled
to dust, but we were rediscovered and are at present inside the
gate of the Ling-ching-ssu of Mt. [Wu]-t'ai." The Regional
Commanders of the three prefectures were amazed and recorded
in detail the appearance [of the apparitions]. Each sent a
messenger to make inquiries, and [they discovered] there were
two Guardian Deities on the left and right of the monastery
gate which in appearance and bearing were exactly like the
apparitions in their own prefectures. The messengers returned
to their provinces and reported this. Thereupon the three prefectures sent messengers here especially to repair the old
images, and there were many divine signs.

THE FIVE TERRACES

However remarkable may have been the marvels of the monasteries of Wu-t'ai, the five terraces themselves were, of course, the most holy places. In typical Chinese fashion, these were named for the four directions and the center. Four of them Ennin visited while he was staying at the Ta-hua-yen-ssu, but he did not climb the Southern Terrace, which was some distance from the others, until he was leaving the Wu-t'ai region on his way to the capital.[48]

Ennin gives a meticulously detailed account of the trails from terrace to terrace and the views from their summits, looking out over unending miles of mountains, with birds circling far below and the sound of flowing waters rising from the unseen floors of "deep ravines and profound valleys." The tops of the terraces were broad level areas, and on three of them there were pools of varying sizes known as Dragon Pools. Typical of these watery mountain tops was the Central Terrace, which Ennin described as follows:

. . . All over the terrace water bubbles up out of the ground and soft grass grows over an inch long, luxuriant and thick, covering the ground. When one treads on it, it gives, but when one raises one's foot, it springs up again. At each step the water dampens [one's feet], and it is as cold as ice. Here and there are small hollows, all filled with water. All over the terrace are sand and stones, and there are innumerable stone pagodas scattered about. The fine and soft grass grows between the moss. Although the ground is damp, there is no mud, and because of the luxuriance of the spreading roots of the moss and soft grass, the shoes and feet of the traveler are not soiled.

Near the southern end of the Central Terrace stood a building containing images of Monju and the Buddha, but the center of the terrace was occupied by a pool of crystal-clear water about three feet deep and forty feet on each side. On a small island in the center of this pool stood a Dragon Hall in which had been placed another image of Monju. A

slightly larger pool occupied the center of the Western Terrace, and in the center of the pool stood another Dragon
Hall with an image of Monju. On the Northern Terrace,
however, the arrangement was different. There was a Dragon
Hall near the southern end of the summit, and inside the
hall was a pool dividing it into three sections. The central
portion was occupied by an image of the Dragon King of
Wu-t'ai, but on either side of him stood images of Monju,
perhaps symbolizing the Bodhisattva's control over the
monarch of the scaly denizens of the mountain. The Eastern
Terrace had no pool, but on it stood a hall of three bays
containing an image of Monju surrounded by a wall of
piled-up stones about ten feet high and possibly symbolizing
a pond. On the Southern Terrace was another hall of three
bays, and in it stood an image of Monju "made of white
jade and riding on a white jade lion."

Ennin repeatedly mentions small stone pagodas which
were scattered over the terrace tops, and he also came upon
iron pagodas on all but the Southern Terrace. These, he tells
us, were erected by the Empress Wu, who, after dominating
the T'ang court for many years, usurped and ruled in her
own name from 690 until shortly before her death in 705.
The three iron pagodas on the Central Terrace Ennin describes as "all without stories, finial rings, or the like. In
shape they are exactly like inverted bells. It would take four
men to reach around them. The central pagoda is square and
about ten feet high, but the two on either side are round, and
both are about eight feet high." The iron pagoda on the
Western Terrace was round and "about five feet high and
about twenty feet in circumference." Another stood on the
Northern Terrace and three more on the Eastern Terrace.

The pilgrim trail around the five terraces was well provided with cloisters and small monasteries where, during the
summer months, the pilgrim could find food and lodging.
On or near the summits of the Northern, Eastern, and
Southern Terraces stood Offering Cloisters (Kung-yang-
yüan). At the first of these Ennin "saw a monk who has not
eaten rice for three years and eats but once a day, consum-

ing mud and earth for his forenoon meal. He has vowed not to come down from the summit of the terrace for three years." The Offering Cloister of the Western Terrace stood about two miles east of the summit on the trail between it and the Central Terrace. The latter had no Offering Cloister but instead had a Ch'iu-yü-yüan, or "Cloister for Seeking Rain," a short distance south of the summit and a P'u-t'i-ssu, or "Bodhisattva Monastery," a short distance to the east. Ennin also came across two small monasteries on the trail from the Ta-hua-yen-ssu to the Central Terrace and a common cloister conveniently placed midway between the Northern and Eastern Terraces, where he stopped for a meal and witnessed one of his miraculous sights.

While the chief cult spots were on the terrace summits, there were many other wonders on their slopes and in the valleys surrounding them. On the side of the Northern Terrace Ennin came to a place which he describes as follows:

. . . Beside the path are many burnt rocks covering the ground. Both square and round, they are in the form of a stone wall which is piled high with burnt stones. This is a place which was turned into a Hell. In ancient times a Prefect of Tai-chou * who was violent in character did not believe in karma. He had heard that there were Hells, but he did not believe it. While he was wandering in appreciation [of nature] around the terraces, looking about, he came to this place. Suddenly he saw violent flames consuming the cliffs and rocks and black smoke billowing up to heaven. The burning rocks and fiery coals, glowing brightly, made a wall around him, and devils appeared before him, angry and lamenting. The Prefect was afraid and submitted to the will of His Holiness the Bodhisattva Monjushiri, whereupon the fierce flames disappeared, but their remains are still here today. The burnt rocks are piled up into a wall, which is about fifty feet in circumference and is filled with black stones.

About two miles west of the summit of the Western Terrace was a spot where Monju had met the ancient Indian layman

---

* The local prefecture in T'ang times.

Yuima, or Vimalakīrti as he is known in Sanskrit, about whom a famous Buddhist scripture has been written. At this place two thirty-foot cliffs faced each other, and on their flat tops were "great stone seats" where the Saint and Bodhisattva presumably had been seated. Monju's leonine mount had left traces on the rocks below the cliff, where Ennin saw "footprints of a lion, trod into the surface of the rock about one inch deep." There was also a building below the cliffs containing an image of Monju riding on a pair of lions and an image of Yuima, which Ennin describes in great detail.

A short distance from the summit of the Eastern Terrace Ennin visited a sacred grotto which, dripping with water and pitch black, "would do for a dragon's hideaway." But he seems to have been more impressed by the storm he saw from this mountain top.

. . . Just before dusk, the heavens suddenly clouded over, and white clouds massed in the bottoms of the valleys to the east. Now red, now white, they swirled upwards, and the thunder sounded, rumbling loudly. The disturbance was in the deep valleys, while we on the high peak lowered our heads to see it.

PILGRIMS AND PATRONS

The many wonders of the Five Terraces and their surrounding monasteries naturally drew throngs of pilgrims during the summer months. As we have seen, Ennin, while traveling through the encircling mountains on his way to the holy region, encountered at one common cloister "a party of more than a hundred monks, nuns, women, and men on a pilgrimage to Mt. Wu-t'ai." Mention has also been made of the fifty Zen monks he found stopping at the Ta-hua-yen-ssu and of the several dozen novices assembled at the Chu-lin-ssu. At the last of the common cloisters on the route to Mt. Wu-t'ai from the east Ennin also saw several dozen pilgrim monks start out for the Central Terrace in clear weather in the early afternoon and return that evening "with their straw hats smashed by hail and their whole bodies soaking." These men were perhaps among the hundred monks who were entertained at a maigre feast at this common cloister the next day. Ennin indicates that some of the pilgrims came from great distances. For example, he encountered four monks from Mt. T'ien-t'ai in the south, who gave him news of his former traveling companion, Ensai, and he learned that three monks from the famous Nālanda Monastery of India had visited the Chu-lin-ssu the preceding summer.[49]

Many of the pilgrims, no doubt, left gifts or offerings of one sort or another at Mt. Wu-t'ai, and some of the richer believers must have contributed substantially to the expenses of the holy establishments. The patron from Shantung who sponsored a maigre feast for 750 monks has already been mentioned. In the Wu-t'ai monasteries Ennin saw many treasures contributed by lay believers. The Imperial court too was a major supporter of the monastic establishments of Wu-t'ai. Many of their treasures Ennin found to be direct Imperial gifts, and, while at the Ta-hua-yen-ssu, he recorded:

>   An Imperial emissary came to the monastery, and the congregation of monks all came out to meet him. As a rule, each year clothing, alms bowls, incense, flowers, and the like are sent on Imperial order. An emissary is sent to the mountain to give to the twelve great monasteries 500 fine robes, 500 packages of silk floss, 1,000 lengths of cloth for Buddhist scarves dyed a blue-green color, 1,000 ounces of incense, 1,000 pounds of tea, and 1,000 hand cloths, and at the same time he goes around the twelve great monasteries with Imperial provisions to arrange for maigre feasts. . . . The Imperial emissary held a maigre feast for one thousand monks.[50]

While many gifts to the monasteries of Wu-t'ai were probably unexpected windfalls, the enterprising monks of the holy mountain did not hesitate to assist the beneficial workings of karma by going out to solicit funds. Ennin received a hint of this when he heard some years later of Egaku, a Japanese monk, who, after visiting Wu-t'ai in 842, had returned to Japan "to seek provisions for Wu-t'ai" and "year after year brought provisions," until defrocked in 845 in the great Buddhist persecution.[51]

Egaku, who was to keep making periodic trips to China until he returned permanently to Japan in 864, was perhaps an unusual example of a fund raiser for the monasteries of the sacred mountain, but Ennin happened to meet another more typical financial agent for Wu-t'ai. This was I-yüan, whom Ennin describes as having been for ten years "a solicitor of offerings for the twelve monasteries and the common cloisters of Wu-t'ai." Ennin also calls him "a mendicant monk," but since I-yüan had a home cloister in the city of Fen-chou in central Shansi some 160 miles air-line southwest of Mt. Wu-t'ai, his mendicancy presumably consisted of wanderings in search of funds for the monasteries of the holy mountain.

I-yüan seems to have brought annually to Mt. Wu-t'ai the fruits of his collecting efforts. He also brought with him groups of pilgrims to the holy region. While in the city of T'ai-yüan-fu, situated between Fen-chou and Wu-t'ai, Ennin was invited out for the forenoon meal several times, twice by individual women and once by a group of three nuns, and all five of these women had at one time or another been members of I-yüan's pilgrim band. Similarly, a monk who accompanied the Japanese at least part of the way to the capital had also been one of I-yüan's followers on a pilgrimage to the holy region. So also may have been three other Chinese who befriended Ennin, two of whom he describes as disciples of I-yüan. These were an official who entertained Ennin in T'ai-yüan-fu, another official who served as his host in Fen-chou, and a third man who housed and fed him and his party in a town between these two cities.[52]

Ennin's association with I-yüan was close and religiously significant. A few days before the Japanese left the Ta-hua-yen-ssu, I-yüan witnessed with them the miraculous sight of a colored, shining cloud in an otherwise cloudless sky. Attributing this sign to the presence of Ennin, the devout solicitor of offerings declared amid tears of joy:

. . . For ten years since I, I-yüan, developed faith, I have yearly delivered offerings to the whole mountain without fail, but I have never before seen a single sign. Now in the company of the foreign Learned Doctor I have seen a shining cloud, and I know indeed that, even though our places of birth are in different regions, in that we have been favored with a manifestation of his Holiness [Monju], we may have the same karma. Henceforth in the future we shall together establish karma affinities and for long shall be the "family" of the Bodhisattva Monjushiri.

When the Japanese moved on to the Chin-ko-ssu, I-yüan followed them there the same day, and on the next he hopefully accompanied Ennin on his sight-seeing tour through the Golden Balcony of that monastery and then up to the summit of the Southern Terrace. It was no doubt his enthusiasm which induced several dozen pilgrims to wait with Ennin on the mountain top until nightfall in the hope of seeing another sign. When none appeared, the group at last withdrew for the night to the Offering Cloister a few hundred yards below the summit. But here I-yüan's faith was at last rewarded by the miraculous appearance of two lights. While the crowd of devout on-lookers "was greatly moved and with loud voices chanted" Monju's name, the lights gradually waxed and then slowly died out around midnight.

Since Ennin was so clearly the cause of I-yüan's first miraculous sights after ten years of waiting, it is small wonder that the solicitor of offerings insisted on accompanying the Japanese as far as his home city of Fen-chou and serving as their host on the way. Actually, business of an unspecified nature forced him to bid them adieu at T'ai-yüan-fu, but he saw to their entertainment in that city and also arranged to have them spend a night in his home cloister in Fen-chou and to be entertained in that city and on the way there by his disciples. In T'ai-yüan-fu, I-yüan lodged the Japanese in the Lower Hua-yen-ssu, which was a sort of city base for the Ta("Great")-hua-yen-ssu of Mt. Wu-t'ai. As Ennin recorded, "All the monks of the Ta-hua-yen-ssu of Mt. Wu-t'ai who come down here from the mountain are under this monastery, and consequently they call it the Lower Hua-yen-ssu."

I-yüan's enthusiasm for his foreign friend and the miracles the latter had inspired actually delayed Ennin's departure from T'ai-yüan-fu. I-yüan had hired an artist to make a painting of one of the "manifestations" they had witnessed together, wishing to send the painting by Ennin to Japan, "that those who see it will develop faith and those with karma affinities will develop these affinities and be reborn together in Monju's great congregation." As might have been expected, the picture was not done on time, and the Japanese were forced to wait eight days for its completion before resuming their journey.[53]

I-yüan saw Ennin off with a final burst of religious sightseeing in the environs of T'ai-yüan-fu, but this was not to be their final parting. Almost two years later the well-traveled solicitor of offerings turned up in the capital and, before leaving, demonstrated his ability as a fund raiser by obtaining from Ennin a contribution sufficient for 150 meals.[54]

THE APOGEE AND DECLINE OF BUDDHISM

Ennin's diary leaves no doubt of the all-pervasiveness of Buddhism in his day. Rich and intellectually vigorous communities of monks were to be found throughout the cities and mountain fastnesses of the land; urban crowds thronged Buddhist festivals; laymen listened eagerly to religious lectures and services; monks and lay believers alike trod the rocky pilgrim trails. There had been earlier periods when the government had given Buddhism more vigorous support, and the Indian religion may have achieved its greatest popular appeal a few centuries later, but Ennin saw China at the moment when the already widespread faith of the masses and the still strong intellectual belief of the ruling classes perhaps combined to bring Buddhism to its apogee in China.

Ennin took the popularity of Buddhism for granted and made little effort to record the numbers of converts or to call attention to the sincerity of their belief. Nonetheless, almost every page of his diary bears unconscious testimony to the hold of Buddhism on the Chinese people. The unquestioning faith of the energetic I-yüan is an example of the passionate sincerity of the churchmen of the time. The complete devotion of the lay convert is illustrated by many nameless commoners who are mentioned casually in the text. For example, we have already noted the villager on the North China Plain who "had become a believer some time ago and had long been preparing maigre meals which he offered to [passing] monks, regardless of their number." [55]

The loyalty and generosity of Ennin's many friends and patrons among the officials of the land indicate the continuing popularity of Buddhism among this class, despite a nationalistic and rationalistic reaction against the foreign religion which had started among intellectuals a few decades earlier. More significant, perhaps, were the officials who demonstrated not merely a willingness to support Buddhist clerics, but a lively intellectual interest in the tenets of the faith. For instance, when Ennin met the Prefect of the coastal city of Hai-chou, he recorded that the man "has a rough understanding of Buddhism and discoursed on it himself to us monks." Again, at the Regional Commandery of Ch'ing-chou in Shantung, Ennin met a high official of whom he wrote, "The Administrative Officer understands the Buddhist Law and is a religious man. He loves discussions [of Buddhism], and, when he sees a monk come from a distance, he is cordial and solicitous." [56]

It is of particular interest that the two greatest officials Ennin was to meet in China—who also happened to be perhaps the two most important political figures of their day—both personally demonstrated to him their strong support of Buddhism. That the powerful eunuch, Ch'iu Shih-liang, should have been a believer and should have befriended Ennin is not surprising, because eunuchs throughout Chinese history tended to represent the antibureaucratic and antischolastic element in Chinese government, which was at the same time more pro-Buddhist than the scholarly civil servants. [57] What is more unusual is that the great Minister of State, Li Te-yü, should have shown himself to be not only

personally friendly to the foreign monks but also an energetic patron of Buddhism while he was the Regional Commander of Yang-chou. This is all the more surprising because Li Te-yü is traditionally given a major share of the
credit or blame, depending on one's point of view, for the
great persecution of Buddhism which was about to strike and
was to draw a sharp line between the religious high-water
mark of Ennin's early years in China and the slow ebbing of
Buddhism ever since.

When Li Te-yü participated in the elaborate religious
ceremony at the K'ai-yüan-ssu of Yang-chou on the anniversary of the death of a former Emperor and again when
he appointed a new Bishop for Yang-chou, he was probably
carrying out ceremonial and administrative functions of his
office which were not necessarily related to his personal religious beliefs. But his part in the carving of a Buddhist image
and the reconstruction of the balcony in which it was housed
appear to have been signs of a personal Buddhist piety not
required by his position.

According to Ennin, four sandalwood images of the historical Buddha, Shakamuni, had come flying to a balcony in
the K'ai-yüan-ssu of Yang-chou in the early seventh century
at the time of the great predecessor of the T'ang, the Emperor Yang-ti of the short-lived Sui dynasty. The building
was consequently renamed the "Balcony of the Auspicious
Images" (Jui-hsiang-ko), and a plaque bearing this name
was written by the Emperor himself and hung on the front
of the structure. While Ennin was in Yang-chou, Li Te-yü
decided to carve a new three-foot white sandalwood image
of Shakamuni, perhaps as a replacement for one that had
been damaged or destroyed, and the day after Ennin heard
of this worthy act the great man himself came to the monastery to inspect the progress of the work. After worshiping
the Buddhas, Li summoned Ennin and Ensai for their first
meeting with him. Ennin was obviously impressed by the
Regional Commander and his large and brilliant entourage,
as well as by the hundred bushels of rice which he donated
on this occasion for monastery repairs.

Some days later the Japanese monks wrote a letter of thanks to Li for his attentiveness to them. When Li again visited the K'ai-yüan-ssu on the following day to worship the "auspicious images" and inspect the new one, he again summoned Ennin and Ensai, this time to the balcony itself. There they were seated on chairs, which were still something of an innovation in China and were not to make much headway in Japan for another thousand years, and, while sipping tea, were questioned by the Regional Commander on the climate, capital, and religious institutions of Japan. Then Li consoled the two Japanese and communicated to them his sympathy, after which the three bowed to each other, and Li went off to inspect some repair work in another cloister of the monastery before leaving.

Some two months later Ennin discovered that Li was now embarked on reconstructing the "Balcony of the Auspicious Images" itself. This apparently was a very expensive project, for the estimated cost was 10,000 strings of cash. Under the Regional Commander's sponsorship, Buddhist lecture meetings were held for more than a month as a fund-raising scheme, and twice Li sent personal invitations to Ennin and Ensai, requesting their attendance at the meetings. As has been mentioned, the members of the Japanese embassy received a request for fifty strings of cash for the good work. Li's interest in the project and perhaps the sincerity of his religious sentiments are best illustrated by his own princely donation of 1,000 strings of cash for the repair of the balcony.[58]

There can be little doubt that in Ennin's day Buddhism was still strong at all levels in Chinese society. And yet, at the same time, there were signs of decline in some quarters— an inner decay that perhaps explains why the blow about to descend on Buddhism, while by no means unique in Chinese history, was to leave a lasting mark. Some of these signs of decay may have been in part the product of the declining fortunes of the T'ang and the resultant growth of internal disorders and decrease in government patronage. But Ennin's diary gives no indication of any general political and economic decline in the regional commanderies and prefectures where he traveled, sufficient to have caused this religious decay. One is forced to assume that, even at the moment when on the surface Buddhism was at the height of its influence in China, a certain lowering of the flame of faith and a debasement of its intellectual vigor were beginning to sap its energies from within.

Ennin gives no indication of any Buddhistic decline in the great cities of Ch'ang-an and Yang-chou or at the cult center of Mt. Wu-t'ai, except for the mention of one ruined monastery on the outskirts of this region. In Shantung and on the North China Plain, however, he saw many signs of decay. The first was when one of the novices of the Korean Cloister at Mt. Ch'ih stole away and "went west," the only direction a man could go on dry land from that spot at the tip of the Shantung Peninsula. Four nights later two more novices, evidently inspired by the action of the first, fled from the cloister and the religious life it represented.[59]

Later in his travels, Ennin came upon several monasteries which had fallen on evil days. The ruined monasteries in a former subprefectural town west of Ch'ing-chou are not a fair example, because in this case the whole town had been deserted for a new subprefectural center. Further out on the North China Plain, however, Ennin on three successive nights lodged first in a monastery in a subprefectural town in which the buildings had become dilapidated and only one discourteous monk remained of the original congregation, then in a monastery in a neighboring subprefectural town where the monks were "common and vulgar" and the establishment "extremely poor," and finally in a village monastery where the monks were "rustics at heart" and the buildings were dilapidated, though the Buddhist images were still "impressive." [60]

On the Shantung Peninsula Ennin came upon one monastery after another which showed signs of serious decline. In a subprefectural town between Wen-teng-hsien and Teng-chou, he stayed for the night in a monastery where the congregation of monks had been reduced to five, "the Buddha halls were dilapidated, and the monks' living quarters were all occupied by laymen and had been converted into ordinary living quarters." At Teng-chou he found the K'ai-yüan-ssu with only about ten monks in residence and with its many cells for monks "all occupied by official travelers." In another prefectural city west of Teng-chou he stayed in the local Lung-hsing-ssu, which had been reduced to two monks who were "common men" and did not know "the proper etiquette toward guests." The base of the thirteen-story brick pagoda of this monastery was "crumbling away," and "the surrounding corridors were dilapidated." The next night he spent in the T'ai Inn, which had once been a monastery and still had a five-storied carved stone pagoda, twenty feet high, and a seven-storied cast iron pagoda, ten feet high, standing in front of it. A few nights later he lodged in a monastery in a subprefectural town where "the Buddha hall and the monks' cells were dilapidated, and the images of the Buddhas were exposed to the elements," and where all but one of the resident monks lived in lay quarters.[61]

Perhaps the saddest case of monastic decline was that of the great Li-ch'üan-ssu on Mt. Ch'ang, west of Ch'ing-chou. Many of the fifteen estates which this monastery had once owned had been lost, the buildings were dilapidated, and the holy sites were "gradually going to ruin," with "no one to repair them." Although about a hundred monks had once resided there, most of them had "scattered in accordance with their destinies," and only thirty-odd remained. Worst of all, Ennin found little "purified eating" at this once great institution, by which he meant that the monks were not observing Buddhist rules limiting both the time of meals and the diet. Perhaps some special calamity had overtaken the Li-ch'üan-ssu, but its sad decline seems symptomatic of the decay which may already have started to undermine Chinese Buddhism from within at a time when outwardly it had achieved its most luxuriant growth.[62]

VII

The Persecution of Buddhism

The Chinese, with their love of classification, speak of the
four greatest persecutions of Buddhism in China as those of
the "Three Wu and One Tsung." These refer to persecutions
under three Emperors who are known by the same posthumous name, Wu-tsung, and one known as Shih-tsung. The
first was in the year 446 under Wu-tsung of the barbarian
dynasty of Northern Wei; the second in 574 under Wu-tsung
of the barbarian dynasty of Northern Chou; the next, which
was the one Ennin encountered, under Wu-tsung of the
T'ang; and the last in 955 under Shih-tsung of the short-
lived Later Chou.

This tabulation of persecutions is even more misleading
than most such efforts at classification. Several other Chinese
Emperors carried out repressive measures against Buddhism
which were almost as severe and in some cases perhaps produced results as lasting as some of the four "great" persecutions. Furthermore, the persecution which reached its
height in 845 when Ennin was in Ch'ang-an was on so much
greater a scale than the other three that to class them together is to underestimate the one or to grossly exaggerate
the others. The T'ang persecution applied to all China; the
other three only to North China or that part of this region
which was under the control of the persecuting Emperor.
The 845 persecution permanently crippled Buddhism and
virtually wiped out the other foreign religions then extant
in China; the other three persecutions had no comparable
lasting effects. In other words, these other persecutions were
merely three of the many incidents in the long history of
Buddhism, but that of the T'ang made 845 one of the great
pivotal dates in the history of religion in China.

ANTI-BUDDHIST SENTIMENTS

It would be a mistake to think of Buddhist persecutions in China in terms of the relentless conflict between Christian and Mohammedan in the West or of the fratricidal strife and inquisitions within Christianity. There has been very little religious conflict in China, compared with Western Asia or Europe, and what religious persecutions have occurred have been motivated more by secular than by strictly religious reasons. Throughout Chinese history the chief cause for overt opposition to Buddhism has been economic rather than religious. As we have seen, Chinese administrators deplored the fact that monasteries not only removed good lands from the tax registers, but also sheltered able-bodied monks who otherwise would support the economy of the state by paying taxes and performing other services. While devout emperors and officials recognized the need for some monks and monasteries to safeguard the spiritual well-being of the state and its rulers, few welcomed an unbridled growth of monastic communities and their holdings. The nonbelieving government official went beyond this and looked upon organized monastic Buddhism as a blight on society and an economic menace to the state.

Governments in need of funds could hardly help casting jealous glances at the treasures of the greater monastic establishments, such as Ennin described at Mt. Wu-t'ai. Their small golden figures and reliquaries, great gilt-bronze images, and bronze bells alone represented a large percentage of the total available supply of gold and copper, the two principal monetary metals. Converted into bulk gold and copper cash, these could go a long way toward restoring a depleted treasury. Small wonder that the Chinese government, when prosperous, usually attempted to restrict the growth of monastic lands and communities and, when impoverished, often set about defrocking monks and confiscating monastic holdings.

Besides the economic reasons for anti-Buddhist sentiments in China, there was also a strong feeling that the Indian religion was antisocial in other ways. In Chinese terms, this charge was undoubtedly true. With its strong other-worldly focus, Buddhism advocated a monastic life of celibacy which struck at the roots of the whole Chinese family system. The chief duty of each Chinese man to his ancestors was to continue the family line. How could one be both a celibate Buddhist and a good Chinese family man? Celibacy was a crime against the family and, if practiced on a mass scale, could be the ruination of the state.

Buddhists also advocated practices of a type abhorrent to Chinese with their concept that the human body, as a gift from one's ancestors, must be preserved intact. Mortification of the flesh, as illustrated by Reisen's icon made from his own body, seemed essentially immoral to many Chinese. So also did the Indian custom of cremation. Moreover, monastic communities and holdings were considered an invitation to tax-evasion by scheming individuals, and rich monks sometimes became dissolute ones, indulging in various carnal sins, from gluttony to sexual perversion.

Another basis for anti-Buddhist feelings in China, which was largely limited to the educated ruling class, was a rationalistic disapproval of Buddhism as merely superstition. Such an attitude was weakest during the four centuries of political disruption and barbarian invasions when Buddhism first established its hold in China, but this view tended to reassert itself during times of stable rule, when the scholar-bureaucrat gained mastery over the state. The T'ang was the first period of prolonged unity and stability in China after the second century A.D., and, with the exception of a half century of political chaos following its collapse, China was to remain for the most part unified and governed by scholastic bureaucrats until the breakup of the empire in the early years of our own century. It is not surprising that during this long period the rationalistic prejudices of these men against Buddhist "superstition" came to dominate Chinese thought. They were schooled in the doctrines of Confucius, who is said to have replied to a query about death with the rebuke, "While you do not know life, how can you know about death?" [1] They naturally had small sympathy for a religion centered on the achievement of Nirvana, which, whether it meant extinction or Paradise to the individual believer, was clearly not of this life.

Still another source of anti-Buddhist sentiment was a rising nationalistic reaction against anything foreign. Even when Buddhism was first introduced to China, there had been those who condemned the Indian religion because it was "barbarian" and not Chinese. Such criticism seems to have increased in intensity during the long period of T'ang decline, when the empire again became subject to barbarian incursions. The nationalistic reaction against Buddhism became even more pronounced during the following centuries, when the Chinese fought a slowly losing battle against their nomadic neighbors to the north, which ended finally in the thirteenth century in the Mongol sweep across China, the first conquest of the whole land by a foreign ruler.

A final reason for anti-Buddhist sentiments in China, which comes closer to paralleling the religious intolerance of the West, was the rivalry and animosity of adherents of other religions. Such opposition came primarily from the Taoists, who, in large part because they had borrowed Buddhist forms of monastic organization and had built up much of their own canon by plagiarizing that of the Indian religion, hated the Buddhists dearly and were in bitter competition with them for the purses as well as the souls of men. In some cases the rationalistic bureaucrats, with fine impartiality, sought to curb Buddhists and Taoists alike. But, in Ennin's time, much of the special ferocity of the persecution was the product of the Taoist fervor of the chief persecutor, the Emperor Wu-tsung. The official histories as well as Ennin's diary make it amply clear that Wu-tsung was a Taoist fanatic. This showed itself not only in the persecution, but also in his addiction to Taoist elixirs of life, which, as with several of his predecessors on the Chinese throne, seems to have hastened his death. That his fanaticism, thus, may have contributed as much to the end of the persecution as to its beginning is a fine example of the Chinese concept of the balancing duality of history: the more of one thing the sooner will come its opposite.

HAN YÜ'S MEMORIAL

The anti-Buddhist sentiments of the Chinese scholar-bureaucrats are perhaps best illustrated by a famous memorial to the throne written in 819 by Han Yü, an illustrious man of letters, in protest against the honor paid by the Emperor to a religious relic, the finger-bone of the Buddha, which the monarch brought to the capital from the Fa-men-ssu of the city of Feng-hsiang, west of Ch'ang-an. This memorial, which resulted in Han Yü's banishment by the enraged monarch, is memorable in Chinese intellectual history because it expressed ideas which were soon to become dominant among the educated classes. Similar points of view had been put forward earlier by other men, but with little lasting effect. In Han Yü, however, these ideas were the first clearly discernible stirrings of a great intellectual reaction against Buddhism, which was to culminate in the Neo-Confucianism of the eleventh and twelfth centuries, when the native philosophy reasserted its complete control over the intellectual life of China, not only by a frontal attack on Buddhism but more significantly by borrowing from it much of its metaphysics and philosophy, thus leaving the Indian religion intellectually emasculated.

Han Yü's memorial, which is still considered a literary masterpiece in China, reads in large part as follows:

Your servant submits that Buddhism is but one of the practices of barbarians which has filtered into China since the Later Han. In ancient times there was no such thing. . . . In those times the empire was at peace, and the people, contented and happy, lived out their full complement of years. . . . The Buddhist doctrine had still not reached China, so this could not have been the result of serving the Buddha.

The Buddhist doctrine first appeared in the time of the Emperor Ming of the Han Dynasty, and the Emperor Ming was a scant eighteen years on the throne. Afterwards followed a succession of disorders and revolutions, when dynasties did not long endure. From the time of the dynasties Sung, Ch'i, Liang, Ch'en, and Wei,* as they grew more zealous in the service of the Buddha, the reigns of kings became shorter. There was only the Emperor Wu of the Liang who was on the throne for forty-eight years. First and last, he thrice abandoned the world and dedicated himself to the service of the Buddha. He refused to use animals in the sacrifices in his own ancestral temple. His single meal a day was limited to fruits and vegetables. In the end he was driven out and died of hunger. His dynasty likewise came to an untimely end. In serving the Buddha he was seeking good fortune, but the disaster that overtook him was only the greater. Viewed in the light of this, it is obvious that the Buddha is not worth serving.

When Kao-tsu † first succeeded to the throne of the Sui, he planned to do away with Buddhism, but his ministers and advisors were short-sighted men incapable of any real understanding of the Way of the Former Kings, or of what is fitting for past and present; they were unable to apply the Emperor's ideas so as to remedy this evil, and the matter subsequently came to naught—many the times your servant has regretted it. I venture to consider that Your Imperial Majesty, shrewd and wise in peace and war, with divine wisdom and heroic courage, is without an equal through the centuries. When first you came to the throne, you would not permit laymen to become monks or nuns or Taoist priests, nor would you allow the founding of temples or cloisters. It constantly struck me that the intention of Kao-tsu was to be fulfilled by Your Majesty. Now even though it has not been possible to put it into effect immediately, it is surely not right to remove all restrictions and turn around and actively encourage them.

Now I hear that by Your Majesty's command a troupe of monks went to Feng-hsiang to get the Buddha-bone, and that you viewed it from a tower as it was carried into the

---

* Five of the relatively short-lived dynasties of the fourth to sixth centuries.

† The first T'ang Emperor.

Imperial Palace; also that you have ordered that it be received and honored in all the temples in turn. Although your servant is stupid, he cannot help knowing that Your Majesty is not misled by this Buddha, and that you do not perform these devotions to pray for good luck. But just because the harvest has been good and the people are happy, you are complying with the general desire by putting on for the citizens of the capital this extraordinary spectacle which is nothing more than a sort of theatrical amusement. How could a sublime intelligence like yours consent to believe in this sort of thing?

But the people are stupid and ignorant; they are easily deceived and with difficulty enlightened. If they see Your Majesty behaving in this fashion, they are going to think you serve the Buddha in all sincerity. All will say, "The Emperor is wisest of all, and yet he is a sincere believer. What are we common people that we still should grudge our lives?" Burning heads and searing fingers by the tens and hundreds, throwing away their clothes and scattering their money, from morning to night emulating one another and fearing only to be last, old and young rush about, abandoning their work and place; and if restrictions are not immediately imposed, they will increasingly make the rounds of temples and some will inevitably cut off their arms and slice their flesh in the way of offerings. Thus to violate decency and draw the ridicule of the whole world is no light matter.

Now the Buddha was of barbarian origin. His language differed from Chinese speech; his clothes were of a different cut; his mouth did not pronounce the prescribed words of the Former Kings, his body was not clad in the garments prescribed by the Former Kings. He did not recognize the relationship between prince and subject, nor the sentiments of father and son. Let us suppose him to be living today, and that he come to court at the capital as an emissary of his country. Your Majesty would receive him courteously. But only one interview in the audience chamber, one banquet in his honor, one gift of clothing, and he would be escorted under guard to the border that he might not mislead the masses.

How much the less, now that he has long been dead, is it fitting that his decayed and rotten bone, his ill-omened and filthy remains, should be allowed to enter in the forbidden precincts of the Palace? Confucius said, "Respect ghosts and spirits, but keep away from them." The feudal lords of ancient times, when they went to pay a visit of condolence in their states, made it their practice to have exorcists go before with rush-brooms and peachwood branches to dispel unlucky influences. Only after such precautions did they make their visit of condolence. Now without reason you have taken up an unclean thing and examined it in person when no exorcist had gone before, when neither rush-broom nor peachwood branch had been employed. But your ministers did not speak of the wrong nor did the censors call attention to the impropriety; I am in truth ashamed of them. I pray that Your Majesty will turn this bone over to the officials that it may be cast into water or fire, cutting off for all time the root and so dispelling the suspicions of the empire and preventing the befuddlement of later generations. Thereby men may know in what manner a great sage acts who a million times surpasses ordinary men. Could this be anything but ground for prosperity? Could it be anything but a cause for rejoicing?

If the Buddha has supernatural power and can wreak harm and evil, may any blame or retribution fittingly fall on my person. Heaven be my witness: I will not regret it. Unbearably disturbed and with the utmost sincerity I respectfully present my petition that these things may be known.

Your servant is truly alarmed, truly afraid.[2]

THE OFFICIAL ACCOUNTS

With their growing contempt for Buddhism as a pack of "superstitions" and their animosity toward it as a foreign religion, later Chinese historians have paid scant attention to the great T'ang persecution, or for that matter to any aspect of Buddhist history. For example, the original official account of the T'ang dynasty, the *Old T'ang History* (*Chiu T'ang shu*), compiled in the middle of the tenth century, has only a few references to the persecution, and there is even less in the *New T'ang History* (*Hsin T'ang shu*), written in the middle of the eleventh century to replace the older and supposedly inadequate first official account of the dynasty. In fact, the compilers of the second work limited their com-

ments on the persecution to the laconic statement, "There
was a great destruction of Buddhist monasteries, and the
monks and nuns were remade commoners." [3]

The *Old T'ang History* and some other sources, while saying more than this, contain relatively little on the persecution compared with the wealth of detailed information and
hearsay which Ennin recorded in his diary. For example,
while they indicate that a persecution of the Manichaen religion started as early as 843, they make no mention of any
measures taken against the Buddhists until 845, though we
know from Ennin that these were under way as early as 842.
These other sources, however, do give some information
which Ennin missed.[4] They tell, for instance, of measures
taken to prevent people from hiding or purchasing former
monastic slaves and of the assignment of the copper acquired
from Buddhist images and bells to the state mint, the iron
to the making of agricultural tools, and the gold, silver, and
jade to the government treasury. One of the more interesting
documents relating to the persecution is a congratulatory
message on the destruction of the Buddhist monasteries addressed by Li Te-yü to the Emperor, in which Ennin's erstwhile friend rejoiced over the destruction of more than 46,600
monasteries and shrines and the defrocking and return to
tax-paying status of 410,000 monks, nuns, and their slaves.
Li also mentioned more than 2,000 Nestorians and Zoroastrians who were secularized.[5]

The most comprehensive single document on the persecution is the Imperial edict issued in the eighth moon of 845,
which Ennin does not mention and may not even have known
about, because he had already been driven from Ch'ang-an
by that time. This document rationalized the persecution in
acceptable Confucian form and also summarized its results
as follows:

We have learned that up through the three dynasties
[of Hsia, Shang, and Chou] there had never been any talk of
Buddhism, and only since the Han and Wei has this idolatrous

religion come to flourish. In recent times its strange ways have become so customary and all-pervasive as to have slowly and unconsciously corrupted the morals of our land. The hearts of our people have been seduced by it and the masses all the more led astray. From the mountains and wastes of the whole land to the walled palaces of the two capitals, the Buddhist monks daily increase in number, and their monasteries daily grow in glory. In exhausting men's strength in construction work, in robbing men for their own golden and jeweled adornments, in forsaking ruler and kin to support their teachers, in abandoning their mates for monastic rules, in flouting the laws and in harming the people, nothing is worse than this religion.

Now, when one man does not farm, others suffer hunger, and, when one woman does not weave, others suffer from the cold. At present the monks and nuns of the empire are numberless, but they all depend on agriculture for their food and on sericulture for their clothing. The monasteries and temples are beyond count, but they all are lofty and beautifully decorated, daring to rival palaces in grandeur. None other than this was the reason for the decline in material strength and the weakening of the morals of the Chin, Sung, Ch'i, and Liang.*

Furthermore, Kao-tsu and T'ai-tsung † put an end to disorders by arms and governed this fair land with literary arts. These two methods suffice for ruling the land. Why then should this insignificant Western religion compete with us? During the Chen-kuan [627-650] and K'ai-yüan [713-742] periods there were also reforms, but they failed to eradicate the evil, which continued to spread and flourish.

We have broadly considered previous statements and widely sought out general opinions and have absolutely no doubt that this evil should be reformed. Our ministers of the court and in the provinces are in accord with Our will. It is most proper that We regulate [the Buddhist church], and We should follow their wishes on this. We are indeed chastising this source of corruption for a thousand years. We yield to no one in fulfilling the laws of the hundred kings [before Us] and in aiding the people and benefiting the masses.

---

* Four successive short-lived dynasties, which together lasted from 265 to 557. All but the first were limited to South China.
† The first two T'ang Emperors.

More than 4,600 monasteries are being destroyed throughout the empire; more than 260,000 monks and nuns are being returned to lay life and being subjected to the double tax;* more than 40,000 temples and shrines are being destroyed; several tens of millions of *ch'ing* † of fertile lands and fine fields are being confiscated; 150,000 slaves are being taken over to become payers of the double tax. Among the monks and nuns are both natives and foreigners. Since [the latter] make manifest foreign religions, We are returning more than 3,000 Nestorians and Zoroastrians to lay life, so that they will not adulterate the customs of China.

Alas that this was never done before! It appears to have waited for Us to do. How could it be called untimely that We have at last wiped them out? We have driven away the lazy and idle fellows to a number of more than ten millions. We have done away with their gorgeous but useless buildings to a number not less than a myriad. Thenceforth, purity will guide the people, who will esteem Our effortless rule. Simplicity will be Our policy, which will achieve the merits of a common culture. We shall have the people of the four quarters all submit to the Imperial sway.

Since this is but the beginning of Our reform of these evils, the time has not sufficed for it to be known. We issue these orders to this glorious court, and it should conform to Our will. Let it be proclaimed in the capital and provinces that all may know.[6]

THE GATHERING STORM

The Imperial edict of the eighth moon of 845 and the other scattered references in Chinese works to the great persecution all give the impression of an Emperor and court resolved on rationalistic grounds to destroy Buddhism and carrying out their determination in one sudden blow. Ennin's diary reveals a vastly more complicated and involved story and one which is obviously closer to the confusions and irrationalities of life.

---

* The chief land tax of the time, collected twice a year.
† A little more than fifteen acres.

Ennin reached Ch'ang-an in the early autumn of 840 only a few months after Wu-tsung had succeeded his brother to the throne, and at first the Japanese monk saw no reason to fear the new ruler. In fact, Wu-tsung seemed to evince a friendly interest in Buddhism. In the ninth moon of 840 he had a monastery rebuilt in the capital and gathered more than fifty monks to form its congregation, seven from the Tzu-sheng-ssu where Ennin was living. Early the next year he revived a custom which had been in abeyance since 835, ordering seven Ch'ang-an monasteries to hold "lectures for laymen" for a full month, and five months later he again ordered ten monasteries to conduct lecture meetings. But this did not mean that Wu-tsung was not at least equally interested in Taoism. On both occasions he ordered two Taoist monasteries to hold lectures, and Ennin learned that, as a preliminary to changing the year period at the beginning of 841, the Emperor went to the official Taoist temple in the capital for what the monk describes as a "maigre feast." [7]

It was not until the sixth moon of 841 that Ennin learned that there might be some difference in Wu-tsung's attitude toward the two religions. The eleventh day of that moon was the Emperor's birthday, and the monarch celebrated it by inviting two Buddhist and two Taoist priests to the Palace to engage in a four-cornered debate on their respective scriptures. Significantly the two Taoists were rewarded by being "granted the purple" to wear, an honor restricted to courtiers of the fifth rank, while the Buddhists received no reward.

This clear sign of the Emperor's coolness toward Buddhism did not mean the end of Imperially sponsored lectures on the Indian religion or of religious debates in the Imperial presence. In fact, only two and a half months later lectures were ordered by the Emperor. Again in the fifth moon of 842 "lectures for laymen" were held in ten capital monasteries. On the Emperor's birthday in 842 a debate was held, and the two Taoists as before "received the purple," while the Buddhists again went unrewarded. Even on the Emperor's birthday in 843, long after the persecution had started, fourteen Buddhist monks were invited to the Palace debate on religion, though as usual "two Taoist Priests were granted purple robes on Imperial decree, but none of the [Buddhist] Reverences was allowed to wear the purple." It ✓ was not until 844 that the Emperor finally excluded the Buddhists from his birthday celebration, and Ennin sadly noted in his diary, "It would appear that hereafter they do not want monks to enter the Palace." Meanwhile the Emperor had been dismissing his Court Priests, discharging forty in the fifth moon of 842 and twenty-four more on his birthday in 843.[8]

These signs of Imperial displeasure with Buddhism were not the only storm warnings which came to Ennin's attention. On the third day of the third moon of 842 he recorded in his diary, "Li, the Minister of State, petitioned the throne to have the monks and nuns regulated, and an Imperial order was issued, dismissing the 'nameless monks without protection' and prohibiting the appointment of boys as novices." The word I have translated as "regulate" was a widely used technical term at this time, with some of the connotations of the phrase "to weed out," and the "nameless monks without protection" were presumably the irregular clergy not entered in the official registers and, therefore, not entitled to official status as clerics.

Since this petition came only seven months before the first major blow against Buddhism, it is natural to assume, as some have, that this petition was the first step in the persecution and that its author, presumably Li Te-yü, was the prime mover in this whole attempt to wipe out the Indian religion. It is not at all certain, however, that this petition should be regarded as the real beginning of the persecution or that Li Te-yü was its author. It called merely for the weeding out of the unauthorized clergy, a routine measure carried ✓ out repeatedly by the Chinese government in order to keep down the number of monks. Such a step would have been advocated by almost any Chinese bureaucrat, including even devout Buddhists. We must assume, of course, that Li Te-yü, as Wu-tsung's chief minister during the years of persecution, was willing to go along with the Emperor in his wholesale attack on the Indian religion. However, what Ennin has to tell us of Li's support of Buddhism while in Yang-chou indicates that he was no fanatical hater of the religion, and we know from another source that he went out of his way to preserve certain Buddhist wall paintings during the persecution.[9] It does not seem likely, therefore, that Li Te-yü was the prime instigator of the persecution as a whole. Even his unctuous message of congratulation to the Emperor on the destruction of the Buddhist monasteries is proof of nothing more than sycophancy or, to put it more generously, political opportunism. Actually, the author of the petition may have been another Minister of State named Li Shen, whom Ennin at first perhaps confused with the great Li he personally knew. This supposition is supported by Ennin's later reference to a petition by Li Shen as having caused the persecution and his statements indicating that the persecution was particularly severe in a part of China where Li Shen was then serving as Regional Commander.[10]

Whoever may have been the author of the petition, the resulting Imperial edict had an immediate bearing on Ennin, for foreign monks were classed among those "without protection." Only two days after Ennin mentioned the petition in his diary, the great eunuch, Ch'iu Shih-liang, who, as the Commissioner of Good Works of the Streets of the Left, was in charge of the clerical population of the eastern half of the capital, sent word to the Tzu-sheng-ssu and two other monasteries where foreign monks resided, reassuring the latter with the statement, "The said foreign monks are all asked to be at ease, as they cannot be dismissed." A few days later a notice was sent on Ch'iu's order by one of his henchmen informing the Tzu-sheng-ssu officially that, despite the order "that 'guest monks without protection' be dismissed and put out of the monasteries," Ch'iu had ruled that the four Japanese were not to be dismissed. A few months later Ch'iu's underling sent around a request for information about the foreign monks under the Commissioner's jurisdiction, and the very next day Ennin made out the required statement, which reads for the most part as follows:

The Japanese monk Ennin of the Tzu-sheng-ssu (aged fifty; versed in lecturing on the Lotus Sutra)* and his disciples, the monk Ishō (aged thirty) and the monk Igyō (aged thirty-one; both are versed in the Lotus Sutra).

They have received a notice inquiring into the country from which they come, the date they reached this city, the monastery they live in, their ages, and what accomplishments they are versed in.

The said Ennin and the others, in order to copy missing scriptures and transmit these to their country, came to Yang-chou with a Japanese tributary embassy in the seventh moon of the third year of K'ai-ch'eng (838). They reached this city on the twenty-third day of the eighth moon of the fifth year of K'ai ch'eng (840) and, on notice from the Commissioner, resided provisionally in the Tzu-sheng-ssu and received instruction.[11]

Exactly a year to the day later and well after the persecution had started, the same inquiry was again circulated, and Ennin replied with a largely identical statement, except for the ages of the monks. Meanwhile Ch'iu had taken another step to reassure the foreign monks under his jurisdiction. Late in the first moon of 843 he summoned them to his offices, where twenty-one gathered, including Ratnacandra and his four disciples from South India, a monk called Nanda from North India, a man from Ceylon, another from the state of Kucha in Central Asia, the three Japanese, and several Koreans. After being served tea, they had an audience with Ch'iu, who "personally consoled" them before sending them back to their monasteries.[12]

PALACE INTRIGUES

Ch'iu Shih-liang's solicitude over the foreign monks indicates clearly that not the whole court was in agreement on the measures being taken against the Buddhists. In fact,

---

* In this heading to the document, as it appears in the diary, the parts given here in parentheses were written in smaller characters.

Ennin noted that, when the first sweeping edict of persecution was issued in the tenth moon of 842, Ch'iu, although his position made him one of the prime executors of the order, "opposed the Imperial edict and did not wish to regulate [the clergy]. Because of the Emperor's desires, this was not permitted, but he was allowed to request a stay of one hundred days." [13]

All this suggests that there may have been some factional disputes involved in the persecution, if not actually behind it. It was not at all unusual for politics and religion to mix in this way. For example, the persecution of the Manichaeans in 843 was very probably in part associated with foreign relations. In the fourth moon of that year Ennin recorded, "An Imperial edict was issued [ordering] the Manichaean priests of the empire to be killed. Their heads are to be shaved, and they are to be dressed in Buddhist scarves and made to look like Buddhist Shamans and are to be killed. The Manichaean priests are highly respected by the Uighurs." The details of this statement are open to doubt, but Ennin is probably correct in his implication that the persecution of Manichaeanism was at least in part because it was the religion of the Turkish Uighurs of Central Asia. The latter had been the T'ang's staunchest allies in that part of the world, but had recently turned against the T'ang and had invaded China. Ennin had first heard of this invasion more than a year earlier, when he reported, with dubious accuracy, the execution of hundreds of Uighurs in Ch'ang-an. Some months later he noted the flight back to the capital of a T'ang princess who had been married to the Uighur Khan, and late in 843 he reported the final defeat of the invaders.[14]

The factional fight involved in the Buddhist persecution seems to have been between Wu-tsung, backed by Li Te-yü and the other scholar-bureaucrats, on one side, and the Palace eunuchs, led at first by the indomitable Ch'iu Shih-liang, on the other. It was perhaps because of this political aspect of the persecution that men like Li Te-yü, who apparently were not fanatical haters of Buddhism themselves, were willing to back the Emperor in his ferocious religious purge. While they may have had mixed feelings about the Indian religion, there was no ambiguity in their attitude toward the eunuchs, their traditional rivals for power and influence at court, and they may, therefore, have welcomed a violent attack on Buddhism as a means of embarrassing and discrediting the eunuchs, who usually were Buddhist believers.

The T'ang court, like any government subject to the whims of a despotic ruler—or perhaps one should say like any government regardless of its leadership—constantly seethed with factional intrigues. Even in Yang-chou Ennin had received an inkling of this when he heard that Wu-tsung's predecessor, Wen-tsung, had killed his son, the Crown Prince, fearing that the latter was plotting against him. The official histories do not explicitly confirm this statement, but their accounts of the Emperor's displeasure with his heir followed by the latter's sudden death sound like the glossing over of a less pleasant story. In Shantung the first thing Ennin heard about Wu-tsung was that "the new Emperor, on ascending the throne, killed over four thousand persons in the capital who had been favored in the time of the preceding Emperor." The number in this case was probably magnified by the geographic and social distance between the throne and Ennin's associates in Shantung, but there is no doubt that Wu-tsung, like many other Chinese Emperors, did get rid of his predecessor's henchmen in order to put his own personal supporters in places of power.[15]

Despite later developments, it seems probable that Ch'iu Shih-liang was in large part responsible for having had Wu-tsung named successor to his brother on the throne. As a result, Ch'iu must have had a very real claim on the new Emperor's favor. This probably explains his subsequent appointment to the high military post of Army Inspector Commissioner (*Kuan-chün-jung-shih*) and Ennin's claim that he was "put in charge of the military affairs of the empire." It also may explain a little incident mentioned by Ennin. In the fourth moon of 841 the powerful eunuch was allowed to erect a monument to his own glory in the precincts of his offices within the grounds of the Ta-ming Palace north of the city walls. The Emperor himself graced the occasion with his presence. The inscription on the monument read, "Stele of the Glorious Record and Virtuous Administration of Lord Ch'iu." [16]

But, whatever Wu-tsung may have owed to the great eunuch, he obviously looked elsewhere for the principal executors of his policies. One of his first acts was to recall Li Te-yü from Yang-chou, and on the fourth day of the ninth moon of 840 he reappointed him as Minister of State. Ennin proved his alertness as a political reporter by noting the new appointment in his diary on the day after it was made, though he mistakenly dated it two days earlier. Another appointment Ennin reported probably had less political significance. This was the selection of a maternal uncle of the new Emperor as a Grand General of the *Chin-wu* Guards, the same unit to which the Japanese Ambassador had been given honorary appointment, and also as Regional Commander of Feng-hsiang, the city from which had come the finger-bone of the Buddha to which Han Yü had taken such exception. This appointment seems to have been primarily humanitarian or, perhaps one should say, nepotal in significance, for Ennin reports that the Emperor's uncle had been "destitute" a year before and had been going around "the city wards and monasteries, carrying turnips, chrysanthemums, violets, and the like to sell." Still another appointment mentioned by Ennin is of note primarily because it shows that Li Te-yü, although Wu-tsung's choice, was able to stand up to his Imperial patron on occasion. When the Emperor shattered precedent by appointing his son-in-law to be a Minister of State, Li Te-yü made a subtle, punning protest, and Wu-tsung apparently accepted the rebuke.[17]

The appointment of Li Te-yü as Minister of State did not necessarily presage any rupture between the Emperor and the eunuchs, and we actually have no evidence of such a break until after the death of Ch'iu in the sixth moon of 843, some months after the start of the Buddhist persecution. Twenty days earlier the failing eunuch had been allowed to resign his official positions only after repeated petitions, and on his death the Emperor made a formal gesture of mourning. However, two incidents which took place almost simultaneously with these events suggest that the Emperor and Li Te-yü had been merely waiting for Ch'iu's decline to strike at his power. The eunuch's two most important posts had been Commissioner of Good Works for the Streets of the Left and Commander of the Left Guard Army of Inspired Strategy (*Tso shen-tse-chün hu-chün chung-wei*). The very day his resignation was accepted he was replaced in both these posts by Yang Ch'in-i, who, as Li's old associate at Yang-chou, was presumably considered by the latter to be a reliable eunuch and who, as Ennin later discovered, was no protector of Buddhism. The other incident occurred two days after Ch'iu's death, when four of his principal henchmen were summarily executed and their households, even to their slaves, were exterminated.[18]

The destruction of Ch'iu's own household followed a little over a year later. Ennin gives the following account of the downfall of Ch'iu's adopted son and heir:

. . . The son of the Army Inspector Ch'iu drank some wine, and getting completely drunk, offended the Imperial person by saying, "Although the Emperor is so revered and noble, it was my father who set him up." The Emperor was angered and struck him dead on the spot, and an Imperial edict ordered that his wife and womenfolk be seized and sent into exile and, with their hair shaved off, be made to guard the Imperial mausoleums. Then the Palace Officers were ordered to take over the wealth of the family. Elephant tusks filled the rooms; jewels, gold, and silver completely filled the storehouses; and the cash, silk, and goods were beyond count. Each day thirty carts transported [the treasure] to the Palace storehouses, but they did not complete transporting it within a month. The remaining treasures and rarities were [still] beyond count. The Emperor went to the Palace storehouses to see [the treasures] and, striking his hands together in surprise, he said, "Our storehouses have never before contained such things," and the high functionaries bowed their heads and did not speak.[19]

This incident alone does not prove any deep rift between Wu-tsung and the Palace eunuchs, for the confiscation of the probably ill-gotten wealth of a deceased eunuch was a common enough occurrence in Chinese history. However, in view of another incident related by Ennin, it appears to have signified more than the posthumous disgrace of merely one eunuch. The power of the Palace eunuchs ultimately rested in no small degree on their control over the Left and Right Guard Armies of Inspired Strategy, which were two of the principal military forces in the capital area. In the fourth moon of 845 Ennin recorded a bold but abortive attempt by the Emperor to transfer the command of these two armies to the civil bureaucracy. Significantly, Li Te-yü's friend, Yang Ch'in-i, as Commander of the Left Army, fell in with the scheme, but it was foiled by the Commander of the Right Army, Yü Hung-chih, who was a doughty eunuch more in the tradition of Ch'iu Shih-liang. Ennin's account of the incident, which has been omitted entirely from the standard histories, runs as follows:

The Left and Right Armies of Inspired Strategy are the Guard Armies of the Emperor. Each year they have 100,000 soldiers. Since olden times the rulers constantly suffered from rebellions by their ministers and so they created these armies, and since then no one has dared usurp the throne. The Emperor gives them seals. Each time a Commander is first appointed, on Imperial command he leads forth his troops and receives his seal. They conduct official business on their own and are not under the civil administration.

At the beginning of the fourth moon of this year there was an Imperial edict demanding the seals of the two armies, but the Commanders were not willing to surrender the seals. There were Imperial edicts demanding them several times. The Emperor's idea was to demand the seals of the Guard Armies and give them to the Imperial Secretariat and Imperial Chancellery so that they would jointly control the two armies, and he intended to have them handle everything. The Commander of the Left Army agreed to surrender his seal, but the Commander of the Right Army was not willing to surrender his

seal. Finally he sent a memorial to the throne, saying that
since on the day he received his seal he had led forth his troops
to receive it, on the day he surrendered his seal he should also
muster his troops to surrender it. The Commander's idea was
that, if the Emperor agreed, through this stratagem he would
muster his troops and start something. He then ordered those
in charge to put his forces secretly in order, but the ruler was
alarmed and gave in, and [the seal] was not surrendered.

We shall probably never know for certain the exact relationship between the efforts of the scholar-bureaucrats to
reduce the power of the eunuchs and the simultaneous attempt of the Emperor to wipe out Buddhism. As has been
suggested, there may have been a close association of the
two undertakings in the mind of Li Te-yü, and his support
of the persecution may have been the result of his desire to
encourage a split between the monarch and his eunuchs.
Certainly both movements were not unconnected with Ch'iu's
death. The plot against the eunuchs might never have been
hatched if he had remained alive and vigorous, nor might
the persecution have reached the extremes it did. In any
case, it seems probable that, without Ennin's candid diary,
the whole plot against the eunuchs as well as its possible
relationship to the Buddhist persecution would have remained entirely concealed beneath the glossy verbal polish
of the standard histories.

THE FIRST BLOWS

The persecution broke from a stormy sky with the issuing
of an Imperial edict on or about the seventh day of the
tenth moon of 842.[20] The edict was aimed in part at slough-
ing off the irregular and less desirable elements in the Buddhist clergy, thus reinforcing the order issued six months
earlier, but what made it more than a routine effort to keep
the number of monks and nuns in bounds was that it also
included provisions for the confiscation of the private wealth
of the clergy and the defrocking of those monks and nuns
who preferred secularization to poverty. The copy of this

document which Ennin says he made has not been preserved, but he fortunately summarized or paraphrased it in his diary as follows:

. . . all the monks and the nuns of the empire who understand alchemy, the art of incantations, and the black arts, who have fled from the army, who have on their bodies the scars of flagellations and tattoo marks [for former offenses, who have been condemned to] various forms of labor, who have formerly committed sexual offenses or maintain wives, or who do not observe the Buddhist rules, should all be forced to return to lay life. If monks and nuns have money, grains, fields, or estates, these should be surrendered to the government. If they regret [the loss of] their wealth and wish to return to lay life [in order to retain it], in accordance with their wishes, they are to be forced to return to lay life and are to pay the "double tax" and perform the corvée.

The two Commissioners of Good Works were responsible for carrying out these measures in the capital, and the various regional commanderies and prefectures in the provinces. As we have seen, however, Ch'iu, as Commissioner of Good Works for the Streets of the Left, protested the order and won a delay of one hundred days in its execution. Actually the purge was not completed in the capital until the eighteenth day of the first moon of 843, which was exactly one hundred days after the seventh day of the tenth moon. During the interim the Commissioners of Good Works ordered the capital monasteries to keep their gates closed and not to let their monks and nuns out. It is presumably because of this enforced confinement that Ennin had nothing else to report during this time.

The final reports to the throne by the two Commissioners, which Ennin quotes, indicated that, "aside from those who were decrepit with age and those who were strict in their observance of the rules," there were in all 1,232 monks and nuns in the eastern half of the capital "who, because they valued their wealth, had voluntarily returned to lay life" and 2,219 * in the western half of the capital. These documents also included some further details on the purge procedures, stating:

. . . those who, because they value their wealth, wish to return to lay life should be handed over to their respective places of origin and should be included among the payers of the "double tax." Hereafter, cases such as this in the various provinces should all be handled in this manner.

As for the slaves they possess, monks may retain one male slave and nuns two female slaves. The others are to be returned and given over to the custody of their original families. Those who have no family should be sold by the government. Likewise, aside from their clothes and alms bowls, the wealth [of the monks and nuns] is to be stored up and its disposition is to await subsequent Imperial decree. If among the slaves retained by monks and nuns there are those who [are versed in] the military arts or understand medicine or the other arts, they may not be retained at all, nor may their heads be shaved in secret. If there are violations [of these orders], the Monastery Administrators and Supervisors are to record them and notify the government. The other property and money should all be turned over to the Commissioners of Good Works to be regulated by them.

This main purge was followed by many minor restrictions on monks and their religion. On the first day of the second moon of 843 Ennin recorded that a notice from the Commissioner of Good Works "stated that the monks and nuns who had already returned to lay life could not go into monasteries or stay there. Moreover the monks and nuns 'without protection' who had been dismissed were not permitted to reside in the capital or enter the garrison areas."

About five months later Ennin noted the outbreak of fires on seven different occasions in the Imperial Palace and capital city, once with serious losses in the Eastern Market, one of the two great bazaar areas of Ch'ang-an. These he attributed to an earlier edict "to burn the Buddhist scrip-

---

* Ennin also gives the figure 2,259 in another place.

tures in the Palace and also to bury the images of the Buddhas, Bodhisattvas, and Heavenly Kings." At about the
same time we also find Ennin making out a document which
illustrated the close check being made on unauthorized residents of monasteries. This document reads in part:

> *The Japanese monk Ennin, his disciple monks Ishō*
> *and Igyō, and his attendant Tei Yūman.*
> Aside from these four, there are no other guest monks,
> novices, or lay guests in their rooms.
> They have received a notice from the monastery of-
> fice saying, "We have received a document from the Commis-
> sioner's office notifying us that we can by no means keep
> [monks] 'without protection,' novices, and lay guests." If sub-
> sequently someone reports that they have concealed [others]
> in their rooms, they will ask for severe punishments.[21]

The remaining clerics also had strict limitations put on
their movements. At some time which Ennin does not specify,
they were restricted to their monasteries in the afternoon,
and in the late spring or early summer of 844 they were
further forbidden to be abroad in the streets at the time of
the bell for the forenoon meal or to spend a single night in
another monastery. If they were to do either, they were to
be judged "guilty of having violated an Imperial edict," with
all the dire consequences this entailed. These restrictions subsequently made it impossible for Ennin to witness a great
official ceremony held in the first moon of 845 at the Altar
of Heaven. Ennin was obviously disappointed at this limita-
tion placed on his sight-seeing activities, but he was able, at
least, to learn about the preparations for this occasion, which
he recorded as follows:

> . . . the officials repaired the bridges, roads, and streets, and
> men, horses, carts, and oxen were kept off them. The Altar [of
> Heaven] in the southern suburb of the city and the special road
> leading to it were rebuilt. Flowered curtains were spread around
> all sides of the Altar, and towers and walls laid out, making it
> look just like the interior of the city. The officials were harassed
> without end.[22]

Some incidents in the persecution Ennin connected with political events. Thus, while he attributed the original purge order of the tenth moon of 842 to a petition by Li Shen, which conceivably may have been the same petition he mentioned in the third moon of that year, he implied that the persecution also resulted from an unfortunate incident involving a Buddhist monk. The latter offered to perform a Buddhist magical practice to aid in the defeat of the invading Uighurs, and, when his efforts produced no results, the Emperor wrathfully ordered him to be decapitated.

A more significant incident was connected with the rebellion of Liu Chen, the nephew of the former Regional Commander of Lu-chou, or Lu-fu as Ennin calls it, in southeastern Shansi. When the old Regional Commander attempted before his death in the fourth moon of 843 to pass on his position to his nephew, the Emperor on Li Te-yü's advice refused to recognize the appointment, thus forcing Liu Chen into rebellion. Some five months later Ennin, after telling about the rebellion and the tremendous strain it was putting on the treasury, recorded that the representative of the Regional Commander of Lu-fu at the capital went into hiding when his arrest was ordered, and the authorities had to content themselves with beheading his wife and children and destroying his house. Someone reported that the man had shaved his head and was hiding among the monks in the city, and Ennin apparently attributed some aspects of the persecution to this fact, pointing out that "monks who had recently [come to] live in the monasteries and whose origins were not clear were all seized by Ching-chao-fu," the prefectural government of the city of Ch'ang-an, and three hundred were executed, while "those who fled and hid did not dare walk in the streets." [23]

A few months later, when Ennin heard that special measures had been taken against certain great Buddhist cult centers, he again attributed these actions in part to the government's fear that the missing representative of Lu-fu was in hiding in one of these places disguised as a monk. Ennin's account of this phase of the persecution runs as follows:

An Imperial edict has forbidden offerings to the teeth of the Buddha. An edict was also issued saying that, whereas festivals had been held for the Buddha's finger [bones] in the monasteries at Mt. Wu-t'ai in Tai-chou, the P'u-kuang-wang-ssu of Ssu-chou,* the "Five Terraces" in the Chung-nan Mountains,† and the Fa-men-ssu of Feng-hsiang-fu, no offerings or pilgrimages [to these places] were to be permitted. If someone presents a single cash, he is to receive twenty strokes of the cane on his back, and, if a monk or nun at the said places accepts a single cash, he is to receive twenty strokes of the cane on his back. If in the various provinces, prefectures, and subprefectures there should be those who make offerings, they are to be seized on the spot and given twenty strokes of the cane on the back. Because of this, no one comes to these four holy areas or makes offerings. In accordance with the Imperial edict, the monks of these places were questioned, and those lacking official credentials were all executed on the spot and their names recorded and presented to the Emperor.[24]

Another incident which seems to have stirred up the Emperor's wrath against Buddhism occurred when some of his courtiers went to various monasteries before his birthday in 843 to arrange maigre feasts "as offerings for [the Emperor's] long life," and one of them, named Wei Tsung-ch'ing, compiled two Buddhist works and presented them to the throne. The Emperor was enraged and took immediate action to punish the unfortunate Wei. Ennin somehow got hold of a copy of the edict issued on this occasion and copied it into his diary as follows:

Wei Tsung-ch'ing . . . stands among those of honorable degree and should conform to the Confucian way of life, but he is drowned in evil doctrines, which stir up depraved customs. He has opened the door to delusions and has gone completely against the doctrines of the sages. How deep is the depravity among those of high office! So much the more should

---

*A city which once stood on the banks of the Huai River about seventy miles northwest of Yang-chou.
† About forty-five miles southeast of the capital.

We proscribe that which is not the words of the sages. Why should foreign religions be propagated?

We should like to overlook [his offense], but this may do injury to public morality. He is to be demoted, and We are still to be called magnanimous [in doing this]. He is to be made the Prefect of Ch'eng-tu-fu * and is to be rushed there by the post stations.

[Wei] Tsung-ch'ing . . . has presented to the throne *The Three Virtues as Culled from the Buddhist Nirvana Sutra* in twenty scrolls and *An Abstract of the Imperially Commissioned Complete Mirror to the Letter "I"* † in twenty scrolls. These have been carefully examined.

The Buddha was a western barbarian in origin, and his teachings spread the doctrine of "non-birth." Confucius, however, was a Chinese sage, and the Classics provide words of profit. Wei Tsung-ch'ing, while being an ordinary Confucianist, a scholar, an official, and [a man of] distinguished family, has not been able to spread [the teachings of] Confucius and Motzu,‡ but, on the contrary, believes blindly in Buddhism and has foolishly made compilations from barbarian writings and has rashly presented them. How much more have the common people of China been steeped for long in these ways! In truth, their delusions should all be stopped, and they should be made to return to their pristine simplicity. But [Wei Tsung-ch'ing] assembles mystical falsehoods and in turn misleads the stupid people. Ranking as he does among the courtiers, should he [not] be ashamed of himself?

The scriptures he presented have already been burned in the Palace. The Imperial Secretariat and Imperial Chancellery are commissioned to find the original drafts and burn them, so that he cannot pass them on to others.[25]

THE EMPEROR AND THE TAOISTS

This verbal castigation of Wei Tsung-ch'ing was a thoroughly Confucianist document which even Han Yü would have applauded. In fact, the whole first stage of the persecu-

---

* The modern capital of the western province of Szechuan.
† A letter in the Sanskrit alphabet.
‡ A Chinese philosopher of the fifth century B.C.

tion, in which the emphasis was on the elimination of the
irregular clergy and the confiscation of private Buddhist
wealth, was entirely in keeping with the attitudes and interests of the scholar-bureaucrats, but in the year 844 the
persecution began to take on a Taoist coloration which could
not have been any more pleasing to the average bureaucrat
than was the religion under attack.

In about the third moon of that year Li Shen and Li Te-
yü, according to Ennin, jointly memorialized the throne, requesting that the moons of long fasts be discontinued.[26]
These were the first, fifth, and ninth moons, when meat was
not to be eaten after noon or, as Ennin puts it, when animal
life, in accordance with Buddhist precepts, was not to be
taken. The official discontinuance of these Buddhist fast
periods was in no way surprising under the circumstances,
but the Emperor's adoption of three annual Taoist observances to take their place must have dismayed his more rationalistic courtiers.

At about the same time Ennin also reported that the
Emperor had a Taoistic "ritual place of the nine heavens"
constructed in the Palace grounds out of "eighty benches
piled up high" and covered with elegantly colored drapes.
Here he had eighty-one Taoist priests, perhaps nine for each
of the heavens, make sacrifices to the heavenly deities of
Taoism at each of the twelve hours into which the Chinese
divided the calendar day. These sacrifices started on the
first day of the fourth moon and continued until the fifteenth
day of the seventh moon, the day of the Buddhist All Souls'
Festival. The whole prolonged ceremony was designed to give
the government spiritual aid in its efforts to suppress the
Lu-fu rebels. Whatever it may have accomplished on this
front, it was not without some ill effects elsewhere, for Ennin
concludes his comments on the incident with the slightly
malicious remark, "Since the place of ritual was not in a
building and the ceremonies were performed in an open
court, when it was clear the sun burned down [on the priests]
and when it rained they were drenched, and many of the
eighty-one men fell sick."

Faced with such evidence of Wu-tsung's preference for Taoism, Ennin concluded that "the present Emperor is a biased believer in Taoism and hates Buddhism. He does not like to see monks and does not wish to hear about the 'three treasures.'" Ennin then noted in his diary that the Buddhist images and scriptures that had "been placed since early times" in one of the Palace buildings had been destroyed and replaced by images of the heavenly deities and Lao-tzu, the supposed founder of Taoism, while, in place of the rotating teams of seven monks each who had continuously performed Buddhist ceremonies, Taoist priests had been assigned to "read Taoist scriptures and practice Taoist arts."

Ennin next reported the exclusion of the Buddhists from the Emperor's birthday celebration that year and went on to explain the Emperor's dislike of Buddhism on the basis of a memorial supposedly presented to the throne by Taoist priests. This memorial had attributed to Confucius the prophecy, "With the eighteenth son of the Li family, its grand destiny will be exhausted, and black-robed Emperors will rule the land." Conceivably some such statement did exist in the Confucian apocrypha, but in any case it was based on a still current pun on the character for Li, the surname of the T'ang Emperors. The graphic elements of this character can be taken apart to make three characters which mean "eighteen sons." Since Wu-tsung could be considered the eighteenth T'ang ruler, if some predynastic ancestors and the Empress Wu were included, the pun could be made to apply to him. The part about the "black-robed Emperors," too, was nothing new, for similar prophecies had been used against the black-robed Buddhist monks several times before in Chinese history. The whole story, even if false, illustrates the hold of the Taoists over Wu-tsung and the state of mind of the harassed Buddhists.

Ennin also reported another rumor which indicates what the Buddhists thought of their persecutor. He claims that Wu-tsung discovered a beautiful priestess in a Taoist nunnery and bestowed on her one thousand bolts of silk and ordered his officers to reconstruct and beautify the institution and connect it with the Palace. Ennin does not press the charge beyond this innuendo, and he at least had the fairness to point out that the Emperor also gave one thousand bolts of silk to a Taoist monastery and, after reconstructing this institution, had a bronze figure of himself placed in it.

Ennin even reports that Wu-tsung's enthusiasm for Taoism went so far that he issued an edict calling on the scholars and learned men of his court to take up the religion. Ennin concluded, with obvious satisfaction, "So far not a single person has done so." This reaction on the part of the scholars is actually more credible than the original edict itself and is balanced by the cool reception the common people gave the Emperor's discriminatory acts in favor of Taoism. During the All Souls' Festival of 844, according to Ennin, the monasteries outdid themselves with their displays of offerings, but the Emperor confiscated these and presented them instead to the favored Taoist monastery. However, when he ordered the people of the city to go to the Taoist institution to see these offerings, "the people cursed him, saying that since he had seized the offerings to the Buddhas and presented them to the spirits, who would be willing to look at them? The Emperor was surprised that the people did not come. The monasteries were extremely distressed because their offerings had been seized."

This sympathy on the part of the common people for the persecuted religion was also illustrated by another story Ennin records:

. . . each time that there was little rain the Commissioners of Good Works, on Imperial command, notified the various Buddhist and Taoist monasteries to read scriptures and pray for rain. But, when in response it rained, the Taoist priests alone received rewards, and the Buddhist monks and nuns were left forlorn with nothing. The people of the city laughingly said that, when they pray for rain, they bother the Buddhist monks, but, when they make rewards, they only give them to the Taoist priests.

One of Wu-tsung's more subtle ways of tormenting the Buddhists was to order the monasteries to make elaborate preparations for his frequent visits to them. The Emperor, according to Ennin, enjoyed going out on trips from the Palace and did so every two or three days, ordering the monasteries "to arrange benches, mats, and carpets, to tie flowered curtains to their towers, and to set out cups and saucers, trays, and chairs. For a single one of his trips with his retinue, each monastery spends more than four or five hundred strings of cash." [27]

Even after Ennin had left Ch'ang-an and had returned once more to the far tip of the Shantung Peninsula, he still heard of the Emperor's fanatical adherence to Taoism. In Shantung he learned that there was an Imperial edict banning wheelbarrows or "single-legged carts," as he calls them, and sentencing to death anyone who used these popular Chinese vehicles. The reason for this was said to be that wheelbarrows break up "the middle of the road," a phrase which could also be interpreted to mean "the heart of Taoism." Ennin heard that another Imperial edict proscribed various black animals, such as black pigs, dogs, donkeys, and oxen, on the grounds that Buddhist monks wore black and Taoist priests yellow, and it was feared that, "if there were much black, it might repress the yellow and cause it to be destroyed." There were also commands that the coastal prefectures and subprefectures should present live otters to the court and that the provinces should present "the hearts and livers of youths and maidens of fifteen years." Ennin did not quite understand the purpose of these orders but presumed them to be the result of the Emperor's delusion by the Taoist priests.[28] Of course, these reports, heard at such great distance from the capital, may have been entirely false, but they at least indicate what Buddhist sympathizers believed to be the Emperor's absurd and pernicious addiction to their rival religion.

THE TERRACE OF THE IMMORTALS

The most interesting series of incidents which occurred between Wu-tsung and the Taoist priests concerned the building of a "terrace of the immortals." It was constructed at the suggestion of the priest Chao Kuei-chen, who appears frequently in the standard historical records of Wu-tsung's reign and as early as the sixth moon of 841.[29] Ennin, however, does not mention him until the ninth moon of 844, when he quotes the following memorial presented to the throne by Chao and some other Taoist priests:

> The Buddha was born among the western barbarians and taught "non-birth." "Non-birth" is simply death. He converted men to Nirvana, but Nirvana is death. He talked much of impermanence, pain, and emptiness, which are particularly weird [doctrines]. He did not understand the principles of spontaneity and immortality.
> Lao-tzu, the Supreme, we hear, was born in China. . . . He roamed about and spontaneously and naturally became transformed. He concocted an elixir and, taking it, attained immortality and became one of the realm of spirits and produced great benefit without limit. We ask that a terrace of the immortals be erected in the Palace where we may purify our bodies and mount to the heavenly mists and roam about the nine heavens and, with blessings for the masses and long life for the Emperor, long preserve the pleasures of immortality.

Ennin reports that in the tenth moon the Emperor set three thousand legionaries of the Left and Right Guard Armies of Inspired Strategy to work on transporting earth to build a terrace 150 feet high. The Emperor was so anxious to see it completed that he failed to give the legionaries the customary seven-day holiday for the Chinese Lent, or "Cold Food Festival," in the spring of 845. Ennin records that the soldiers "were resentful and, holding their tools, they bowed down, and all three thousand of them raised their voices together. The Emperor was afraid and bestowed on each one three bolts of silk and gave him a three-day holiday." In connection with this big construction project, Ennin also tells the following story, which reflects on Wu-tsung's sanity:

. . . The General Supervisors of the two armies held sticks and oversaw [the work]. When the Emperor went to inspect it, he asked the Great Officials of the Palace who the men holding sticks were. They told him that they were the General Supervisors of the Guard Armies, managing the construction of the terrace. The Emperor told them, "We do not want you to hold sticks and manage [the work]. You yourselves should be carrying earth." And he had them transport earth. Later the Emperor went again to the place where the terrace was being built and he himself drew a bow and for no reason shot one of the General Supervisors, which was a most unprincipled act.[30]

Ennin, of course, was neither a firsthand nor an unprejudiced observer of the Emperor's actions, but he tells enough stories of irrational conduct by Wu-tsung to indicate that there were many rumors current which cast doubt on the ruler's mental stability. Thus, he reported earlier that when the Emperor decided to go to Lo-yang, the Eastern Capital, he issued an edict stating that, "if a courtier admonished him [against doing so], he would be executed and his family wiped out." Other rumors were that Wu-tsung had poisoned an Empress Dowager who protested against his persecution of Buddhism and that he had personally shot to death with an arrow another Empress Dowager who appears to have been his stepmother, because the lady had rejected his advances.[31]

Ennin seems to have attributed two other cases of flagrant misgovernment to Wu-tsung's extreme unreasonableness, if not outright insanity. He reports that the soldiers sent against the Lu-fu rebels, fearful of the Emperor's wrath because of their lack of initial success, seized innocent farmers and herdsmen of the border region and sent them as captured rebels to the capital, where the Emperor had them cut into three pieces "right in the streets" by the soldiers of the Armies of Inspired Strategy. Ennin, with

somewhat doubtful accuracy, even reported that the legionaries, "each time they killed a man, cut out his eyes and
flesh and ate them," and he stated that "the slaughtered
corpses constantly littered the roads, while their blood flowed
forth and soaked the ground, turning it into mud. Spectators
filled the roads, and the Emperor from time to time came
to see, and there was a great profusion of banners and
spears." [32]

A somewhat similar occurrence took place when three
thousand legionaries from T'ai-yüan-fu, who had been guarding the frontiers against the Uighurs for three years, were
ordered out again against the Lu-fu rebels immediately after
their return home. When their protests went unheeded, they
mutinied against the local Regional Commander, who seized
them and sent them to the capital. Here the Emperor, despite recommendations for clemency by the official investigators of the incident, had the unfortunate legionaries
slaughtered in the same manner as the supposed Lu-fu
rebels. [33]

Despite Ennin's obvious indignation at these unreason-
able acts of the Emperor, his diary discloses a trace of
amusement when he turns to recording the trials of the Taoists with their too sincere and fanatical Imperial convert:

> The construction of the terrace of the immortals was
> about to be completed, and an Imperial edict ordered the Tao-
> ist priests to concoct an elixir. Chao Kuei-chen, the head of the
> Taoist priests, sent a memorial to the throne, saying that there
> was a certain drug of immortality which does not exist at all in
> this country but was to be found in the land of Tibet, and he
> asked to go to Tibet himself to get the drug. The Commanders
> of the two [Guard] Armies [of Inspired Strategy] would not
> permit this, memorializing the throne to send another man to
> get it, for Chao Kuei-chen was the head of those who sought
> immortality and it would not be proper for him to go himself.
> The Emperor, in accordance with the memorial from the Com-
> manders, did not let him go. [34]

In the next incident which Ennin records, he may be sus-
pected of having purposely made the ingredients of the

Taoist elixir of life sound more ridiculous than they actually were. The story as he tells it runs as follows:

> An Imperial edict inquired what drugs were used in the search for immortality and [ordered the priests] to record their nature and report on them. The Taoist priests reported the names of the drugs [as follows]: ten pounds of plum skins, ten pounds of peach fuzz, ten pounds of the membranes of living chickens, ten pounds of tortoise hairs, and ten pounds of rabbit horns. The Emperor ordered that these be sought in the medicine stalls of the markets, but they all said that they had none. Consequently documents were issued for [the merchants] to be beaten. But [the Emperor's] worry was not assuaged, and they finally looked [for the drugs] in various places to no avail.

The terrace was eventually completed in the third moon of 845, and Ennin describes it in the following terms:

> I have been told that the terrace of the immortals is 150 feet high. The area on top is level and [big enough] for the foundations of a seven-bay building, and on top rises a five-peaked tower. People inside and outside [the grounds] can see it from afar, soaring high like a solitary peak. They have brought boulders from the Chung-nan Mountains and have made mountain cliffs on the four [sides] with grottoes and rocky paths. It is arranged most beautifully, and pines, arbor vitae, and rare trees have been planted on it.[35]

The Emperor was "overjoyed" with the results and at once ordered seven Taoist priests to concoct an elixir and "seek immortality on the terrace." The two eunuch Commanders of the Armies of Inspired Strategy, however, appear to have been somewhat less credulous, for Ennin records with obvious enjoyment that, when the Emperor, accompanied by the two Commanders and the high officials and Taoist priests, first mounted the terrace, the two martial eunuchs said to Chao and his associates, "Today we have come to the terrace of the immortals. We wonder if you, my lords, will seek to become immortals?" The unhappy Chao could only lower his head and remain silent.

The next time the Emperor mounted the terrace he was again rumored to have demonstrated his mental instability and also, for that matter, his hostility to the eunuchs, which was shortly to result in the incident of the seals of the two Guard Armies. While on top of the terrace he ordered a singer to push Yang Ch'in-i, the Commander of the Left Army of Inspired Strategy, off the terrace. When the singer demurred, "the Emperor asked him, 'When We have you push him, why don't you obey?' The singer said, 'The Commander is an important minister of the land. I dare not push him down.' The Emperor became angry and gave him twenty strokes of the cane on his back."

The Emperor, according to the story Ennin heard, then said to the Taoist priests, "Twice We have mounted the terrace, but not a single one of you, Our lords, has as yet mounted to immortality. What does this mean?" The Taoists explained that the existence of Buddhism alongside of Taoism in the land blocked the way to immortality. The Emperor then turned to the two Commissioners of Good Works and said, "We wonder if you realize, Our lords, that We do not want any [Buddhist] teachers at all, whoever they may be."

The most absurd incident involving the terrace of the immortals and one which, if correct, best proves Wu-tsung's insanity, was the final story Ennin recorded about it. The Emperor, it seems, announced to his officials:

> "The pit from which they took the earth [for the terrace] is very deep and makes people afraid and uneasy. We wish that it could be filled up. On a day for sacrifice to the terrace, you should falsely state that a maigre feast is being held to pay reverence to the terrace and should gather all the monks and nuns of the two halves of the city at the Left Army [of Inspired Strategy] and should cut off their heads and fill the pit with them."

The Emperor was only dissuaded from this mad act by one of his officers who argued:

> "The monks and nuns basically are ordinary people of the state, and if they are returned to lay life and each makes

his own living, it will benefit the land. I submit that you need not drive them [to extinction]. I ask that you order the offices concerned to force them all to return to lay life and to send them back to their places of origin to perform the local corvée."

It is not surprising that Ennin concluded the story with the comment, "When the monks and nuns of the various monasteries heard about this, their spirits lost confidence, and they did not know where to turn."

THE FULL ONSLAUGHT

In the second half of 844 the Buddhist persecution began to enter a new phase. The earlier objectives seem to have been primarily the weeding out of the irregular clergy and the confiscation of the private wealth of the monks and nuns, who supposedly were pledged to a life of poverty. For this phase the term "regulating" was not at all inappropriate, but in the latter part of 844 the persecution began to turn into an outright effort at extermination of the Indian religion. The chief reason for this change, no doubt, was Wutsung's fanatical espousal of Taoism and his apparently progressive insanity. Ennin, however, seems to have attributed it also in part to the financial needs of the state, for at this point he again mentions the great costs of the campaign against the Lu-fu rebels, which, he claims, amounted to the fantastic sum of 200,000 strings of cash a day. He also says that a sort of temporary income tax was assessed on the officials, who paid into the treasury "much or little money in accordance with their rank." [86]

The first sign of the intensification of the persecution was an Imperial edict ordering the destruction of all the small Buddhist temples and shrines throughout the empire which were not registered as official government monasteries and the return to lay life and to the tax registers of all the monks and nuns associated with them. The order also called for the destruction of all Buddhist stone pillars and grave monuments. In Ch'ang-an alone, Ennin reports, three hundred Buddhist institutions were destroyed as a result of this edict.[37] A few months later another edict broadened the attack to "the small monasteries of the land":

. . . Their scriptures and images were taken to the large monasteries, and their bells were sent to the Taoist monasteries. Those monks and nuns of the destroyed monasteries who were unrefined in their conduct or did not observe the rules, regardless of their age, were all forced to return to lay life, were sent back to their places of origin, and made to perform the local corvée. Those who were old and observed the rules were assigned to the great monasteries, but those who were young, even though they observed the rules, were all forced to return to lay life, going back to their places of origin. In the city thirty-three small monasteries were destroyed and their monks regulated, exactly in accordance with the Imperial edict.

At about the same time the strain on the Imperial treasury was greatly eased not only by the confiscation of the treasures of Ch'iu's adopted son, but also by the sudden collapse of the Lu-fu rebellion and the resultant acquisition of Liu Chen's vast wealth. But Wu-tsung showed no sign of relaxing his attack on the Buddhists. According to Ennin, the Emperor, seated in a tower above one of the Palace gates, gloated over Liu Chen's head,[38] as it was borne about the city on the end of a spear, and laughingly announced, "Now that [Liu Chen] has been smashed, the only ones that We have not yet got rid of are the monasteries of the land. We are not yet completely finished regulating the monks and nuns. Are you aware of this, Our lords?"

In the third moon of 845 Ennin recorded further edicts aimed at the confiscation of the slaves and other property of the remaining monasteries:

Another Imperial edict was issued to the monasteries of the land prohibiting them from establishing estates and also ordering that an inventory be made of the number of slaves of the monasteries of the land and their money, grain, and textile [holdings], which were to be ascertained in detail, recorded, and reported to the throne. The Commanders of the two armies were ordered to make an inventory of the monasteries in the city, and the inventory of those in the various prefectures and commanderies was entrusted to the Imperial Secretariat and Imperial Chancellery.

The slaves of the monasteries in the city were in three classes: those with skills were handed over to the military; those who lacked skills but were young and strong were sold; and those who were old and feeble were joined to the Palace slaves. This, alas, was a time when fathers went north and sons south. The Commissioners of Good Works notified the monasteries that [every] five slaves were to constitute a single mutual guaranty group and that, if a single one of the group fled, it would be fined two thousand strings of cash. The money of the monasteries and the payments for the slaves that were sold were all taken by the government to be applied to the officials' salaries.[39]

At about the same time the government started a wholesale defrocking of the remaining clergy. In previous "regulatings," as Ennin says, the purges had been limited largely to "those of unrefined conduct and those who did not conform to their own religion," but now the blow fell on the remaining monks of the large, officially recognized monasteries, regardless of their religious sincerity or official status. This great purge was arranged in successive stages and was executed by the Commissioners of Good Works in the capital, and in the provinces by the local governments under orders from the Imperial Secretariat and Chancellery.

The first stage in the capital was the defrocking and return to their places of origin of all monks and nuns under forty. This occurred between the first and fifteenth days of the fourth moon at the rate of three hundred clerics per day, according to Ennin. Next came the turn of the monks and nuns under fifty, who were all defrocked and returned to their places of origin between the sixteenth day of the fourth moon and the tenth day of the fifth moon. On the following day started a selective purge of the monks and nuns over fifty. All those who lacked documents from the Bureau of Sacrifices (*Tz'u-pu*), a government office in charge of the clergy, were immediately returned to lay life and sent back to their places of origin. Ennin records of the others:

. . . Those with documents from the Bureau of Sacrifices were all taken to the military and questioned, and if there were the slightest smudge on their documents from the Bureau of Sacrifices or if the birth year differed from that entered by the offices of the Commissioners of Good Works on their "protection documents," they were put among those to be returned to lay life. [The documents which] showed no discrepancies were taken by the military offices and were not returned, thus putting the monks and nuns of the various monasteries in the position of lacking credentials. Everyone said that the failure to return the credentials was a plot to get rid of the monks and nuns and the taking of the slaves and money of the monasteries was a foreshadowing of their destruction.

Ennin, of course, knew directly only about the procedures in the capital, but he understood that "the scheme is generally the same throughout the land." He also reported that Wu-tsung took a personal interest in the course of the purge and urged his officials on with repeated inquiries regarding the results. As a special precaution during the purge period, the Commissioners of Good Works again restricted the monks and nuns to their respective monastic establishments and dispatched five or six men to each monastery and convent to guard the gates and prevent the inmates from leaving. The Commissioners also warned that, if there were a violation of this rule, the monastic officers "as well as the men guarding the gate would each be sentenced to twenty strokes of the cane on the back, and the monk or nun who had gone out of the monastery would be executed on the spot." Naturally any cleric who tried to resist defrocking was also to be summarily condemned to death.

Foreign monks had hitherto been exempted from the purge, perhaps because of Ch'iu's intervention in their behalf before his death, but now "the Commissioners of Good Works made special inquiry of the throne, and a decision was made, and an Imperial edict stated that, if they lacked documents from the Bureau of Sacrifices, the foreigners too were to be forced to return to lay life and were to be sent back to their homelands." The Japanese, naturally, lacked the necessary documents, as did also Ratnacandra and his four disciples from South India, Nanda from North India, and most of the Korean monks in the capital.

For Ennin this, of course, was the climactic stage in the clerical purge, but one more was soon to follow which was to be the last both temporally and logically. On his way to Yang-chou Ennin fell in with an official court scholar who had been degraded and was on his way to a minor post in a distant prefecture. This man had left Ch'ang-an on the twenty-ninth day of the fifth moon, only two weeks after Ennin, but he reported that, before he left the city, "the return to lay life of the monks and nuns in the city was completed. In accordance with an Imperial edict, the monastery officers were left in each monastery to make an inventory of its money and wait until the government had collected it, after which they were to be returned to lay life." He also reported that the destruction of the monasteries themselves had started and that three of the most famous were being "incorporated into the Imperial parks." [40] When the great edict on the persecution which has been preserved in the official accounts finally appeared in the eighth moon, there was little for it to do but to record what had already been accomplished and to justify it in sanctimonious Confucian terms.

ENNIN'S EXPULSION

The order of deportation was not an unmitigated tragedy for Ennin, or, as he himself says, there was "both sorrow and joy" in it. He had been trying for almost four years to obtain permission to return to Japan, and he was glad to receive it at last, even if it had to come in the form of official deportation orders.

Ennin had first made application to return home in the eighth moon of 841. Mindful of what had happened to the Indian Ratnacandra when he had tried to bypass the Commissioner of Good Works, the Japanese monk circumspectly addressed his letter to Ch'iu himself. Ennin says no more of this request, which obviously was refused, and not until almost exactly two years later does he again mention the subject. At that time he called on a certain Li Yüan-tso at his home in the city to enlist his aid in the matter. Li, who was a devout Buddhist of Korean origin, was a Guard Officer of the Left Army of Inspired Strategy and held many high court ranks and offices. Ennin wrote of him, "He was most friendly at heart and always helped me whenever, far from home, I was in want of something." However, since by this time the irreligious Yang Ch'in-i had already replaced Ch'iu as Commissioner of Good Works, Li proved unable to obtain the permit his friend sought. This was not because of any lack of effort on his or Ennin's part. Ennin claims that in the four years between 841 and 845 he himself wrote to the Commissioner of Good Works more than one hundred times, asking to be allowed to return to his homeland, and at various times used bribery and the influence of patrons, but all to no avail.[41]

Ennin was not the only foreign monk who found his movements hampered by the growing restrictions on the Buddhist clergy. There was, of course, the case of Ratnacandra, and subsequently Ennin heard of the difficulties his former traveling companion, Ensai, was having in the Mt. T'ien-t'ai region. Late in 843 Ennin had heard that Ensai had been able to gain permission to send his two disciple monks back to Japan, but, when Ensai early in 844 sought permission for himself to go to Ch'ang-an, he was completely unsuccessful. A local military officer had gone to the capital to deliver medicines to the court, and Ensai had commissioned him to obtain the permit for him, but the Chinese officer was not even allowed to present the request.[42]

As things began to look worse for the remaining Buddhist monks in 845, Ennin seems to have redoubled his efforts to gain permission to return to Japan, for at this time he admits writing to the Commissioner of Good Works, asking to be defrocked and allowed to return home, but no action was taken even on this request. Finally, on the thirteenth day of the fifth moon of that year, the names of Ennin and Ishō appeared on the official list of thirty-nine monks from the Tzu-sheng-ssu who were being returned to lay life because they lacked documents from the Bureau of Sacrifices.

Knowing of the decision regarding foreign monks, Ennin had already begun to prepare for departure. As he wrote shortly before the official order came through:

. . . I bound up my written materials, wrapping up all the scriptures I had copied, the teachings on devotion, and my *mandara*. In all I had four hampers of writings and clothes. Then I bought three donkeys and waited for a decision [on my case]. I do not regret my return to lay life. I merely regret that I shall not be able to take with me the holy teachings I have copied. Buddhism has been proscribed on Imperial order, and I fear that, [were I to take the writings with me], on my way the various prefectures and commanderies would examine me and, discovering the truth, would accuse me of disobedience to an Imperial edict.

Actually, Ennin had relatively little trouble in taking his religious possessions with him, and his Chinese friends rallied around to help with his baggage and to assist in other ways. A defrocked monk who had been one of the members of Igyō's funeral procession offered to accompany the Japanese as far as Pien-chou, the modern K'ai-feng, near the head of the Pien River leading eastward into the Huai River system, and Ennin, "seeing how great was his concern, did not oppose his desire." One of the remaining monks of the Tzu-sheng-ssu gave the Japanese a farewell present of a sandalwood box and image, and the monastery officers philosophically remarked to them:

. . . Since ancient times until now those in search of the Law have indeed had their troubles. We beg you to remain calm. If it were not because of this difficulty, there would be no way for you to return to your land, and we rejoice that you will be able to return to your land with the holy teachings, as was your original intention.

Early on the fourteenth, the day after they had received their defrocking and expulsion orders, the Japanese left the monastery which had been home to them for almost five years and went to Ching-chao-fu, the prefectural government of the capital, to obtain travel credentials. There they met seven monks "from the Western Lands" bent on the same purpose. The prefectural officials made out for the Japanese the necessary documents to see them through the two provinces lying between the capital area and the Eastern Sea.

The next morning the Japanese were escorted from the prefectural government to Wan-nien-hsien, one of the two subprefectural offices of the city. On the way they stopped for a farewell call on a high Chinese official named Yang who had been their patron and who now gave them a parting gift of a string of brick tea. At the subprefectural offices Ennin also received a tragic letter with "veiled words of parting" from a former Court Priest who was now in hiding in Yang's home. Two other prominent defrocked monks also called on Ennin, and his patron Li Yüan-tso turned up with a nephew. These loyal friends also bought the Japanese hats made of felt to cover their shaved pates and went back to the monastery to take charge of their hampers.

That same evening Ennin and his two attendants left the city under guard on the first leg of their long journey eastward. Li and one of the defrocked clerics accompanied them outside the city gate, where they ran into a veritable farewell delegation. Yang had sent a man to deliver a letter saying, "I, your disciple, have written five documents and notes in my own hand for the officials I have known of old in the prefectures and subprefectures on your route. If you take these letters, they should help you get through." Another official who had often come to the monastery to call on Ennin and had given him woolen shirts and trousers and pieces of silk was there in person with his son and presented the departing Japanese with "two bolts of silk, two pounds of tea, a string of brick tea, two strings of cash, and two letters" for persons on the way, as well as a letter for Ennin himself. A merchant patron of the Japanese had sent a man to give the

Japanese "one bolt of silk, one length of woolen cloth, and one thousand cash." There were also others there to bid the Japanese farewell and to call after them, "Stay a while longer."

Li and the man sent by Yang were not willing to quit the Japanese even then and spent the night with them at their first stop a couple of miles east of the city. Here Li gave Ennin munificent farewell presents, consisting of ten bolts of damask, a piece of fragrant sandalwood, two sandalwood boxes with images, a bottle of incense, a five-pronged silver *vajra* (a Buddhist weapon symbolizing a thunderbolt), the two felt hats Ennin had mentioned before, one scroll of the *Diamond Sutra* (*Kongō-kyō*) in silver characters, which later became a Palace possession in Japan, a pair of soft slippers, and two strings of cash. Li also asked for and received from Ennin the latter's Buddhist robe and scarf, wishing to "take them home and burn incense and make offerings to them for the rest of my life." Li's farewell speech was particularly touching:

. . . Your disciple has had much good fortune in his life in having met you who came from afar in search of the Buddhist Law and in having made presentations to you for several years, but my heart is not yet satisfied, and I do not want to be separated from you my whole life. You now have encountered this difficulty with the ruler and are going back to your homeland. Your disciple believes that it is not likely that he will see you again in this life, but certainly in the future in the paradises of the various Buddhas I shall again be your disciple, as I am today. When you attain Buddhahood, please do not forget your disciple.

ON THE ROAD AGAIN

The next morning the Japanese continued on their way in the company of nineteen other monks. In the group was a young man of twenty "who was a native of the city of Ch'ang-an and whose parents, brothers, and sisters were still alive." He had been an attendant to a Korean monk and, when the persecution had started, had managed to avoid defrocking by palming himself off on the authorities as a Korean. But now poetic justice had overtaken him, and he was being deported to Korea despite all his protestations and the loud wailing of his relatives. The young man, however, managed to slip away before the party started out that morning, and his absence was not discovered until evening. Immediately guards were sent out to search for him, and word was sent back to the prefectural government of Ch'ang-an to be on the lookout for the fugitive.

What happened to the pseudo-Korean monk Ennin never learned, for he and the rest of the party moved on the next day. In the towns and cities along the way Ennin delivered his letters of introduction, receiving one or two bolts of cloth from at least three of the officials he met in this way. In one city he also ran into an official who had been an old patron of his at the capital and who now entertained him and presented him with a bolt of silk, a stomach wrap, light shirts, and woolen shirts. When Ennin was forced to leave the city before this man could make his last farewells, the latter followed him on horseback, overtaking the party about five miles from the city. After having tea together, the Chinese made a little farewell speech:

. . . Buddhism no longer exists in this land. But Buddhism flows toward the east. So has it been said since ancient times. I hope that you will do your best to reach your homeland and propagate Buddhism there. Your disciple has been very fortunate to have seen you many times. Today we part, and in this life we are not likely to meet again. When you have attained Buddhahood, I hope that you will not abandon your disciple.[43]

After almost a month on the road the Japanese reached Pien-chou, where there were two officials for whom Ennin had letters. One of these men proved very friendly and hired a boat for the first part of their trip down the Pien River, though subsequently the Japanese had to pay for their own boats. Nine days later they reached Ssu-chou, but an uncooperative Subprefect in the town across the river from this

city forced them to go overland from there to Yang-chou
instead of continuing on down the river to Ch'u-chou as they
had intended. In Yang-chou, however, the judicious use of
bribery induced the officials to route them back up the
Grand Canal to Ch'u-chou, which they reached on the third
day of the seventh moon.[44]

In Ch'u-chou the Japanese immediately looked up their
old friend, the Korean Interpreter Yu Sinŏn, and the General Manager (*Tsung-kuan*) of the Korean ward, Sŏl Chŏn.
Through the influence of these two, the Japanese sought
permission from the subprefectural government of the city
to be allowed to stay there, waiting for a ship bound for
Japan, but the officials ruled, "At this prefecture you are
not yet out on the sea, and, since you are being sent through
on Imperial order, we dare not detain you, and therefore you
should be sent to the land's end in Teng-chou, where you can
board ship and return home."

The Japanese had no desire to make the long and arduous
trip to the tip of the Shantung Peninsula. Yu and Sŏl did
their best to persuade the subprefectural officials to reverse
their decision, but even bribes produced no results. They also
tried to induce the prefectural government to overrule the
subprefectural order, but again without avail. At the subprefectural offices they were told that "this was an area of
law and order and within the jurisdiction of the Minister of
State, Li Shen, and it would be a violation of the Imperial
edict if those being sent through on Imperial command
should tarry a day or two."

The subprefectural officials, however, did offer to send
the Japanese either north or south, depending on their preference, and Ennin, realizing that "there was nothing more
to be said in words," elected to go north to Shantung where
he had still other Korean friends. The necessary documents,
accordingly, were issued and some government hirelings assigned to escort the Japanese on their way. The latter proved
to be more susceptible to bribery than the officials and were
persuaded by 300 cash to delay the departure of the Japanese three days while the weary travelers rested in Yu's home.

Ennin, apprised of the "evil hearts" of the people in the lightly populated area ahead of them and fearful of what might happen if they were found carrying icons and texts of the proscribed religion, decided to leave behind with Yu "all four of the hampers of holy teachings, pious pictures, and clerical clothing." But his baggage was somewhat replenished by gifts of three pairs of socks from the General Manager Sŏl and nine bolts of silk, ten Korean knives, five pairs of socks, and "a lot of provisions" from Yu, from whom Ennin also received letters to the Koreans along the way.

The three Japanese set forth from Ch'u-chou on the appointed day and went to Lien-shui-hsien, a short distance down the Huai River. Here, armed with one of Yu's letters, they went to the Korean ward but found scant sympathy until they ran into a Korean named Ch'oe, whom Ennin had first met six years earlier at the Mt. Ch'ih Cloister in Shantung. Ch'oe had written his name down for Ennin to keep and had told him that, when he was ready to return to Japan, he should look him up in Lien-shui and he, Ch'oe, would give the monks passage home on his ship. In the meantime, however, Ch'oe had fallen on less prosperous days and apparently had lost his vessel. But he could at least intercede in behalf of the Japanese with the local Koreans and officials. The latter, who took pity on the Japanese and served them tea and food, agreed to let them stay in the Korean ward to await a ship bound for Japan, provided that the local Koreans would grant them official recognition as members of their group. Probably under Ch'oe's influence, the General Manager and most of the others agreed to give the required recognition, but one of the group blackballed the Japanese, and the Koreans, therefore, finally refused to make out the necessary affidavit.

The subprefectural officials permitted the Japanese to tarry for three days longer in a local monastery, while Ch'oe paid their expenses. Then, provided with fresh documents from the local government and a boat and provisions supplied by Ch'oe, Ennin and his companions started off again down the Huai River to Hai-chou, the prefectural city near its mouth. Ch'oe's parting message was: "Your disciple wishes that he were able to keep you and send you home from here, but, because the group refused and the official document has expired, my efforts have been to no avail, and I cannot fulfill my wish. After the autumn I intend myself to go to the Teng-chou region, and I hope to see you then."

At Hai-chou the Japanese made one final effort to win permission to settle down, arguing very plausibly in the document they presented to the subprefectural offices:

> The ships of the Japanese tributary embassy landed here and started back to Japan from here. We, Ennin and the others, came with the embassy to China and are now returning to our homeland and have been sent here in due course. Since this is the sea-coast, we humbly beg to stay for a little while in this prefecture to look for a ship on which to return home.

The Subprefect, however, pointed out that he could not grant this petition since the Prefect of Hai-chou had already refused a similar request from a Korean monk who was being deported from the capital. The next day the Japanese made their appeal directly to the Prefect, whose blunt reply was, "You are to be sent on, in accordance with the Imperial edict. The prefectural government does not dare keep you. You have been notified." [45]

The following day the Japanese started out on the long overland trek northward to Teng-chou, which they reached about a month later. From there they proceeded eastward to Wen-teng-hsien and from this easternmost subprefecture, at their own request, to the Office in Charge of Korean Affairs situated on the seacoast not far from their old home, the Mt. Ch'ih Cloister. Here they were cordially received by their former friend and benefactor, Chang Yŏng, the Guard Officer "in charge of the Korean population of the Wen-teng-hsien area," who, when apprised of the situation, made the following speech:

> . . . From the time you set off from here until now, I have had no news of you, and in my heart I thought that you had returned to Japan earlier. I did not think that you would come

here again and to have met you again is very strange, very strange. Your disciple has great affinities with you. I shall strive to see that nothing untoward happens to you within my jurisdiction. Please be at ease and rest yourself. There is no need to worry. I wish to provide you myself with provisions for your forenoon meals each day until you return home, so eat your fill and sleep.[46]

Chang informed the subprefecture of the arrival of the Japanese, typically referring in his letter to the full documentation of the case:

We have received a document from Wen-teng-hsien, which says, "The two Japanese monks, Ennin and Ishō, have each been granted covering documents from Ching-chao-fu and, in accordance with the Imperial edict, are being sent to their homeland and in due course have been sent to this subprefecture. They ask to go to the Office in Charge of Korean Affairs to seek [sustenance] whereby to prolong their lives and to await a ship bound across to Japan, on which they would hope to return home." They are at present at this inlet.

Ten days later came the reassuring reply, "Let the monks be at ease. If there is a ship bound across to Japan, then they may go at their discretion." At last, almost four months after they had been escorted out of the capital, Ennin and his attendants had found a haven where they could stay.

This, of course, was not the end of Ennin's deportation, for he was still on Chinese soil, but the rest of the story develops into one of those absurd contradictions which official procedures and particularly those concerned with travelers from abroad produce all too frequently even today. A few months after the Japanese had settled down with Wang Chŏng, they learned that, although they were condemned to deportation, a new edict had now placed restrictions on their further movements. A Tibetan monk on his way back to his native land from Ch'ang-an had stopped at Feng-hsiang, the home of the famous finger-bone of the Buddha. Here the Regional Commander had requested and received permission to take charge of the man, who was accordingly relieved of

the necessity of climbing back to his original home on the
roof of the world. The Imperial ruling may have been a special favor arranged by the Regional Commander of Feng-
hsiang for this one Tibetan monk, but it raised the question
of what should be done with the other foreign monks who
were being deported. Perhaps to resolve these doubts regarding his own clerical guests, Wang Chŏng requested the local
prefectural government to issue them a passport, but after
some discussion the officials replied, "This would be to oppose
the text of the Imperial edict. We are not willing to give
them official credentials." Ennin and his companions now
were indeed ensnarled in red tape, with one scarlet band
dragging them toward deportation and another tying them
down to their stopping place in Shantung.[47]

THE PERSECUTION IN THE PROVINCES

However uncomfortable this position may have been for
Ennin, it at least kept him in China long enough to see the
persecution of Buddhism through to its end. His lengthy
journey from the capital to Yang-chou and Ch'u-chou and
finally to Shantung and his prolonged stay there enabled
him to round out his account of the great persecution both
temporally and spatially. In Ssu-chou on the Huai River,
for example, he learned the fate of the great P'u-kuang-
wang-ssu. More than a year earlier Ennin had mentioned the
banning of the festival for the finger-bone of the Buddha at
this famous monastery, and now he discovered that "its estates, money, and slaves have all been confiscated by the
government, and the monastery is desolate and no one comes
there. The prefectural government is about to destroy it in
accordance with an Imperial edict." [48] A few days later in
Yang-chou Ennin recorded:

We . . . saw the monks and nuns of the city being
sent back to their places of origin with their heads wrapped up.
The monasteries are to be destroyed, and their money, estates,
and bells are being confiscated by the government. Recently a

document came on Imperial command saying that the bronze and iron Buddhas of the land were all to be smashed and weighed and handed over to the Salt and Iron Bureau [*Yen-t'ieh-ssu*] and a record made of this and reported to the throne.[49]

Ennin's storing of his religious baggage with the Korean, Yu Sinŏn, in Ch'u-chou was an indication of the severity of the persecution in that part of the empire. He later learned from Yu that when a further edict was issued ordering the burning of all Buddhist paraphernalia and specifying that violators of this order would be "punished to the limit of the law," the Korean had burned all his own Buddhist materials and Ennin's *Double Great Taizō and Kongō Mandara*, which probably were paired paintings of huge dimensions and therefore particularly hard to conceal.[50]

In Teng-chou Ennin heard of an Imperial edict, "saying that prefectural and subprefectural governments are to peel the gold off the gilt bronze Buddhist images throughout the land and are to weigh it and present it to the throne." Of Teng-chou he also recorded:

. . . Although it is a remote place, it has been no different from the capital in the regulation of monks and nuns, the destruction of the monasteries, the banning of the scriptures, the breaking of the images, and the confiscation of the property of the monasteries. Moreover they have peeled off the gold from the Buddhas and measured their weight. What a pity! What limit was there to the bronze, iron, and gold Buddhas of the land? And yet, in accordance with the Imperial edict, all have been destroyed and have been turned into trash.[51]

Even at the haven provided for them by Wang Chŏng, the Japanese witnessed further results of the persecution. They had hoped to stay once again in the Mt. Ch'ih Cloister, but they found that it had been destroyed by the authorities "in accordance with the Imperial edict" and that not a single habitable building remained. Since Wang's home was constantly full of "official guests" and the Japanese desired quieter quarters, Wang finally placed them in a house on the cloister's former estate. Here they met one of their former Korean acquaintances from the Mt. Ch'ih Cloister. This now defrocked monk had once lived for several years in Japan and consequently was now serving as an interpreter, apparently for occasional Japanese merchants passing that way.[52]

Ennin, while in relative seclusion at the tip of the Shantung Peninsula, also learned several more details about the persecution in general:

Recently there was an Imperial edict [saying]:
"The black clothing of the monks and the nuns of the land who have been returned to lay life should all be collected and burned by their respective prefectures and subprefectures. It is feared that the officials . . . have used their power to hide [monks and nuns] in their private homes and that in secret they wear their black robes. These should be ruthlessly confiscated and all burned, and the matter reported to the throne. If after the burning there be monks or nuns who wear their black robes and have not given them all up and there be those who protect [monks and nuns] at the time of the investigation, they shall be sentenced to death in accordance with the Imperial edict."

The prefectures and subprefectures, in accordance with the Imperial edict, have notified the city wards and the cantons to collect the clothing of the monks and nuns and bring it to the prefectures and subprefectures for all of it to be burned.

There also was an Imperial edict ordering that the rarities, treasures, jewels, and gold and silver of the monasteries of the empire be confiscated by the prefectures and subprefectures and presented to the throne.

Again, there was an Imperial edict, saying that the copper utensils, bells, gongs, caldrons, pans, and the like, used by the monks and nuns of the monasteries of the land, should be collected into the government storehouses by the Commissioners of Salt and Iron of the various provinces and the matter recorded and reported to the throne.

. . . .

The monks and nuns of China are naturally poor. Throughout the land they have all been returned to lay life, and, now that they have been secularized, they lack clothes to wear and food to eat. Their hardships are extreme, and they cannot assuage their cold or hunger, so they enter the cantons and villages and steal the property of others, and their transgressions are very numerous. Those whom the prefectures and subprefectures are arresting are all monks returned to lay life. Because of this, the check on monks and nuns who have been regulated and have already returned to lay life is still more [severe].[53]

Ennin learned, however, that there was at least one part of China in which the persecution was not strictly enforced. In recording in his diary his own summary of the results of the persecution, he noted that in four regional commanderies north of the Yellow River, Lu-fu in southeastern Shansi and three others on the North China Plain,

. . . where Buddhism has always been honored, they have not destroyed the monasteries, the monks and nuns have not been regulated, and Buddhism has not been in the least disturbed. There have repeatedly been Imperial Commissioners to investigate and punish them, but they say, "If the Emperor himself were to come to destroy [the monasteries] and burn [the scriptures], it could be done, but we are unable to do it." [54]

It was also in Shantung that Ennin finally learned of the death of Wu-tsung, the Imperial nemesis of Buddhism. This happy event occurred on the twenty-third day of the third moon of 846, and Ennin heard of it twenty-one days later. At the same time he heard the rumor that the Emperor had died "because his constitution had been ruined," perhaps a reference to the results of the Taoist elixirs of life which the Imperial convert had been taking. Wu-tsung's uncle and successor, Hsüan-tsung, almost immediately set about undoing his nephew's work, even before changing the name of the year period to Ta-chung at the beginning of the next year.

In the fifth moon of 846 there was a great amnesty, which, Ennin learned, was proclaimed in Ch'u-chou on the twenty-second day of that moon. According to Ennin, the amnesty was accompanied by

. . . an Imperial edict that each prefecture of the land was to build two monasteries and that the regional commanderies were permitted to build three, and each monastery was to have fifty monks. The monks over fifty years of age who had been returned to lay life last year were allowed to take Buddhist orders as of old, and on those who had reached eighty years were bestowed five strings of cash by the state. The moons of the three long [fasts] were re-established, and, as before, butchering was proscribed [during these moons].[55]

The government obviously was returning to the more usual practice of "regulating" rather than persecuting Buddhism, and Ennin, though still defrocked and far from home, must have uttered a heartfelt sigh of relief.

VIII

The Koreans in China

Ennin remained in China for more than a year after the end of the Buddhist persecution, but during this time his personal contacts seem to have been primarily with Koreans rather than with Chinese. This had also been the case during his earlier stay at the Mt. Ch'ih Cloister. In fact, although his diary recounts the travels of a Japanese in China, in its pages Koreans rival Chinese in number and decidedly overshadow the Japanese. Then as now, some eleven centuries later, these three people were the major national groupings of that part of the world, and of the three the Koreans played the least known but, as we see in Ennin's diary, perhaps the most interesting role.

THE LAND OF SILLA

Korea at this time was already the same country it is today—geographically, linguistically, and in some ways culturally. This makes it one of the oldest countries of the modern world. In fact, the only contemporary nation which can claim a longer continuity of language, people, and boundaries is China, and Japan is among the very few other countries that can boast a national identity of an age comparable to Korea's. Certainly no modern European nation emerged on the maps of the world with roughly its present borders until long after Korea had taken shape.

Korean unity was first achieved by the southeastern Korean kingdom of Silla, and throughout Ennin's diary it is the name Silla which he uses for the whole country. In the middle of the seventh century the T'ang, after several unsuccessful

Chinese attempts, had once again invaded Korea. With the aid of Silla, the T'ang armies destroyed the southwestern Korean kingdom of Paekche in 663 and the northern kingdom of Koguryŏ in 668, despite the aid given these states by Japanese forces. Allied with T'ang and recognizing its suzerainty, Silla fell heir to virtually the whole of the peninsula, which, except for a few brief periods of disruption, has remained a politically and culturally unified land ever since.

Silla gave way between 918 and 935 to a new dynasty, which modified the earlier name of Koguryŏ to Koryŏ and thus gave the Western world its name for the country. In 1392 Koryŏ was succeeded by the I dynasty, which lasted until 1910, finally being replaced by a Japanese colonial administration. During the long period from 668 until the present, Korea has usually been under the domination of some foreign power—strong Chinese dynasties to the west, ascendant barbarian tribes to the northwest, or more recently, the Japanese to the east. The present political and military pressures on the peninsula from these three directions, therefore, are hardly new in Korean history. But, despite changing native dynasties and foreign suzerains, Korea has remained a remarkably homogeneous and stable unit for more than twelve hundred years.

Korea in an earlier day had been the first cultural offspring of China and, until the Japanese took over the peninsula, was the most closely imitative and most loyal of China's spiritual descendants. During the important stage in world history when the culture of the ancient centers of civilization seeped outward to neighboring lands, it was at first largely through Korea that Chinese civilization came to Japan. Far closer and more intimately connected with China than were the Japanese, the Koreans during this period had a long head start on the Japanese in civilization. But in both these lands, Chinese influence resulted in a cultural rise which was far more rapid and spectacular than was the slow cultural growth of their tribal counterparts in North Europe under civilizing influences from the Mediterranean world.

THE KOREANS AND WORLD TRADE

Ennin, as we have seen, was perhaps the last major figure
in this first great period of cultural borrowing by Japan from
China, but the Koreans he met on the continent were part of
a new and even more dramatic phase of world history. They
were taking part in the early stages of the period of world
maritime commerce, the age in which, for all the progress of
air transportation, we still are living. Man long before had
mastered the Mediterranean Sea and other relatively small,
land-locked bodies of water, but only slowly did he dare to
venture forth on the unbounded oceans. A limited trade had
existed for some time along the ocean fringes of the southern
coast of Asia, and men from the Near East, claiming to
represent the Roman Emperor, had come by sea to the
southern borders of China as early as the second century A.D.
But not until the time of the T'ang did world maritime trade
grow to such proportions that it began to modify substantially the economy of mankind and ultimately, through that
economy, our political and social life as well.

The Persians and Arabs seem to have been the spearhead
of the rapidly growing commerce of the oceans and some
centuries later were perhaps the first to utilize for man's
mastery of the sea an important invention which may have
developed from a bit of ancient Chinese lore—the compass.
The Chinese themselves took scant part in maritime navigation during these early centuries, but it was the rich load-
stone of T'ang prosperity that drew the Near Eastern
traders on beyond India and far around the southward trail-
ing land barrier of Malaya to the coasts of distant Cathay.
Thus, the role of the Chinese initially was passive, but without the unparalleled wealth of the T'ang, world commerce
might not have been born so early or have reached such great
proportions by Ennin's time. On the other hand, the tremendous economic and cultural growth which took place in
China between the seventh and thirteenth centuries perhaps
would have been impossible without this foreign trade. Thus,

domestic developments in China probably helped produce world maritime commerce and at the same time were themselves in part the product of this trade. Here again we have the familiar chicken and egg situation, which is so typical of man's progress.

It is a tribute to the stability and excellence of traditional Chinese political and social institutions that, despite the vast economic growth of the centuries following the rise of the T'ang, the principal political forms of earlier days as well as much of the social structure survived intact, to solidify into apparent permanence at the end of this period of rapid growth. It was left for latecomers to world trade to undergo first the more extreme social and political changes growing at least in part out of this economic revolution. Through the crusades and Marco Polo the relatively poor and backward peoples of the European Peninsula, jutting westward from the great land mass of Asia, learned something of the riches and glories of the civilizations participating in oceanic commerce. Only slowly did the side currents of this flow of goods reach up into Europe, but the results were relatively drastic in the unstable feudal society of that part of the world. Somewhat the same picture of rapid change and instability appeared in the feudal society of Japan, which also began to take significant part in world trade in the thirteenth century.

In Europe economic growth and the resultant political and social changes were greatly accelerated by the rapid mastery gained during the fifteenth and sixteenth centuries by the peoples of Western Europe over the oceans of the world and the commerce that had existed on these oceans for centuries. We rightly date the beginning of the modern West from that time, but in a broader view of world history one might with some justice begin the modern period with the growth of world trade during the T'ang and make the joining in this world trade by the Europeans the start of a significant subperiod within the modern age. The long delayed political and social upheaval in our own day in Asia would then mark the beginning of another important subdivision in this period of world maritime commerce.

Ennin had one small and indirect contact with the main stream of world trade while in China. It is known that in the latter half of the T'ang there were large communities of Near Eastern traders in Yang-chou and Canton, China's two greatest ports at this time. Unquestionably the Persians who, at Li Te-yü's suggestion, donated one thousand strings of cash for the repair of the Balcony of the Auspicious Images in Yang-chou, were either individual members or more probably the official representatives of the Near Eastern commercial community in that city. They were probably not Buddhists themselves, but, like good businessmen anywhere, realized the value of charitable contributions in keeping on good terms with the local authorities. The men of Champa, the kingdom on the southeastern coast of the modern Indo-china, who gave two hundred strings of cash for the balcony, may have been members of an embassy, but it seems more probable that they too were merchants carried to Yang-chou on the strong tide of commerce flowing from the west past their shores and on to China.[1]

In the Korean traders of China Ennin was not encountering the main stream of world commerce but a significant side flow. The Near Eastern merchants apparently went no farther east or north than Yang-chou, and at this point the Koreans took over for the last leg of the trade to the easternmost corners of the known world. From what Ennin tells us, it seems that commerce between East China, Korea, and Japan was for the most part in the hands of men from Silla. Here in the relatively dangerous waters on the eastern fringes of the world, they performed the same peripheral functions as did the traders of the placid Mediterranean on the western fringes. This is an historical fact of considerable significance but one which has received virtually no attention in the standard historical compilations of that period or in the modern books based on these sources.

KOREANS AT THE COURT

Ch'ang-an during the T'ang dynasty was the seat of what was perhaps the greatest empire, both in geographic size and in population, that the world had as yet seen. Naturally the metropolis, which itself numbered its population in the millions, drew to it large numbers of foreigners from all parts of the known world, except Europe, which at the time was partially isolated from the rest of civilization by barbarian invaders. Year after year embassies came to the Chinese capital in large numbers from virtually all parts of Asia, and the city was also the chief eastern terminus of the great overland trade routes. The large Nestorian, Zoroastrian, and Manichaean communities which Wu-tsung wiped out were probably made up almost exclusively of men from Central Asia and the Near East who had been drawn to Ch'ang-an by its diplomatic and commercial magnetism.

It is not at all surprising that there were many Koreans among the foreigners thronging the streets of the Chinese capital. In fact, Ennin's diary and many other historical sources give the impression that Koreans were among the most numerous of the foreign peoples there and had worked their way into Chinese life more thoroughly than most. Many members of the conquered Paekche and Koguryŏ ruling families and courts had been transplanted to China, and the unification of the peninsula by Silla under the T'ang aegis led to a steady stream of embassies going from Korea to Ch'ang-an. Sometimes more than one embassy was dispatched in a single year, and there seem to have been no less than forty-five in the thirty-six-year period between 703 and 738.[2]

These embassies, like the much less frequent ones from Japan, were often accompanied by scholars and monks, as well as by courtiers and junior members of the ruling house. Some of these men settled down in China for many years, where a few even passed the civil service examinations and many more served in the Imperial guards. Probably the great majority of the Koreans sooner or later returned to their homeland, but some remained permanently in China, and a few of these carved out impressive careers for themselves as servants of the Chinese Emperors.

Among the various men of Korean origin who became so famous that they were given official biographies in the dynastic histories of the T'ang, the greatest of all was Kao Hsien-chih.[3] In 747 this Korean led a Chinese army of ten thousand men across the Pamirs and Hindukush Mountains to the upper waters of the Indus in a successful effort to keep the troublesome Tibetans and invading Arabs of the west from joining forces against the Chinese overlords of Central Asia. This expedition across passes in some cases as high as 15,000 or 16,000 feet at a distance of well over 2,000 miles of deserts and mountains from the seat of Chinese power is one of the most amazing military feats of history. Unfortunately for Kao Hsien-chih's reputation, he is also known as the general who in 751 was defeated by the Arabs at Talas in what is now Russian Turkestan on the far side from China of the great central mountain mass of Asia. This again was one of those pivotal dates of history, for it marked the start of a long decline in Chinese power and was the prelude to the Mohammedan conquest of the Central Asian regions, which hitherto had been the imperial domain of China and the spiritual domain of the Buddha.[4]

Many of the Korean monks who went to China to study also turned into permanent immigrants, and several became famous members of the Chinese Buddhist church. A great Chinese churchman and translator of Buddhist scriptures, I-ching, who himself sailed for India from Yang-chou on board a Persian ship in 671 and returned by sea to Canton twenty-four years later, has left us an account of the trips to India of fifty-six clerics in his own day or shortly before, and of these no less than seven were Koreans rather than Chinese. After I-ching's time other Koreans continued to make this perilous trip. For example, in 1908 the famous French scholar, Paul Pelliot, discovered a manuscript which proved to be a fragment of the travel record of Hui-ch'ao, a monk of Korean origin, who some time around the year 723 went by sea from China to India and returned about six years later by way of Central Asia.[5]

In contrast to these nine successful Korean pilgrims, only one Japanese is known to have attempted in these early days the long and hazardous trip to the home of the Buddha. This was Prince Takaoka, who for a while in his youth was heir apparent to the Japanese throne, but was subsequently demoted and became a monk and the disciple of Ennin's famous predecessor, Kūkai. Years later in 862, when in his seventies, the hardy Prince set out for China and three years later reached Ch'ang-an. There he met Ensai, Ennin's former traveling companion, who aided him in obtaining permission to go on to India. In 866, leaving his tardy entourage behind, he set sail alone from Canton for the holy land and, as it turned out, for oblivion, for he perished short of his goal, apparently somewhere in Malaya.[6]

With so many Koreans drawn to the Chinese capital, it is not surprising that Ennin encountered some there. Actually his patron, Li Yüan-tso, the court functionary and officer of the Left Guard Army of Inspired Strategy, was the only official of Korean origin whom he mentions, but he does write of several Korean monks, even if briefly. There were apparently ten Koreans among the twenty-one foreign monks residing in the eastern half of Ch'ang-an whom Ch'iu assembled at his quarters at the beginning of the Buddhist persecution. Another indication of the relatively large number of Korean monks in the city was the fact that the young Chinese disciple of a Korean monk, of whom Ennin tells us, was able to pass so successfully as a Korean himself that he was finally sentenced to be repatriated to Korea.[7]

Ennin also met or heard of several other Korean monks who had been in Ch'ang-an or other parts of North China. Pŏpch'ŏng, the Prior of the Mt. Ch'ih Cloister, had lived in the Chinese capital some thirty years before Ennin first met him, and other members of this Korean monastic community had also traveled to Ch'ang-an as well as to Mt. Wu-t'ai. In a monastery in the vicinity of T'ai-yüan-fu, Ennin also ran into a local tradition involving a Korean monk who had lived in the capital in the seventh century. This Korean and a Chinese monk, who was to become one of the great church fathers, were rival disciples of the famous Buddhist traveler, Hsüan-tsang. Once the Korean listened surreptitiously to a lecture Hsüan-tsang was giving on a certain scripture espe-

cially for the benefit of the Chinese disciple, and the Korean
stole a march on his rival by immediately assembling a congregation and delivering a lecture on the scripture himself.
But Hsüan-tsang comforted his crestfallen disciple by im-
parting to him further lore which the Korean did not know,
and, according to Ennin, the Chinese monk then came to this
distant monastery to lecture on the scripture, free of the embarrassing presence of the tricky Korean cleric.[8]

Ennin encountered no Korean embassies in China, but he
had direct or indirect dealings with two embassies bound the
other way. At the Mt. Ch'ih Cloister in 839 he met more
than thirty members of an embassy on its way from China to
Korea to check on a newly enthroned King. In the early part
of 847 members of an embassy bound for Korea, reportedly
to conduct somewhat tardy mourning ceremonies for Wu-
tsung and to re-enfeoff the Korean King, prevented Ennin's
Korean patron, Wang Chŏng, from building a ship on which
to take Ennin back to Japan. Ennin also saw further indications of the flow of embassies between Korea and China in
the presence of a Korean Inn at Teng-chou and Korean
Cloisters in a Ch'ing-chou monastery and at the Li-ch'üan-ssu
west of that city.[9]

As we have seen, there was also a P'o-hai Inn in Teng-
chou, presumably for embassies going from and to that East
Manchurian kingdom. The people of P'o-hai were Tungusic
ancestors of the later Manchu Emperors of China and like
the Koreans were busily engaged at this time in creating a
small replica of the T'ang Empire in their far northern
forests. Laymen and monks from P'o-hai streamed to China,
where Ennin naturally met some of them. The day before he
reached Ch'ing-chou, he encountered "on the moors a P'o-hai
embassy returning home from the capital," and a few days
later in Ch'ing-chou itself he was entertained at a maigre
feast by a Prince of P'o-hai, who probably was a straggler
from this embassy. At Mt. Wu-t'ai Ennin discovered the
panegyric poem and inscription put up after Reisen's death
by his devoted disciple from P'o-hai. The most surprising
thing Ennin has to tell of this Manchurian kingdom is his

statement in the autumn of 839 that a "P'o-hai commerce ship" was anchored near the tip of the Shantung Peninsula, but this is his only mention of a Manchurian vessel in these waters which were normally dominated by the Koreans.[10]

TRADERS ON THE COAST

While many sources tell of Korean monks in the monasteries of China and Korean courtiers and soldiers in the service of the T'ang Emperors, there are only hints in other works of the flourishing communities of Korean traders which Ennin found on the eastern littoral of China. One such hint is a reference to a Korean merchant who bought every poem he could find by Ennin's great contemporary, the poet Po Chü-i. Another is found in a work on the famous painters of the T'ang, probably written during the very years when Ennin was in China. In this text reference is made to a Korean who some four or five decades earlier had "bought up at good prices several tens of scrolls" of paintings by a certain contemporary artist in the Ch'u-chou and Yang-chou area and had taken them back to Korea.[11] But such a statement takes on full significance only when read in the light of what Ennin has to tell of the Koreans in China.

The Korean trading communities seem to have been concentrated along the southern coast of the Shantung Peninsula and the lower stretches of the Huai River, which together formed the natural water route between Korea and the heart of the T'ang Empire. The chief terminal port for the trade between China and its eastern neighbors apparently was the city of Ch'u-chou, strategically located at the juncture of the Grand Canal and the Huai River, where ocean-going vessels could meet smaller boats from Yang-chou and the Yangtse River system to the south and the river craft of the upper Huai and Pien Rivers, leading westward toward the capital region.

In Ch'u-chou, as we have seen, there was a large Korean colony—so large in fact that there was a Korean ward under its own General Manager (*Tsung-kuan*). Another indication

of the size of the Korean community was that in the spring
of 839 Kim Chŏngnam, one of the Korean Interpreters of
the Japanese embassy, was able to hire at Ch'u-chou sixty
Korean sailors to man the nine ships he had obtained there
for the returning embassy. Some of these men came from
the town of Lien-shui-hsien, a short distance down the Huai
River from Ch'u-chou. When Ennin visited this town for the
first time in 845, he found that it too had a Korean ward
under its own General Manager.[12]

Ennin makes no reference to Korean colonies in any of
the other towns or cities he visited in China, but he does indicate that large numbers of Koreans lived along the coast
from the mouth of the Huai northward to the tip of the Shantung Peninsula. One of the largest of these communities must
have been the one in the neighborhood of the Mt. Ch'ih
Cloister, near the usual landfall for ships bound from Korea
to China and the point from which they left the Chinese coast
on the homeward voyage. Here the Korean Cloister with its
twenty-nine Korean inmates stood high on a hill, guarding,
as it were, the open-water crossing between China and Korea,
and around it lived a large number of Korean laymen under
the general supervision of Ennin's patron, Chang Yŏng.

The Mt. Ch'ih community seems to have been a bit of
Korea transplanted to the shores of China. For example, on
the fifteenth day of the eighth moon, Ennin found the cloister
beginning the observance of a national Korean festival, in
which all the local Koreans apparently joined. According to
Ennin, they served noodles and cakes on this occasion and
made music and danced gaily. Moved by the scene, he wrote,
"They prepare all sorts of food and drink, and sing, dance,
and play instrumental music for three days before stopping,
continuing from the daylight hours into the night. Now, in
this mountain cloister, in memory of their homeland, they
are today observing this festival." The celebration, he understood, was to commemorate a great victory of Silla over P'o-
hai. Actually it was the anniversary of the destruction of
Koguryŏ, the last of Silla's rivals in the Korean peninsula,
but there is some reason for Ennin's statement, because flee-

ing remnants of the Koguryŏ forces merged with the tribal group which subsequently founded the kingdom of P'o-hai.[13]

Ennin has scattered references to individual lay members of the Mt. Ch'ih community, but its size is best indicated by the number of Buddhist believers who attended the lecture meetings on the *Lotus Sutra* held during the winter at the cloister. These, Ennin tells us, were conducted for the most part in the Korean language and according to the customs of the Buddhist church of Korea, and the congregation, which numbered two hundred fifty and two hundred on the last two days, was entirely Korean, except for the four Japanese in Ennin's party.[14]

This was by no means the only Korean community along the coast. The strong desire of the Korean sailors of the returning Japanese embassy to go to a certain area southwest of the modern Tsingtao in order to repair their ships and the plan Ennin made with the aid of the Korean Interpreter, Kim Chŏngnam, to leave the ships of the embassy at that same spot and hide in a private home ashore both indicate that there may have been a Korean colony of some size in that area. Subsequently when the embassy ship on which Ennin was a passenger came ashore northeast of Tsingtao, it was visited by a Korean in a small boat and later by a local official accompanied by a Korean. After sailing a very short distance southwestward down the coast, the Japanese were visited by a group of more than thirty Koreans who approached the shore mounted on horses and donkeys, and later the local Guard Officer himself arrived on a Korean boat and treated with the Japanese through their Korean Interpreter. Ennin had the latter inquire of the local Korean residents whether it would be possible for the Japanese monks to reside safely ashore, and the reply was in the affirmative, though in the end nothing came of these negotiations. Evidently here again was a large Korean community, and the Guard Officer himself, like Chang Yŏng further up the coast, may well have been a Korean.[15]

The possession of horses and donkeys by these coastal Koreans and of a wagon by one member of the Mt. Ch'ih community with whom Ennin later traveled part way down the peninsula suggests that these Koreans were not merely maritime transients but were permanent settlers. This conclusion is underscored by what Ennin tells us of the boatmen transporting charcoal from Shantung to Ch'u-chou, whom he encountered when he and his companions were put ashore by the Japanese embassy north of the mouth of the Huai River. These boatmen claimed that they were of Korean origin, but they obviously no longer spoke the language, for they apparently were duped by the claim of the Japanese that they too were Koreans. It would appear that some Koreans had even moved inland a ways and become farmers, because, when the Japanese that same day reached a village across a range of hills from the sea, they rested briefly in the home of a Korean villager, and their little deceit was immediately detected by the village elder, who realized that they were speaking neither Korean nor Chinese to each other.

While the Korean traders seem to have lived primarily in the cities of the lower Huai and along the southern coast of Shantung, they no doubt extended their commercial activities to many other parts of China. Several times Ennin writes of Korean ships or ones presumably Korean owned and operated which visited Yang-chou and even ports south of the Yangtse. In Yang-chou Ennin also met a Korean who, in the company of some Chinese, had been wrecked on the coasts of Japan and, because of his long enforced stay there, still understood the Japanese language very well. Far inland at Ch'ang-an Ennin also encountered Koreans from Ch'u-chou. One brought him a letter from his friend Yu Sinŏn early in 843, and one of the two other times Yu wrote to Ennin in the capital the message may also have been taken by one of the Ch'u-chou Koreans.[16]

At least some of the Korean communities on the Chinese coast appear to have enjoyed a certain degree of extraterritorial privileges. The same is known to have been true of the Moslem communities in the cities of the southeastern coast of China, which were allowed to manage their own affairs autonomously and according to their own customs. It is, therefore, not at all surprising to find that the Korean traders were granted the same autonomous status.

In Ch'u-chou and Lien-shui the units of Korean self-government were, of course, the Korean wards, and the headmen of these were the General Managers. Korean Interpreters appear to have been the next ranking officers of these communities, for Yu Sinŏn, who originally held this post, became Sŏl Chŏn's successor some years later when the latter either resigned or was dismissed from the office of General Manager of the Korean ward of Ch'u-chou. In the Mt. Ch'ih community the posts and titles were a little different. Chang Yŏng was not only the local Korean Interpreter but was also the headman of the Korean colony. His chief title seems to have been that of Guard Officer of Teng-chou, and his official quarters were called the Office in Charge of Korean Affairs. According to Ennin, he was in charge of Korean embassies as well as the Korean population of the Wen-teng-hsien area. Despite the difference in title between Sŏl Chŏn and Chang Yŏng, which perhaps represented the difference between their respective urban and coastal areas of authority, the two men may have been of comparable rank. Ennin notes that Sŏl had the honorary title of Assimilated Colonel, as I have translated the Chinese term *T'ung-shih-chiang* ("Same as the Ten Generals") in order to retain its very vague and purely honorific military flavor, and Chang also was "an Imperially appointed Assimilated Colonel" of one of the regional commanderies of the Shantung area.[17]

The autonomy of the Korean colonies in China, no doubt, was the fundamental reason why Ennin, when in 839 he was being forced by the Chinese authorities to return to Japan, sought to find shelter among the coastal Koreans for himself and his attendants and also the reason why, when he did go ashore without authorization, he attempted to pass as a Korean. It also explains how he finally managed to stay in China under Chang Yŏng's protective wing. Apparently, if the Koreans were willing to accept the Japanese as members of their extraterritorial group, the Chinese authorities were willing to overlook the fact that as members of a returning

Japanese embassy they were not supposed to stay longer in China.

Much the same situation developed again several years later when the subprefectural officials of Lien-shui agreed to permit the defrocked Japanese monks to settle down there, if the local Korean community would make out an affidavit officially recognizing the Japanese as members of their group. But there were limits to the extraterritorial privileges of the Korean traders. In Ch'u-chou, when official recognition was extended to Ennin and his companions by the Korean community, the local Chinese officials still refused to let them stay.[18]

While there were limits to the influence of the Koreans along the eastern coast of China, there can be no doubt of their dominance over the waters off these shores. There were many ships which Ennin encountered off the coast of China or heard were engaged in trade between China and Japan, but few of these appear to have been manned by either Chinese or Japanese. While the ownership of some of the ships and the nationality of many of the mariners cannot be established with certainty, Ennin clearly labeled several of the ships and merchants as Korean, and judging from the context in which they appear, many of the others too seem to have been Korean. In contrast to this, Ennin identifies only one of the international traders as Chinese, and the ship on which this man was traveling also carried three Koreans, one of whom seems to have been either the owner or the captain. Ennin also mentions four Japanese who apparently were engaged in international trade. One of these came with his ship to Ming-chou, the modern Ningpo in Chekiang, south of the Yangtse. The other three, one of whom had been all the way to Canton, hired a ship of unspecified flag in Ming-chou for the return voyage.[19]

While Ennin's diary, as well as other sources, shows that the Japanese were starting to compete with the Koreans in the maritime trade of the Far East, their challenge was still feeble. Even if one makes due allowance for the bureaucratic inefficiency and confusion of the Japanese embassy, Ennin's

crossing to China and his subsequent voyage up the south
coast of Shantung on Japanese ships as well as the whole
catastrophic maritime record of the embassy contrast sharply
with the speed and efficiency with which Korean vessels
whisked him up and down the Shantung coast and finally
back home to Japan. Another indication of the discrepancy
in navigational skill between the Koreans and Japanese at
this time was the employment by the Japanese embassy of
sixty Korean helmsmen and sailors to help get the main party
safely home. The role of the Korean Interpreters on each of
the original embassy vessels is also a case in point. These men
were not only very useful in dealings ashore but, from what
Ennin tells of his own crossing to China, apparently were the
chief navigational experts on board the ships.[20] The days of
Korean maritime dominance in the Far East actually were
numbered, but in Ennin's time the men of Silla were still the
masters of the seas in their part of the world.

CHANG POGO

While men like Chang Yŏng and Sŏl Chŏn were, in a sense,
Korean consular agents in China, it would be a mistake to
think of them as representatives of the Korean government.
They did enjoy official status with the Chinese government
but not with their own. Chang, and possibly Sŏl too, instead
of serving the King of Korea, seem to have been representatives of a private Korean trader, the fabulous adventurer
and merchant prince, Chang Pogo. This man's name turns
up in several variant forms in the official histories of China
and Japan as well as in the Korean chronicles,[21] and, although he never appears in person in Ennin's diary, he frequently looms in the background as the master of more than
one of Ennin's Korean friends and patrons.

The various references to Chang Pogo in the chronicles of
the Far East are somewhat contradictory, but the main
course of his life is clear. He was a man of obscure origin
who migrated to China and made his fortune there, serving
as a military officer in the lower Huai area and very possibly

rising to become the recognized headman of one of the Korean colonies, in much the same way as the semimilitary officials, Chang Yŏng and Sŏl Chŏn, of Ennin's day. Returning to Korea in 828 a rich and powerful man, he established his headquarters on Wando Island at the southwestern extremity of Korea, an excellent vantage point from which to control the trade routes from China down the west coast of Korea and around the southwestern corner of the peninsula to the capital region of Silla and to Japan. While in China, Chang Pogo had discovered that many Koreans were being abducted and taken to China by slavers, and, after he returned to Korea, he requested the King of Silla to permit him to guard the coasts against these slaving depredations. The King accordingly appointed him Commissioner of Ch'ŏnghaejin, the administrative center on Wando Island, and reportedly gave him a force of ten thousand men, though this last part of the story seems most improbable.

Conceivably because of this royal favor, but more probably because of his control over the lucrative trade between China and its eastern satellites, which itself was no doubt the reason for this royal indulgence, Chang grew to be an important figure in Korean politics. In 837 he became embroiled in a struggle over the royal succession when Ujing, the son of an unsuccessful contender for the throne, fled to him for protection. The following year the men who had killed Ujing's father and had set his rival on the throne killed their own royal puppet, and one of them usurped his crown. Ujing, declaring that he could not "live together under the same heavens" with the murderers of his father, asked Chang to help him gain the throne. The latter, according to the official chroniclers, quoted the *Confucian Analects*, nobly stating, "The ancients had a saying, 'To see what is right and not to do it is want of courage.' [22] Though I am without ability, I shall follow your orders." He then assigned five thousand of his soldiers to Ujing's cause and put them under the command of Chŏng Yŏn, a younger compatriot who had likewise emigrated to China but had fared less well than Chang and had eventually been rescued by the latter from destitution in Lien-shui.

Chŏng Yŏn, who reportedly was able to swim incredible distances under water, now distinguished himself on dry land and, with some other military men who had joined Ujing's cause, fought a series of successful battles against the royal armies. Eventually the victorious forces captured the capital and killed the usurper, and in 839 Ujing ascended the throne as King Sinmu, the forty-fifth ruler of Silla. The new King naturally rewarded Chang for having sheltered him and for having contributed so decisively to his victory, giving him a high military title and a fief of two thousand households.

It was during this crucial phase of Chang Pogo's life that Ennin first heard of him. News of Ujing's efforts to win the throne had come to China, and in the early spring of 839 a member of the returning Japanese embassy pointed out to his colleagues that "Korea was having troubles with Chang Pogo and was at war with him," using this as an argument for crossing to Japan directly from the mouth of the Huai River, rather than first going up the coast to Shantung, where they would be closer to the hostile shores of Korea. A few weeks later Ennin was informed by a Shantung Korean that Chang's forces had been victorious and that he had put his candidate on the throne of Korea. Only a few days later Ennin learned that a Chinese embassy was being dispatched "to bestow the title of King" on Ujing. Chang's victory had occurred only four months earlier, and the speed with which news of it had reached China and the alacrity with which the Chinese court gave recognition to the new King are indications of the efficiency of communications along the sea routes between Korea and China and the respect of the Chinese for the Korean master of these sea lanes.[23]

At the Mt. Ch'ih Cloister Ennin came under Chang Pogo's direct though distant patronage. Chang had built the cloister, probably to give spiritual protection to his ships and religious guidance to his agents, and he had endowed it with an estate which yielded an annual income of five hundred Chinese bushels of rice. Chang Yŏng, who was in charge of the cloister and the whole local Korean community, was apparently Chang Pogo's man, as were probably many of the other Koreans in the neighborhood. For instance, the monk at the cloister who had lived in Japan for several years and whom Ennin met again during his second sojourn in Shantung had been brought back to China from Japan by one of Chang Pogo's ships.

It was at the Mt. Ch'ih Cloister in the summer of 839 that Ennin first met Ch'oe, whom he described as "an agent sent by Chang Pogo to China to sell things." Ch'oe, who also had the title of Guard Officer, had brought two of Chang's ships over from Korea. When he came back up the Shantung coast the next spring on the return voyage to Korea from Yang-chou, Ennin sent him a very polite letter, attributing to Ch'oe the kind treatment he had received from the monks at Mt. Ch'ih and thanking the Korean profusely for having offered to donate a ship to take the Japanese back south by way of Lien-shui so that they could go to Mt. T'ien-t'ai as they had originally intended. Ennin also explained to Ch'oe that, after his pilgrimage was completed and he had started back to Japan, which he optimistically estimated would be "about the autumn of next year," he intended to visit Chang Pogo at Ch'ŏnghaejin to "explain the whole situation to him." He concluded with the request that Ch'oe be so kind as to order his men and ships to keep a special lookout for the returning Japanese, who depended solely on Ch'oe for their return home. At the same time, Ennin wrote the following letter for transmission by Ch'oe to Chang Pogo, whom he addressed as "the Commissioner":

Although I have never in my life had the honor of meeting you, I have for long heard of your great excellence, and I humbly respect you all the more. With mid-spring already turning warm, I humbly hope that a myriad good fortunes will bless the Commissioner's person and actions.

I, Ennin, have received your benevolence from afar and am overwhelmed with gratitude. In order to carry out long-cherished hopes, I remained in China. By great good fortune to my insignificant self, I have been sojourning in the area blessed by the vow of the Commissioner, and I find it difficult to express in words anything but my great happiness.

When I left home, I was entrusted by the Governor of Chikuzen * with a letter for the Commissioner, but, since our ship unexpectedly sank in a shallow part of the sea and our things floated away, the letter with which I had been entrusted sank in the waves, which causes me greater sorrow every day. I humbly beseech you not to blame me.

I do not know when I shall have the honor of meeting you, but in my humble way I think of you all the more from afar. Respectfully I write to inquire after you. Respectfully written in brief.

Presented on the seventeenth day of the second moon of the fifth year of K'ai-ch'eng by the Japanese monk in search of the Law of the Dentō-hosshi Rank, Ennin.

To Chang, the Commissioner of Ch'ŏnghaejin (His Excellency, with humble respect).† [24]

The story of Chang Pogo's rise to power is clearer than that of his subsequent downfall. His biography in the Korean chronicles blandly states that King Sinmu summoned him to the capital and made him a Minister of State and had his faithful lieutenant Chŏng Yŏn succeed him at Ch'ŏnghaejin. This is simply the Korean version of "they lived happily ever after," and even the compilers of the biography admit that this account "differs greatly from that of the Silla records." [25] These presumably are the source of two other accounts of Chang Pogo's end, which, while differing on the date and the details, tell approximately the same story of his downfall in connection with his efforts to marry his daughter to the Korean King.

According to one account, Sinmu died only a half year after ascending the throne, but his son and successor continued to honor Chang, declaring, "The Commissioner of Ch'ŏnghaejin . . . formerly aided Our saintly father with his military power and destroyed the great bandits of the preceding reign. How can We forget his great accomplish-

---

* A province in North Kyūshū in Japan.
† The words in parentheses are written in small characters in the letter as copied into the diary.

ments? Therefore, We appoint him General of Ch'ŏnghaejin and bestow on him the garments of an official." However, in 845, when the King desired to take Chang's daughter as a secondary consort, his ministers dissuaded him from taking such a step, pointing out the importance of marriages in the fate of the rulers of China. They concluded with the contemptuous remark that, since Chang "was an islander, how could his daughter be assigned to the King's chamber?" When this slight induced Chang to rebel the next year, the court was thrown into consternation, but a certain Yŏm Chang boldly proposed to cut Chang down singlehanded and deliver his corpse to the King. Yŏm then pretended to be a rebel and fled to Chang, who, liking hardy men and completely duped by his visitor, took him in as an honored guest, only to be murdered while in his cups by the treacherous courtier.[26]

According to another account, Ujing, while a refugee with Chang, promised, if successful in his bid for the throne, to make the latter's daughter his consort, but, once he had become King Sinmu, he was dissuaded from going through with the agreement by his ministers, who asserted that Chang "was of trifling account, and it would not do for the King to take his daughter as a consort." Since it was feared that Chang might take umbrage at this and revolt, the doughty Yŏm volunteered to get rid of him for the King. Proceeding to Ch'ŏnghaejin, he claimed to bear a grudge against the King and asked protection from Chang, but the latter, greatly incensed, accused Yŏm of being one of the group that had ruined his daughter's chances at court. Yŏm, however, explained that he personally had opposed the other officials in this matter, and Chang finally took him in with the unfortunate results described above.[27]

These two stories are not actually as incompatible as they may at first appear. It is not unlikely that the agreement for a marriage alliance between the throne and the merchant prince was first made by Ujing and that, because of the latter's untimely death, Chang sought to force his successor on the throne to make good the promise his father had made.

If Chang's downfall had occurred before Sinmu's death, Ennin most certainly would have heard of it before he left the Mt. Ch'ih Cloister in 840. On the other hand, his failure to record anything more about Chang after he had returned to the coastal Korean colonies again in the summer of 845 suggests that the latter's death had occurred at some earlier date. It seems altogether probable that the murder of Chang and the collapse of his organization were the "political difficulties" which forced Ennin's old friend, Ch'oe, to flee from Korea back to Lien-shui, where Ennin found him in 845. Unfortunately, Ennin did not date these "political difficulties," but they must have happened some time between the spring of 840 and the summer of 845.[28]

The Japanese histories supply the missing date with considerable credibility. Early in 842 they report the arrival in North Kyūshū of a Korean who had come as the representative of Yŏm Chang to report that Chang Pogo was dead and that one of his lieutenants had revolted and been subdued by Yŏm but that the Koreans feared that some of the rebels would "escape the net" and, fleeing to Japan, cause trouble there. Yŏm, therefore, requested the Japanese not to deal with any such fugitives and also asked them to send back with his representative several of Chang's former underlings who were known to have reached Japan.

The response of the Japanese courtiers to this request was not at all favorable. They distrusted Yŏm's representative because they knew he had once been a subordinate of Chang Pogo and they felt that merchants would try any stratagem for the sake of trade. They even objected to the form of the letter he brought, and they felt that to hand over the Korean fugitives to him would be like "casting stray animals to a hungry tiger." The men, they decided, should be free to do as they wished about the matter.

The visit of Yŏm's representative, of course, brought into prominence the case of these fugitives. They had described themselves as "islanders under the rule of Chang Pogo," who, after their master's death in the eleventh moon of 841, had found life unsafe in Korea and had therefore come to Japan.

Their hope was to receive permission to settle down there, but, perhaps because of the notoriety of the case, they were eventually ordered to return to their homeland.[29]

Taking together all our material on the end of Chang Pogo, we can conclude that he died in 841 and that Yŏm Chang played an important part perhaps in Chang's demise and certainly in the destruction of his organization. Whatever may have been the exact steps leading up to Chang's downfall, his death and the subsequent disappearance of his maritime commercial empire very probably marked the passing of the high-water mark of Korean mastery over the seas lying between China, Korea, and Japan.[30] Control over the ocean commerce of this part of the world began to shift to the hands of the Chinese and then some centuries later to traders and pirates from West Japan.

IX

Homeward Bound

Even though Chang Pogo and his maritime empire had disappeared before Ennin returned to Shantung in 845, the three Japanese travelers depended almost completely on the Koreans for means by which to return to Japan. They not only relied for food and lodging on Chang Yŏng, the generous headman of the Korean community at Mt. Ch'ih, but also looked to him for passage home. Ennin, in view of the unhappy months he had spent off the shores of Shantung in 839, probably never wished to see that particular coast again, and, after his long trek from the capital to the tip of the Shantung Peninsula, he no doubt hoped and expected to return directly to Japan from there. But things did not work out quite so simply. More travels up and down the coast of Shantung were in store for the Japanese before they at last were able to sail eastward for Japan.

When one of Chang Yŏng's servants was sent by ship to Ch'u-chou in the ninth moon of 845, Ennin commissioned him to bring back the religious paraphernalia he had left there in the home of Yu Sinŏn. Two months later the obliging Chang told his Japanese pensioners that he would build a ship the following spring to take them home. Ennin must have felt that their return to Japan was now imminent, but his hopes were quickly and thoroughly dashed. Chang was refused passports for the Japanese because of the Imperial edict banning the further movement of foreign monks, and in the first moon of 846 his servant returned from Ch'u-chou with Yu Sinŏn's reply that he did not dare to send on Ennin's baggage because of the severity of the measures against Buddhism. Chang's servant also reported the arrival in China of two Japanese monks, come to look for Ennin, and their defrocking at the hands of the Chinese authorities.[1]

Ennin was determined at least to recover his baggage, and two months later he persuaded Chang to arrange passage to Ch'u-chou for Ennin's own servant, Tei Yūman, who was to bring it back. In the fourth moon, a Korean traveler arrived from Yang-chou with a letter from Shōkai, the head of the party searching for Ennin, and, when the Korean returned to Yang-chou a few days later, Ennin sent a letter by him inviting Shōkai to join him in Shantung. In the sixth moon Ennin received a letter from Sŏl Chŏn, the General Manager of the Korean ward of Ch'u-chou, saying that Tei Yūman was about to return to Shantung and that the Korean traveler had reached Ch'u-chou twenty-odd days after leaving the Mt. Ch'ih area and had gone on to Yang-chou. Later, the same moon, Tei himself returned. Since the persecution of Buddhism had been ended the previous moon by the new Emperor, Tei had been able to bring the missing baggage, but Ennin now learned that Yu Sinŏn had been forced to burn the "*Double Great Taizō and Kongō Mandara* in full colors" left with him. Early in the tenth moon Shōkai joined Ennin, restoring the number of the party to four, as it had been before Igyō's death.[2]

With many restrictions on the Buddhists now lifted, Chang Yŏng renewed his plan to build a ship on which to send his Japanese guests to their homeland. Starting work on the vessel in the winter of 846, he completed it by the second moon of 847, but a new disappointment lay in store for Ennin. The Vice-Ambassador and an Administrative Officer of an embassy on its way to Korea, perhaps wishing another ship for themselves or perhaps merely out of pique, as Ennin suggests, put an end to the whole project. According to Ennin:

. . . Someone treacherously [said] that the Assimilated Colonel Chang, ignoring the national regulations, intends to dispatch men from a foreign land and has been selfishly building a ship for them and has not come to greet the Imperial envoys. The

Vice-Ambassador and the other, on hearing these [slanderous] words, were very indignant and notified him that the regulations of the whole land did not permit anyone to send travelers on ships across the sea. The Commissioner Chang did not dare specifically oppose them, and so our plan to return home across the sea from the Wen-teng region has come to nought.[3]

If Ennin were ever to get home, it was obvious that he would have to find a ship elsewhere. Accordingly, he decided to go far south to Ming-chou, where a Japanese ship was reported to have arrived. Starting out on a wagon hired from a local Korean early in the intercalary third moon of 847, the Japanese followed the coast southwestward until they finally found a Korean ship bound for Ch'u-chou loading charcoal on the coast southwest of the modern Tsingtao. Although held up for several days at a time by adverse winds, the ship made the mouth of the Huai on its fifteenth day at sea and, after another long delay, when bad weather prevented it from entering the river, finally arrived at Ch'u-chou on the fifth day of the sixth moon. Here a special representative of Yu Sinŏn, who had recently been made the General Manager of the Korean ward, took care of their baggage and also settled the Japanese in a government building.[4]

Despite Yu's courteous reception, the news which greeted Ennin and his companions at Ch'u-chou was discouraging. The Japanese vessel had already left Ming-chou. But four days later word came of another ship bound for Japan. The monks learned about it from a letter from a Korean called Kim Chin, two other Koreans, and a Chinese. These men were on board a ship from Su-chou which had cleared the mouth of the river on which Shanghai now stands on the eleventh day of the fifth moon. After reaching the Shantung coast northeast of Tsingtao, these merchants had learned that there were some Japanese monks awaiting passage to Japan at Mt. Ch'ih, but, fortunately, just before the traders sailed on up the coast, a man told them that the monks had gone south to look for a ship. The merchants now offered to wait for the Japanese if the latter would come back up to Shantung to join them.

Ennin and his companions of course jumped at the chance and were lucky enough to find the ship of a Ch'u-chou Korean sailing for Shantung only nine days later. Yu attended to the provisions for their trip, and a brother of Chang Yŏng and the latter's daughter as well as Sŏl Chŏn, the former General Manager, all saw them off. A seven-day run down the Huai River and up the coast brought them to the anchorage where Kim Chin's ship had been, but they found that the traders had gone, leaving word behind for the Japanese to come on to Mt. Ch'ih. But now a long spell of adverse winds set in. Ennin, apprehensive that Kim's ship would sail without them, dispatched his servant Tei Yūman to hurry on by land to Mt. Ch'ih. This is the last that we hear of Tei in the diary, and it is possible that, missing the ship at Mt. Ch'ih, he stayed on in China. In any case we know from Ennin's rival, Enchin, that Tei Yūman once again went to Ch'ang-an in the year 855, where he was recognized by a Chinese priest as Ennin's former servant.[5]

The long-delayed winds finally came, and Ennin's ship started out again up the coast and on the second day caught up with Kim's vessel. The Japanese then changed ships and on the following day reached Mt. Ch'ih, where Chang Yŏng came on board to greet them and later presented them with farewell letters and gifts. Kim's ship, however, stayed at Mt. Ch'ih for almost a month and a half, waiting for the good weather and westerly winds of early autumn. During this time Ennin, after more than two years in defrocked status, once again shaved his head and donned his black robes. In preparation for the dangerous crossing he also worshiped the Shintō spirits, as he had often done on board the ships of the Japanese embassy. Finally, at noon on the second day of the ninth moon, Kim and his associates decided that the time had come to set forth. Heading out of the sheltering bay, they set their sails due eastward for Korea as Ennin looked his last upon the receding coastline of the great land of T'ang, which for more than nine years had been both home and prison to him.[6]

One afternoon and a night of steady sailing eastward brought Ennin and his companions in sight of the islands off the west coast of Korea, at this point only 110 miles from Shantung.[7] The wind then conveniently shifted to north, and the Korean vessel trimmed sails to run southeastward. All day and all night they sailed on and the next dawn found themselves again in sight of land off the southwestern coast of Korea. Still sailing southeastward, they threaded their way among the many coastal islands, finally tying up that night at a small island near the southwestern tip of the peninsula.

The next day they were held up by adverse winds, but at midnight they started again and early the next morning tied up at another island, from which they could see far to the southeast the 6,400 foot summit of Quelpart Island, some seventy miles distant. Although they were reportedly a day's sail from the mainland, the travelers found an island guard and two falconers who told them the news of the land. "The nation was at peace," and "an Imperial Chinese Embassy of over five hundred men in all was at the capital." Also, during the earlier part of the year, six Japanese fishermen from the large island of Tsushima in the straits between Korea and Japan had been stranded on the shores of Korea. These men were being held in confinement, pending their repatriation, and one of them had sickened and died.

Lacking reliable winds, the travelers stayed at this island anchorage for two whole days, but then they "heard bad news and were extremely frightened," perhaps by a report that pirates were in the vicinity or possibly that government forces were still on the lookout for the survivors of Chang Pogo's maritime empire. Unable to start out because of the calm, "the group on board cast away mirrors and the like in sacrifice to the spirits to obtain a wind," while the monks read the *Diamond Sutra*, "burned incense, and recited prayers on behalf of the spirits of the soil of this island and the spirits of the great and the lowly, praying that we might safely reach our homeland." Finally, in the early morning hours they "started out even though there was no wind. Scarcely had we gotten out of the mouth of the inlet when a west wind suddenly blew up, so we hoisted sail and headed east. It seemed as though the spirits were aiding us."

Making their way eastward between the coastal islands for a day and night, they reached an island the next morning some 110 miles to the east of their starting point and about midway along the southern coast of Korea, from which high Quelpart was still visible far to the southwest. Shortly after noon, they set out again and presently headed southeastward away from the shores of Korea and out onto the open sea. At dawn the next morning the low-lying coast of the southern end of Tsushima was visible to the east, and at noon they saw ahead of them "the mountains of Japan stretching out clearly from the east to the southwest." That night they reached an anchorage on one of the islands off the north-western coast of Kyūshū—home at last in Japan. It was the tenth day of the ninth moon, and on the morning of the second day of that same moon they had still been at anchor off the coast of Shantung.

At dawn on the following day a representative of one of the local provincial officials and the headman of the island came to visit the ship, and a few days later the travelers sailed on eastward along the Kyūshū coast, arriving on the seventeenth day at Hakata Bay, from which Ennin had set sail for China nine years and three months earlier. Two days later Ennin and his followers were settled in the official quarters maintained there for embassies from abroad.

Ennin had obviously promised to pay the fare for himself and his party when they reached Japan, and so now in partial payment he "borrowed eighty bolts of silk and two hundred packages of silk floss from the official storehouse for winter clothing for the forty-four men on board the ship." Meanwhile notice of Ennin's return had been sent to the capital where, according to the entry in the official history, it must have arrived on the second day of the tenth moon. On this day the Japanese chronicles record, "Ennin, the Tendai Scholar Monk who had been sent to China, two disciples, and forty-two Chinese arrived from China." [8] The disappearance of two of the crewmen in the Japanese chronicles is no doubt the result of calligraphic carelessness by a copyist, but the transformation of Kim Chin and his at least partially Korean crew into Chinese is more significant and suggests that many of the other "Chinese" traders mentioned in the Japanese records may actually have been men from the Korean colonies on the Chinese coast.

On the first day of the tenth moon the local provincial government started to furnish Ennin's living expenses, and on the nineteenth word came from the Council of State in Kyōto, instructing Ennin and his companions to hasten on to the capital and ordering Dazaifu, the local government headquarters, to pay off Kim Chin and his forty-three associates. A week later, however, Ennin noted that he still had not received "the documents for going to the capital," indicating that travel orders were as necessary in Japan as in China. Early in the eleventh moon a delegation of three monks arrived from Mt. Hiei to welcome Ennin back to his own monastic community, and a week later instructions came from the Council of State that "the Chinese travelers, Kim Chin and the others," be provided for generously.

The remaining month of the diary is devoted almost exclusively to brief remarks by Ennin on the various ceremonial readings of Buddhist scriptures which he performed in behalf of the Great God of Sumiyoshi and the major Shintō deities of North Kyūshū, who had obviously watched over him with care during his perilous voyages on the waters that stretched from the shores below their shrines to the distant coast of China. Some local monks who had aided Ennin in these pious acts he rewarded with two hundred packages of white silk floss.

On the fourteenth day of the twelfth moon of 847 Ennin jotted down a brief entry telling about the arrival of an unidentified fellow monk from an unspecified place. Here the diary ends with disconcerting abruptness, and we have come to the time to say farewell to Ennin. He is safely home again in Japan. He is standing on the threshold of a dazzling career as the leading cleric of Japan, extravagantly honored by the court and devotedly venerated by his fellow monks.

The persecuted pilgrim is about to become the triumphant church father. The faithful diarist, whose picture of himself reveals in clear detail a strong and determined but still humble figure, is about to have his portrait painted in the heroic proportions and brilliant colors used by the court chroniclers and biographers to transform living men into the huge but lifeless figures of official history.

NOTES

[1] As given in *The Travels of Marco Polo* ("The Broadway Travellers" Series, London: Routledge & Kegan Paul, 1950), pp. 224–25. Translated into English from the text of L. F. Benedetto by Professor Aldo Ricci.

[2] Fortunately the life of Hsüan-tsang and his great travel work are readily available to the Western reader. There are two excellent accounts in English of his life and travels: Arthur Waley, *The Real Tripitaka and Other Pieces* (London: Allen & Unwin, 1952), and René Grousset, *In the Footsteps of the Buddha* (London: George Routledge, 1932). The *Hsi-yü-chi* itself has been translated in two volumes by Samuel Beal under the title of *Si-Yu-Ki. Buddhist Records of the Western World. Translated from the Chinese of Hiuen Tsiang* (A.D. *629*) (London, 1906) and in fragmented form sandwiched between long commentaries in a two-volume work by Thomas Watters entitled *On Yuan Chwang's Travels in India* (London: Royal Asiatic Society, 1904 and 1905).

[3] Printed in the *Dainihon Bukkyō zensho* (*Complete Works of Japanese Buddhism*) 113.286–95.

[4] Printed in the *Dainihon Bukkyō zensho* 115.321–487 and reproduced photographically from an early manuscript in 1937 as No. 7 of the *Tōyō bunko sōkan* series. Jōjin eventually died in China in 1081, but his diary does not cover the later years.

[5] There are some eighth- and ninth-century accounts of Moslem traders who went to the Far East by sea, but these are extremely sketchy compared to Ennin's diary. Cf. Gabriel Ferrand, *Relations de voyages et textes géographiques arabes, persans et turks relatifs à l'extrême-orient du VIII⁴ au XVIII⁴ siècles* (Paris: 1913) and Jean Sauvaget, *'Ahbār as-sīn wa l-hind. Relation de la Chine et de l'Inde rédigé en 851* (Paris: 1948).

[6] Arthur Waley devotes a section of *The Real Tripitaka and Other Pieces* (pp. 133–68) to Ennin and his original traveling companion, Ensai, based on a few scattered portions of Ennin's

diary and also on Enchin's *Gyōryakushō*, which tells something
of Ensai's later life in China.

[7] Published in 1926 as a Supplement to No. 7 of the *Tōyō bunko
ronsō* series.

[8] Okada's studies are entitled *Jikaku Daishi no nittō kikō ni
tsuite* and appeared in the journal, *Tōyō gakuhō* 11.461–86;
12.147–86, 273–95; 13.1–28. Many other scholars have used
Ennin's diary for studies of specific subjects. Notable among
these is the work by the Buddhist churchman and scholar,
Ōtani Kōshō, entitled *Tōdai no Bukkyō girei* (Tōkyō, 1937), in
which he uses Ennin's detailed descriptions of Buddhist religious services as his major source for a study of the Buddhist
ceremonies of T'ang times.

[9] As translated by Arthur Waley in *Three Ways of Thought in
Ancient China* (London: Allen & Unwin, 1939 and 1946),
pp. 18–20.

[10] I have consulted three of these editions and have found the
1918 printing in the *Dainihon Bukkyō zensho* (113.169–82)
the most useful and reliable.

[11] In *Kokuyaku issai kyō* (*The Complete Scriptures in Japanese
Translation*) (Tōkyō, 1939) A24.1–154.

[12] In an effort to make the diary and quotations from it in this
volume as readable as possible, I have translated almost all
official titles into English, attempting where possible to indicate
something of the holder's duties as well as the literal meaning
of the title. Japanese, Korean, and Indian proper names, although uniformly written in Chinese characters, I have rendered
according to the accepted transcriptions for the respective
languages. Buddhist terms, which with equal validity could be
put in their Sanskrit, Chinese, or Japanese forms, I have
usually transcribed according to their Japanese pronunciations
because it is only the Japanese religious and scholarly tradition
which has kept alive the type of Buddhism that Ennin knew.

[13] The specialist who wishes to ascertain the character equivalents for the Chinese, Japanese, and Korean proper names and
terms used in this book can find them in the companion volume,
*Ennin's Diary—The Record of a Pilgrimage to China in Search
of the Law*. Most of these character equivalents can be located
through the Index, and the remainder will be found in a special
Character Glossary preceding the Index.

CHAPTER II

[1] The early Japanese annals were collected and edited in six volumes known as the *Rikkokushi*, or *The Six National Histories*. The last three of these, covering the years 833–887, contain information on Ennin, and his biography is in the sixth and last, which is the *Sandai jitsuroku*, or *Annals of Three Reigns*. Since all these annals are organized chronologically, I have made my references to them as well as to Ennin's diary by date. The fourteenth day of the first moon of 864 (or 864 I 14 as I have written such date references in these notes) was February 24, 864, according to the Occidental calendar. The year in the Far Eastern lunar calendar usually began about a month later than in the Western calendar.

[2] This biography is called simply the *Jikaku Daishi den*, or *The Biography of Jikaku Daishi*, which was Ennin's posthumous title. The text is printed in chapter 211 of the *Zoku gunsho ruijū* (*Continuation of the "Classified Collection of Texts"*; Tōkyō, 1904) 8.684–700 and in the *Shiseki shūran* (*Collection of Historical Works*; Tōkyō, 1902) 12.58–73. According to the colophon of one transmission of the text, it was compiled in 912 by a man with the two posts of Acting Great Counselor (*Dainagon*) of the Council of State (*Dajōkan*) and Minister of Civil Affairs (*Mimbu no kami*). This is believed to have been Minamoto no Noboru, the second son of the more famous Minamoto no Tōru (822–895). According to the colophon of a second transmission of the text, it was started by the Emperor Uda's third son, Prince Nariyo (who became a monk under the title of Kampyō Nyūdō Shinnō); it was continued after the Prince's death in 927 and on his express orders by his eldest son Minamoto no Hideaki, who had it copied by the famous calligrapher Ono no Michikaze (popularly known as Ono no Tōfū); and it was finally completed after Hideaki's death by his younger brother Moriaki (in 929 according to the colophon, though presumably some time later, since Hideaki was still alive at that time).

These two versions of the origin of the text are discussed in detail and an ingenious theory reconciling them is put forth in an article by Washio Junkei in *Jikaku Daishi* (pp. 102–9), a volume of articles and studies about Ennin published in Tōkyō in 1914 by the Tendai Sect.

Lengthy biographies of Ennin, based for the most part on these earlier works, are also to be found in the various collections of biographies of famous Japanese monks, as for example in the *Nihon kōsō den yōmon shō* compiled in the years 1249–1251 (*Dainihon Bukkyō zensho*, 101.32–42), the *Genkō shakusho* of 1322 (*ibid.*, 101.170–74), and the *Honchō kōsō den* of 1702 (*ibid.*, 102.115–19). The *Dainihon Bukkyō zensho* also contains fifteen works attributed to Ennin, including his diary and catalogues of the books and sacred paintings he brought back with him from China; and the *Tendai kahyō*, a compilation of the eighteenth and nineteenth centuries, contains seventy-four lesser works and documents either by him or relating to him (as listed in the index to this work in *ibid.*, 126.372–74).

[3] The *Jikaku Daishi den* records the date as 794, and this has been accepted by virtually all the authorities. The *Sandai jitsuroku*, however, states that he was seventy-two at the time of his death, which would make his birth date 793, and this date is confirmed by two documents (dated 842 V 26 and 843 V 26) in Ennin's diary which give his age in these two years as fifty and fifty-one respectively. Ages, as traditionally computed in the Far East, are from one to two years higher than they would be as computed in the West, however, because a person is counted as being one during the calendar year of his birth and two as soon as the next calendar year starts.

[4] Corresponding to about five feet, eight inches in our system.

[5] The *Sandai jitsuroku* biography records this breakdown as having occurred at the time of Saichō's death, when Ennin was thirty.

[6] Ennin's lonely hermitage eventually grew into the Shuryōgon-in, also known as Yokawa, one of the three main divisions of the flourishing monastic establishments on Mt. Hiei.

[7] The rank was *Dentō-hosshi*, or "Ecclesiastic Transmitter of the Light," but this was probably a reissue of an earlier patent, for Ennin's age is given in the document as fifty, which was his age in 842, and in his diary he refers to himself as already having this rank in his first months in China.

[8] Ennin's appointment as a *Naigubu* is dated in the seventh moon of 849 in the *Sandai jitsuroku*.

[9] Cf. *ibid.* under the date 864 II 16.

[10] *Ibid.*, 864 III 27.

CHAPTER III

[1] As recorded in the *Hou Han shu* (*History of the Later Han*), chapter 115, which is on "The Eastern Barbarians." The sections telling of Japan in this and the subsequent dynastic histories of China have been conveniently brought together in English translation by Ryūsaku Tsunoda and L. Carrington Goodrich in *Japan in the Chinese Dynastic Histories. Later Han through Ming Dynasties* (South Pasadena: P. D. & Ione Perkins, 1951).

There is some doubt about the exact significance of the two characters which are generally interpreted as standing for "Japan" and "Nu" in this text. The former is usually pronounced "Wa" by the Japanese, and conceivably it and "Nu" are to be read together as a single name. In any case the character for "Nu" means "slave," and that for "Wa" also has pejorative implications. The Japanese in later centuries indignantly rejected this name for their land in favor of the newly coined term Nihon or Nippon, which has come to us through a South Chinese pronunciation as "Japan."

[2] *Sui shu* (*Sui History*), chapter 81, as translated in Tsunoda and Goodrich, *op. cit.* 32.

[3] *Nihon shoki* (*Records of Japan*, the first of the *Six National Histories*) 608 VI.

[4] *Ibid.* 608 IX 11.

[5] Tsuji Zennosuke, *Zōtei Kaigai kōtsū shiwa* (Tōkyō, 1933), 67–80, and Kimiya Yasuhiko, *Nisshi kōtsū shi* (Tōkyō, 1912), 1.120–28, have convenient tables of all the embassies sent from Japan to the T'ang.

[6] As recorded in chapter 220 of the *Hsin T'ang shu* (*New T'ang History*) and translated in Tsunoda and Goodrich, *op. cit.* 39.

[7] Listed as the twelfth embassy by Tsuji but as the eighteenth by Kimiya, who lists more categories of missions, including those that never reached China.

[8] He has a short biography in the *Shoku Nihon kōki* (hereafter abbreviated as *SNK*) under his death date, 840 IV 23.

[9] He has a biography in the *Montoku jitsuroku* (*Annals of Montoku*), the fifth of the *Six National Histories*, under his death date, 852 XII 22.

[10] *SNK* 835 II 2 and V 13.

[11] These ages, which are given according to Far Eastern count and would be approximately a year less in our system, are all computed from the ages given in their respective biographies under their dates of death. For the last four men these biographies are to be found in *Montoku jitsuroku* 852 XI 7, *Sandai jitsuroku* 867 X 4 and 879 XI 10, and *Montoku jitsuroku* 857 IX 3.

[12] 839 II 20. Subsequent references to *Ennin's Diary* are simply by date.

[13] *SNK* 834 VI 22; 835 X 27 and XI 20; 836 IV 29; 837 III 5.

[14] 838 VII 19 and VIII 10.

[15] 839 IV 8 and *SNK* 836 Intercalary V 13. Intercalary moons were added from time to time to the usual twelve moons of the year to keep the lunar calendar in line with the solar year.

[16] 838 VIII 21; 839 II 20 and IV 8.

[17] 838 XI 29; 839 I 3 and VII 21.

[18] 839 V 27.

[19] 838 XII 23; 839 Intercalary I 4 and 5.

[20] 838 VII 2, 12, and 20, and VIII 1 and 4; 839 II 20 and 22, and III 22.

[21] 839 III 1, IV 1, and *SNK* 836 IV 28; 839 III 16 and VIII 25; 841 I 23; 834 XII 19; 836 Intercalary V 8.

[22] 838 X 4; 839 IV 4; *SNK* 839 VIII 25 and X 1; *Montoku jitsuroku* 853 VI 2.

[23] *Sandai jitsuroku* 867 X 4. According to his biography Sadatoshi's encounter with Liu Erh-lang took place in the Chinese capital; Ennin's diary, however, indicates that Sadatoshi never went to Ch'ang-an but remained in Yang-chou with Ennin (see 838 XI 29 and XII 9).

[24] *SNK* 836 VIII 2 and 20. *SNK* merely states that there were more than 600 men on the embassy, but the *Teiō hennenki* (*Shintei zōho kokushi taikei* 12.194) gives the figure as 651 men.

[25] *SNK* 840 IX 26.

[26] 842 V 25.

[27] *SNK* 834 II 2, V 13, and VIII 4 and 10.

[28] *SNK* 835 III 12; 836 Intercalary V 14.

[29] *SNK* 836 III 14.

[30] *SNK* 835 XII 25; 837 II 13.

[31] *SNK* 836 II 17 and Intercalary V 13.

[32] *SNK* 835 XII 2; 836 IV 29 and V 2.

[33] *SNK* 834 VI 22 and XII 19; 835 I 7, X 16 and 27, and XI 20; 836 II 9, III 30, IV 28, V 2, and Intercalary V 8; 837 III 5.

[34] *SNK* 835 II 2 and X 27; 836 IV 29.

[35] *SNK* 836 I 25.

[36] *SNK* 836 II 1 and 7, IV 25, and V 9.

[37] The bolts of silk were *hiki* (*p'i* in Chinese), equivalent to almost forty feet in T'ang times; the lengths of the linen-like cloth (*sayomi no nuno*) were *tan* (*tuan* in Chinese), equivalent to almost fifty feet. In this passage the Scholar Monks are called *Gengaku-sō*, an alternate term for *Shōyaku-sō*.

[38] *SNK* 836 Intercalary V 13.

[39] *SNK* 836 VII 15, 17, and 24 and VIII 1, 4, 20, and 25.

[40] *SNK* 836 VIII 25 and XII 3.

[41] *SNK* 839 IX 25.

[42] *SNK* 837 III 19, 22, and 24. The last item is recorded in *SNK* between notices concerning 837 V 7 and 21, but the cyclical signs for the date correspond to IV 5.

[43] *SNK* 837 IX 21.

[44] *SNK* 838 III 27. Two men were assigned to each of the four shrines, the Kashii and Munekata Shrines in Chikuzen, the province in which Dazaifu was located, the Aso Shrine of central Kyūshū, and the Hachiman Shrine of Usa in northeastern Kyūshū. The ninth man was assigned to "the Minister of State," meaning the protohistoric figure, Takeuchi no Sukune, who was one of the deities worshiped at the Kashii Shrine. Hachiman, though a Shintō deity and commonly described as the God of War, is termed in this document "the Great Bodhisattva Hachiman," a thoroughly Buddhist name by which he was popularly known at this time.

[45] *SNK* 838 IV 5. The *Kairyūō-gyō* tells how the Buddha preached to the Dragon-King of the Sea.

[46] The fuller name of this famous scripture in Sanskrit is *Mahā-prajñā-pāramitā-sūtra*.

[47] *SNK* 838 VI 22 and VII 5 and 29. The true story of the Vice-Ambassador's failure to go to China can be pieced together from the judgment handed down in his case and recorded in *SNK* 838 XII 15 and from Takamura's biography in *Montoku jitsuroku* 852 XII 22.

[48] Recorded in *SNK* 838 VIII 3.

[49] *SNK* 839 III 16.

[50] *SNK* 839 III 1.

[51] 838 VII 3 and 24, and VIII 8, 17, 24, and 25.

[52] 838 VIII 10 and IX 11; 839 II 20, IV 6 and 8, and VI 9.

[53] 839 III 1–3.

[54] Cf. *Hsin T'ang shu* 220 and *Sung shih* (*Sung History*) 491 (Tsunoda and Goodrich, *op. cit.*, pp. 42, 52).

[55] Ennin's chief notices about this aspect of the embassy are to be found under the dates 838 X 4 and XII 18; 839 I 21 and II 6, 8, 20, and 24–27.

[56] 838 X 19, XI 29, and XII 9.

[57] *Montoku jitsuroku* 857 IX 3.

[58] 839 II 8 and 20–22.

[59] 838 VII 2, 14, 18, and 30, VIII 4, 9, and 26, IX 28 and 29, and XI 16 and 17; 839 I 25, II 17, 20, and 27, and III 3 and 22.

[60] 838 VII 14 and 23, VIII 9 and 26, and XI 17; 839 II 6 and 20, and III 23; also *SNK* 839 X 25.

[61] 838 XII 18; 839 III 17.

[62] 839 Intercalary I 19.

[63] 839 III 5, 22, and 23.

[64] 839 IV 8, 11, 12, 24, and 26.

[65] 842 V 25. A report Ennin received on 839 VIII 13 that the Ambassador's nine ships were still on the Shantung coast must have been false, as he surmised at the time.

[66] *SNK* 839 VIII 20.

[67] *SNK* 839 VIII 24 and 25.

[68] *SNK* 839 X 9; 840 III 3 and IV 8.

[69] 842 V 25; *SNK* 840 IV 15, VI 5 and 18, and VII 26; *Montoku jitsuroku* 853 VI 2; *Sandai jitsuroku* 879 XI 10.

[70] *SNK* 839 X 25.

[71] The passage seems to say that one received the third rank, two the fourth rank, 134 the fifth rank, 129 the sixth rank, 59 the seventh rank, 39 the eighth rank, and 12 the ninth rank. However, there are some doubts about this statement. For one thing, it seems most improbable that 134 members of the embassy received appointments to the fifth rank, which would have made them courtiers. What specific appointments we know show that only the higher officers of the embassy achieved this rank. Furthermore, the usual term for "rank" is not used; the numbers add up to 381 instead of 391; and the ranks are listed in reverse order, with the ninth coming first and the third just

before the statement that five men received no ranks. Perhaps a better interpretation would be that 12 men were promoted nine degrees, 39 eight degrees, and so on. Since all the lower ranks were divided into four grades and each of these could be subdivided into two further degrees, a promotion of nine degrees from no rank at all might have been only to the Junior Eighth Rank Lower Grade. In any case, it would seem certain that either 376 or else 386 members of the embassy ended up with some sort of court rank, which must have been a great honor for such humble folk as the common sailors.

[72] *SNK* 840 II 14 and VI 17; 841 Intercalary IX 19; *Montoku jitsuroku* 852 XII 22.

[73] *SNK* 839 IX 23; 840 VI 3.

CHAPTER IV

[1] 839 I 17.

[2] 839 XI (or XII) 17 and 22.

[3] 839 VII 23 and IX 1.

[4] 839 VI 7; 840 I 20 and II 17; 845 VIII 27.

[5] 839 VI 28.

[6] This document appears out of place in the diary under 840 II 17 (or 19).

[7] Although the document was not presented until III 5, it is dated 840 III 3 in the *Tōji* manuscript.

[8] The term is *chai* in Chinese and *sai* in Japanese.

[9] 840 IV 13 and 14. Chü-chou, which is the modern town of Ch'ing-ho, is incorrectly written in the text of the diary as we now have it, but from Ennin's route we can be certain that this was the city where he stopped.

[10] 840 IV 24 and 25.

[11] 840 IV 23.

[12] 840 VII 15. The T'ang T'ai-yüan-fu is the present T'ai-yüan-hsien, about twelve miles southwest of the modern city of T'ai-yüan-fu.

[13] 840 VIII 1, 2, 4, 5, and 13.

[14] 841 XII 3.

[15] 840 IX 14 and 18.

CHAPTER V

[1] See the first days of the years 839–842.

[2] 842 II 19; 840 III 28; 847 VI 19; and also 838 XI 27; 839 XI 9; 840 XI 26 (perhaps an error for XI 20); 841 XI 1.

[3] 845 I 3.

[4] 840 II 22 (where Ennin mistakenly states that Wen-tsung died on I 3); 846 IV 15 and VII 22.

[5] *Tzu-chih t'ung-chien* (*Complete Mirror for Aid in Government*), chapter 246.

[6] 838 VIII 26 and XI 17.

[7] 839 XI (or XII) 22; 840 I 21.

[8] See, for example, 839 VI 29, VII 23, and VIII 16; 840 VII 6 and VIII 5.

[9] 839 X 15 (Nov. 24); 842 VIII 16 (Sept. 23); 845 XI 15 (Dec. 17); 846 XII 2 (Dec. 23).

[10] 841 XII 4 (Jan. 19, 842); 841 XI 1 (Dec. 17); 838 X 22–23 (Nov. 12–13).

[11] 838 XI 24; 839 Intercalary I 4 and 5.

[12] 844 VII 15; 840 IV 3.

[13] 838 XI 16–17.

[14] 845 V 14–15.

[15] 845 V 22, and VI 1 and 9.

[16] 845 V 14, VI 28, and VII 3 and 5.

[17] Cf., for example, the reported route and distance of 2,990 *li* from Mt. Ch'ih to Mt. Wu–t'ai, recorded by Ennin on 839 IX 1, with his actual route and calculated distance of 2,300 *li*, recorded on 840 IV 28.

[18] 840 VIII 10.

[19] 838 IX 13.

[20] See, for example, 838 XI 18; 839 IV 7; 840 III 13 and 14, IV 2, 5, 6, and 22, V 16 and 22, and VII 1; 843 I 28; 845 V 15, VI 9, and VII 9.

[21] 838 VII 20 and 25; 839 III 23; 845 VI 13.

[22] 847 Intercalary III.

[23] 840 III 17.

[24] 840 III 1.

[25] 838 VII 26, IX 29, and X 3 and 4; 839 III 22.

[26] 840 III 2.

[27] 845 VI 23.

[28] 838 VII 24.

[29] 839 II 24; 840 II 25 and 26.

[30] 840 II 29 and III 1, 13, and 14.

[31] 840 III 18, IV 3 and 20, VII 12, VIII 5, 6, and 9.

[32] 840 III 21, VII 11, and VIII 3, 4, 5, 8, 9, 12, 13, 17, 18, 19, and 20.

[33] 838 VII 26 and VIII 24; 840 VIII 15; 845 V 15 and VI 9.

[34] 840 III 14 and VIII 18.

[35] 845 VI 13.

[36] 840 III 17 and 20.

[37] 840 III 13, 14, and 18.

[38] 840 II 27 and IV 4.

[39] 840 III 19 and IV 9, 10, 12, 19, 20, and 21.

[40] 840 IV 22 and 16.

[41] 838 VII 26; 840 IV 17.

[42] 845 VIII 16.

[43] 840 IV 7 and 21.

[44] 838 VIII 26 and 29, and XI 19 and 24; 840 III 5 and 6.

[45] 840 VII 27 and 29, and VIII 2.

[46] 840 IV 21.

[47] 838 VII 3, 12, 13, and 23.

[48] 839 IV 8.

[49] 840 III 24, and IV 6.

[50] 840 III 2 and 7.

[51] 840 II 27.

[52] 840 III 16.

[53] 840 IV 23.

[54] 840 V 22 and 23, and VII 5–12.

[55] 840 VII 27, and VIII 7 and 8.

[56] 838 VII 2, 21, 22, and 23; 839 IV 7.

[57] 839 IV 18.

[58] 839 IV 5; 847 Intercalary III 17.

[59] 839 IV 1, and V 27.

[60] 845 VIII 16.

[61] 840 V 20, and IV 27.

[62] 840 V 21.

[63] 840 IV 23 and 24.

[64] 840 IV 4, and VII 12 and 26.

[65] 838 VIII 26 and X 14; 839 IV 5 and II 27.

[66] 842 V 25 and X 13; 846 X 2.

[67] *SNK* 842 III 6 and IV 12.

[68] 840 IV 28, V 17, and VII 1.
[69] 840 VII 3.
[70] 838 VIII 26 and X 14.
[71] All these statements and documents occur in the diary under 841 IV 28.
[72] 838 XI 2
[73] 841 IV 13–V 3.
[74] 840 XII 22; 841 II 8.
[75] 838 X 9 and 24.
[76] 838 X 14 and XI 19.
[77] 838 VIII 26, XI 19 and 24, and XII 9; 839 III 3.
[78] 839 IV 7; 840 IV 11; 847 Intercalary III and Intercalary III 17.
[79] 840 III 2, 15, 19, and 25 and IV 10.
[80] 839 I 7 and Intercalary I 5.

CHAPTER VI

[1] 840 III 2 and 6.
[2] 838 VII 23, VIII 26 and 29, XI 24 and 29, and XII 8.
[3] 842 X 9; 843 I 17 and 18; 843 VII 29; 844 VII 15; 845 V 13.
[4] 839 Intercalary I 19.
[5] 840 V 2 and 16, and VI 6 and 8.
[6] 839 VI 7 and 8, and XI 1; 840 I 15, IV 6 and 7, and VII 12; 845 IX 22.
[7] 840 I 15 (see also 838 VII 24); 839 IX 28.
[8] 838 XI 24.
[9] 839 I 18; 841 I 9 and II 8.
[10] 840 VIII 24; 844 IV 1.
[11] See for example 841 I 9, II 8, V 1, and IX 1; 842 V.
[12] 838 X 13 and 19, and XII 2 and 18; 839 VIII 16.
[13] 838 XII 2 and 18.
[14] 840 IV 13 and 14.
[15] 840 V 1, 2, and 14. These days are duplicated in scrolls two and three, with the fuller statements on the ordinations in scroll three.
[16] 838 VIII 3; 839 II 26 and III 3; 841 VI 11.
[17] 838 X 14; 840 I 15, IV 22, and V 17.
[18] 838 XII 9; 839 I 3, VI 7, and XI (or XII) 16 and 22; 840 I 15.
[19] 840 V 16 and 17.

[20] 839 VII 23; 840 V 16 and 23, and VI 29.

[21] 839 II 27; 840 V 17 and 18.

[22] 840 VIII 26, IX 5 and 6, X 13, 16, 17, and 29; 841 II 8 and 13, and IV 28.

[23] 841 IV 4, 7, 13, 28, and 30 and V 1 and 3; 842 II 29, III 12, and V 16 (following V 26).

[24] 838 VIII 26 and 29, and XI 19 and 24; 839 II 25; 840 III 5 and 28.

[25] 838 XI 29 and 30, and XII 5 and 9; 839 III 1–3 and 5.

[26] 838 XI 19 and 24, and XII 8; 840 IV 1 and VI 11.

[27] 838 XII 23; 839 Intercalary I 3; 840 II 15 and 28, and VII 1.

[28] 840 V 5 and 7 (second scroll), and VI 6–8.

[29] 838 XII 8.

[30] 839 XI (or XII) 22.

[31] 841 I 9, V 1, and IX 1; 842 V 1.

[32] 838 IX 1; 839 VI 7 and XI (or XII) 16, 17, and 22; 840 I 15, and V 16 and 17.

[33] 841 II 8, II (or III) 15, and IV 1.

[34] 843 VII 24–29, VIII 15 and 29, IX 13, and XI 3.

[35] 840 V 5.

[36] 841 II (or III) 8 and III 25; 842 III 8 and 11.

[37] 840 IV 6.

[38] 839 I 3.

[39] 840 II 14.

[40] 840 VII 26.

[41] 840 IV 28.

[42] This and the following materials are found under the dates 840 V 20 and 21 and VII 2.

[43] 840 V 1 and 23, and VII 6.

[44] 840 V 16 and VII 2.

[45] This and the following sights are all recorded on 840 V 16 and 17, Ennin's first two days at the Ta-hua-yen-ssu.

[46] 840 VII 2.

[47] 840 VII 2–4.

[48] Ennin's descriptions of the first four terraces come on 840 V 20–23 and that of the Southern Terrace on VII 2.

[49] 840 IV 23, 25, 28, and 29, and V 2 and 17.

[50] 840 V 5 and 17, and VI 6 and 8.

[51] 845 VII 5.

[52] 840 VI 21, VII 17, 19, 22, 23, 26, and 29, and VIII 1 and 2.

[53] 840 VI 21 and VII 1, 2, 3, 13, 18, and 26.
[54] 842 III 12.
[55] 840 IV 22.
[56] 839 IV 8; 840 III 23.
[57] 842 III 8 and X 9 (following X 13); 843 I 28.
[58] 838 XI 7, 8, 16, 17, and 18; 839 I 6 and 7, and Intercalary I 5.
[59] 840 II 7 and 11, and VII 3.
[60] 840 IV 9, 17, 18, and 19.
[61] 840 II 27 and III 2, 6, 15, 16, and 19.
[62] 840 IV 6.

CHAPTER VII

[1] As translated by James Legge from *The Confucian Analects* in *The Chinese Classics* (Oxford, 1893) 1.241.

[2] Translated by Professor James R. Hightower of Harvard for a forthcoming history of Chinese literature. The original is the second item in the thirty-ninth scroll of the compendium of Han Yü's writings, the *Ch'ang-li Hsien-sheng chi.*

[3] *Hsin T'ang shu* 8 under the date 845 VIII 7.

[4] Chia Chung-yao, "T'ang Hui-ch'ang cheng-chiao ch'ung-t'u shih-liao," *Shih-huo* 4.18–27 (No. 1, July 1936), has collected most of the main references to this Buddhist persecution, including many of the passages from Ennin's diary. Okada Masayuki, *op. cit.* 12.147–86, has a detailed study of the persecution based largely on Ennin's statements. Y. P. Saeki, *The Nestorian Monument in China* (London, 1916), also gives some material on the persecution, including the full original texts of certain key documents.

[5] The standard texts have "more than twenty" in place of "more than 2,000." This document is the third item in the twentieth scroll of the compendium of Li's writings, the *Li Wen-jao wen chi* and is also quoted in Saeki, *op. cit.* 285–86.

[6] The text appears at the end of the forty-seventh scroll of the *T'ang hui yao*, a great political and social encyclopedia on the T'ang period, compiled largely in the ninth and tenth centuries, and also in a slightly variant form in the *Chiu T'ang shu* 18A. Saeki, *op. cit.* 87–89 and 281–82, gives the latter text and a rough translation of it.

[7] 840 IX 6 and 7; 841 I 7 and 9, and V 1.

[8] 841 IX 1; 842 V, V 29, and VI 11; 843 VI 11; 844 IV 1 and X. Ennin notes, however, that Buddhist monks were allowed to participate in a great ceremony on 842 IV 23 when the Emperor's ministers presented him with an honorific title.

[9] Cf. Alexander Coburn Soper, *Kuo Jo-hsü's Experiences in Painting (Tu-hua chien-wên chih)* (Washington, D. C.: American Council of Learned Societies, 1951), p. 83. The case against Li Te-yü is given in Okada, *op. cit.* 12.150–52. Arthur Waley in *The Life and Times of Po Chü-i 772–846* A.D. (New York: The Macmillan Co., 1949), 205–6, comes to the conclusion that Li Te-yü was not responsible for the anti-Buddhist measures.

[10] 842 X 9 (following X 13); 845 VII 3; 846 VI 29 and X 2.

[11] 842 III 8 and 12, and V 25.

[12] 843 I 27 and 28, and V 25.

[13] 842 X 9.

[14] 842 III 12; 843 II 25, IV, and IX 13.

[15] 838 IX 29; 840 II 22; *Chiu T'ang shu* 17B and *Tzu-chih t'ung-chien* 246 under the date of 838 IX 7.

[16] 841 IV 9; 842 II 1. The latter is the date under which Ennin mentions Ch'iu's new military appointment, but the *Tzu-chih t'ung-chien* 246 records it in 841 VIII.

[17] 840 IX 5; 841 I 6; 843 IX 13; 844 VII 15.

[18] 843 VI 3, 23, and 25; 845 V 14.

[19] 844 IX.

[20] Ennin at one point says it was the ninth day and at another refers to edicts of the seventh and sixteenth days. Of these dates, the seventh seems the most probable. The materials on this phase of the persecution are to be found under 842 X 9, and 843 I 17 and 18.

[21] 843 VI 27, 28, and 29, and VII 2.

[22] 844 IV 1 and XI; 845 I 3.

[23] 843 IX 13.

[24] 844 III.

[25] 843 VI 11.

[26] This and the following incidents are all recorded in the diary between 844 III and VII 15.

[27] 844 X.

[28] 845 VIII 27.

[29] Cf. *Tzu-chih t'ung-chien* 246–248, especially under the dates 841 VI, 844 IV, 845 VII, and 846 IV, and *Chiu T'ang shu* 18A under 845 I.

[30] 844 X and 845 I 3.

[31] 844 III and VIII.

[32] 844 VII 15.

[33] 844 VIII.

[34] This and the following incidents are all told under the date 845 I 3.

[35] This description and the following incidents are all recorded under the date 845 III 3.

[36] 844 VII 15.

[37] Ennin's comments on this edict are recorded under the date 844 VII 15 and those about the next edict under 844 X.

[38] Actually Ennin says it was the head of Liu Chen's uncle, who had died almost a year and a half earlier. Ennin seems to have consistently confused the uncle with the nephew, writing all that he has about the Lu-fu rebellion as if the uncle were alive and leading it.

[39] This and the following materials occur under the dates of 845 III 3, IV, and V.

[40] 845 VI 23.

[41] 841 VIII 7; 843 VIII 13; 845 V 14.

[42] 843 XII; 844 II.

[43] 845 V 22, and VI 1 and 9.

[44] 845 VI 13, 22, 23, and 28, and VII 3.

[45] 845 VII 15 and 16.

[46] 845 VII 17 and VIII 16, 21, 24, and 27.

[47] 845 XI 3 and 15.

[48] 845 VI 22.

[49] 845 VI 28.

[50] 845 VII 5; 846 I 9.

[51] 845 VIII 16.

[52] 845 IX 22.

[53] 845 VIII 27.

[54] 845 XI 3.

[55] 846 IV 15, V 1, and VII 22; 847 I.

CHAPTER VIII

[1] 839 I 7.

[2] As tabulated from materials in the *Chōsen shi* (Keijō, 1933), the voluminous official history of Korea compiled by the Japanese Government General.

[3] Cf. for example *Chiu T'ang shu* 104, 106, 109, and 124.

[4] Cf. Sir Aurel Stein, "A Chinese Expedition Across the Pamirs and Hindukush A.D. 747," *The New China Review* 4.161–83.

[5] Cf. Walter Fuchs, "Huei-ch'ao's Pilgerreise durch Nordwest-Indien und Zentral-Asien um 726," *Sitzungsberichte der Preussischen Akademie der Wissenschaften (Philosophisch-historische Klasse)* 1938.426–69. I-ching's famous work has been translated by the French Sinologist, Edouard Chavannes, under the title, *Mémoire composé à l'époque de la grande dynastie T'ang sur les religieux éminents qui allèrent chercher la loi dans les pays d'occident* (Paris, 1894).

[6] Cf. Tsuji Zennosuke, *op. cit.* 90–97.

[7] 843 I 28 and VIII 13; 845 V, and V 14 and 16.

[8] 839 VII 23, and IX 1 and 12; 840 VII 26.

[9] 839 VI 28; 840 III 2 and 24, and IV 6; 847 Intercalary III.

[10] 839 VIII 13; 840 III 2, 20, and 28, and VII 3.

[11] Cf. Arthur Waley, *The Life and Times of Po Chü-i 772–846* A.D. 160 and Alexander C. Soper, "T'ang Ch'ao Ming Hua Lu. The Famous Painters of the T'ang Dynasty," *Archives of the Chinese Art Society of America* 4 (1950).11.

[12] 839 III 17 and 25; 842 V 25; 845 VII 3, 5, 8, and 9; 847 VI 5.

[13] 839 VI 7 and VIII 15; 840 I 15.

[14] 839 XI (or XII) 1, 16, and 22; 840 I 15 and II 14; 847 Intercalary III.

[15] 839 IV 1, 5, 20, 24, 26, and 29.

[16] 839 I 8; 840 II 15; 842 V 25; 843 I 29 and XII; 845 VII 5; 846 IV 27, V 1, and VI 17; 847 VI 9.

[17] 839 III 22 and 23; 840 II 19; 845 VII 3, and VIII 24 and 27; 846 VI 17; 847 VI 5 and 10.

[18] 839 III 22 and 23, IV 5 and 29, and VI 7 and 29; 845 VII 3 and 9, and VIII 27.

[19] 839 V 25; 842 V 25; 843 XII; 845 VII 5 and IX 22; 846 I 9, II 5 and 9, IV 27, V 1, VI 17 and 29, and X 2; 847 Intercalary III, III 17, and VI 9, 10, 18, and 27.

[20] 838 VI 28.

[21] Cf. for example *Hsin T'ang shu* 220 and *SNK* under the dates 840 XII 27, 841 II 27, and 842 I 10. The chief historical materials on Chang Pogo are to be found in the twelfth-century Korean chronicle, the *Samguk sagi (Historical Records of the Three Kingdoms)* 10, 11, and 44 and the thirteenth-

century Korean record, the *Samguk yusa* (*Memorabilia of the Three Kingdoms*) 2.

[22] Cf. Legge, *op. cit.* 1.154. The account of this part of Chang's life is taken from the *Samguk sagi* 10 (828 III ff.) and 44 (Biographies of Chang Pogo and Chŏng Yŏn).

[23] 839 IV 2, 20, and 24.

[24] 839 VI 7, 27, and 28; 840 II 15 and 17; 845 IX 22.

[25] *Samguk sagi* 44.

[26] *Samguk sagi* 11 (839 VIII to 846 spring).

[27] *Samguk yusa* 2 (under the heading "Great King Sinmu").

[28] 845 VII 9.

[29] *SNK* 842 I 10.

[30] *Samguk sagi* 11 (851 II).

CHAPTER IX

[1] 845 IX 22, and XI 3 and 15; 846 I 9.

[2] 846 II 5, III 9 and 13, IV 27, V 1, VI 17 and 29, and X 2.

[3] 847 I, II, and Intercalary III.

[4] 847 Intercalary III to VI 5.

[5] Cf. *Gyōryakushō* in *Dainihon Bukkyō zensho* 113.291.

[6] 847 VI 5 to IX 2.

[7] This section is based on the concluding materials in the **diary** between the dates 847 IX 2 and XII 14.

[8] *SNK* 847 X 2.

Index

Date Due

JAN 6 '61		
JAN 2 7 '61		
MAR 3 1 '61		
JAN 1 1 '63		
JAN 1 0 '64		
𝒢𝐵	PRINTED	IN U. S. A.	

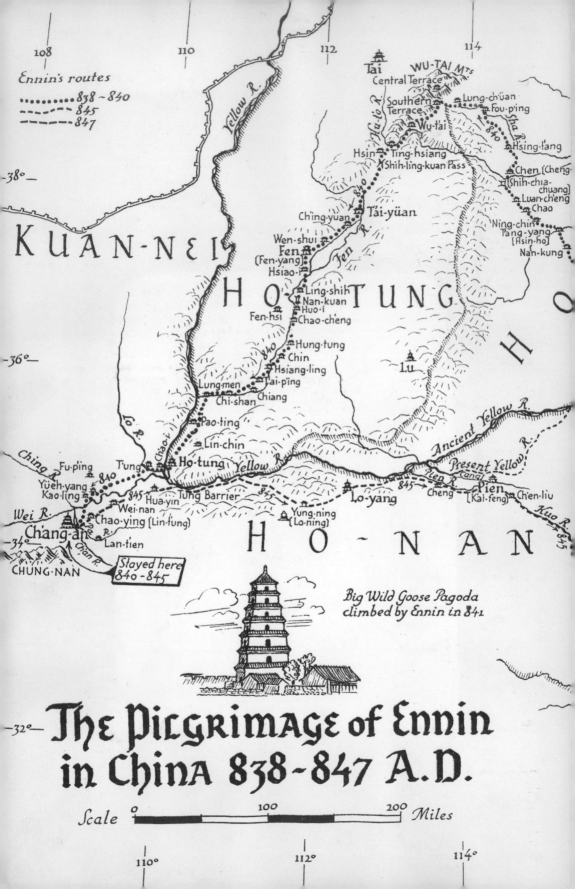

The Pilgrimage of Ennin in China 838-847 A.D.

Ennin's routes
········· 838-840
- - - - - 845
—— —— —— 847

108   110   112   114

-38°-

KUAN-NEI

Yellow R.

Tai
WU-TAI Mts
Central Terrace
Southern Terrace
Wu-tai
Lung-ch'üan
Fou-p'ing
Hsin
Ting-hsiang
Shih-ling-kuan Pass
Hsing-t'ang
Ch'ing-yüan
T'ai-yüan
Chen (Ch'eng-
Shih-chia-
chuang]
Luan-ch'eng
Chao
Wen-shui
Fen
(Fen-yang)
Hsiao-i
Ling-shih
Nan-kuan
Huo-i
Chao-ch'eng
Ning-chin
Tang-yang
[Hsin-ho]
Nan-kung
Fen-hsi

HO - TUNG

Hung-tung
Chin
Hsiang-ling
T'ai-p'ing
Lu
Lung-men
Chi-shan
Chiang
Pao-ting
Lin-chin

HO

Ancient Yellow R.

Ch'ing R.
Fu-p'ing
T'ung
Ho-tung
Yellow R.
Present Yellow
Canal
Pien
[Kai-feng]
Ch'en-liu
Yüeh-yang
Kao-ling
Hua-yin
Tung Barrier
Lo-yang
Cheng
Wei R.
Wei-nan
Chao-ying (Lin-t'ung)
Yung-ning
(Lo-ning)
Ch'ang-an
Lan-t'ien

HO - NAN

Kuo R.

CHUNG-NAN
Stayed here
840-845

Big Wild Goose Pagoda
climbed by Ennin in 841

-36°-

-34°-

-32°-

Scale   0   100   200   Miles

110°   112°   114°